THE REMINISCENCES

of

Admiral Alfred C. Richmond
U. S. Coast Guard (Retired)

U. S. Naval Institute
Annapolis, Maryland
1976

PREFACE

Herein is a transcript of some taped interviews with Admiral Alfred C. Richmond, USCG (Ret.) They were obtained under sponsorship of the U. S. Coast Guard and are part of the on-going program in Oral History of the U. S. Naval Institute. The interviews were given by Admiral Richmond to John T. Mason, Jr. during a number of visits to the Admiral's home in Claremont, California in the week of November 17, 1975.

Admiral Richmond read the initial transcript from the tapes. He made some corrections and they have been incorporated in the re-typed version that appears here. A subject index has been added at the end of the volume for the convenience of researchers.

The Admiral's career in the Coast Guard is a distinguished one. It reached its climax during the years 1954-62 when he served as Commandant of the Coast Guard. Prior to that, however, Richmond was engaged in a number of assignments that have historic significance. As a junior officer he was part of the Special Patrol Force operating against rum runners off the Atlantic and Pacific Coasts. Early in his career he earned a Juris Doctor degree (with distinction) from the George Washington University (1938). His knowledge of the Law proved invaluable to him during the balance of his career. One can cite especially the major role he assumed in the establishment of the Coast Guard Reserve before World War II; in his vital part in bringing into being the Merchant Marine Hearing Units of World War II and especially his command of those Units in various parts of the United Kingdom; in his strenuous role at various International

Conferences; in his years as Chief of Program Planning at Headquarters; in his frequent appearances before Congressional Committees in pursuit of legislation. Finally, one should not overlook the yeoman service Admiral Richmond rendered the Coast Guard during a period of over sixteen years in which he was charged with the task of presenting the annual Budget to the Congress.

A letter of Admiral Richmond (July 2, 1976) is attached as an appendix to this volume. It deals with various questions about the Coast Guard Academy presented to him by a Professor at Indiana University.

John T. Mason, Jr.
Annapolis, Maryland

November 1976

Public Information Division
U. S. Coast Guard Headquarters   Biographical Sketch
Washington, D.C., 20226

ADMIRAL ALFRED C. RICHMOND, USCG
COMMANDANT
OF THE UNITED STATES COAST GUARD
1954-1962

Alfred Carroll Richmond was born at Waterloo, Iowa, on January 18, 1902, and at the age of 10 moved with his family to Cherrydale, Virginia. After receiving a certificate from the Massanutten Academy of Woodstock, Virginia, he entered the George Washington University college of engineering of Washington, D.C., at the age of 16. At the same time he was employed at the U. S. Naval Observatory.

Appointed a cadet at the U. S. Coast Guard Academy, New London, Connecticut, in July 1922, he was graduated senior man in his class and commissioned an Ensign on October 1, 1924.

Subsequently he advanced in rank to Lieutenant (jg), October 1, 1926; Lieutenant, October 1, 1928; Liet. Commander, October 16, 1932; Commander, July 17, 1942; Captain, June 1, 1943; Rear Admiral (when he took oath of office as Assistant Commandant) March 10, 1950; Vice Admiral and Commandant, June 1, 1954; Admiral, June 1, 1960. Retired June 1, 1962.

From November 1924 to September 1926, he served as aide to the Commandant of the Coast Guard at headquarters in Washington, D.C.. During this time he also performed temporary duty from May to July of 1925 as an aide to the commanding officer of the Special Patrol Force operating against "rum runners" off the coast of New York State, and of the Special Service Squadron off the coast of Massachusetts. He was commended for efficient work in this connection.

Beginning in September 1926 he was assigned for two years as a member of the Coast Guard Academy staff. During this period he served temporarily with the Cutter MOJAVE from June to September of 1927, and took part in the cadet practice cruise aboard the Destroyer SHAW during the summer of 1928. In October 1928 he was assigned a course of instructions at the Sperry Gyro Compass School at Brooklyn, N.Y., after which he became navigator aboard the Cutter PONTCHARTRAIN stationed at Quincy, Mass. From July to November of 1930, he served as executive officer of the Destroyer WAINWRIGHT in the Gulf Division.

He then reported to the Coast Guard Representative at Philadelphia Navy Yard, and was assigned as executive officer of the Destroyer HERNDON, Flagship of Division III, Destroyer Force, when the ship was commissioned and assigned to Boston for permanent station.

In May 1932 he transferred to Coast Guard Headquarters to undertake duties in connection with the small arms training of a Coast Guard Detachment which he helped assemble at Camp Curtis Guild, Wakefield, Mass., then later accompanied to such places as Cascade, Maryland, and Quantico, Va., for the National Rifle Association regional shooting matches and the national matches held at Ft. Sheridan, Illinois. Completing this tour in August he returned to Headquarters and two months later became executive officer of the Cutter HAIDA stationed at Cordova, Alaska, in which he performed patrol duty in the Bering Sea and Arctic waters.

In September 1935 he again was assigned to Coast Guard Headquarters at which time he began taking a resident law course at the George Washington University. He was graduated on June 8, 1938, and awarded a degree of Juris Doctor "with distinction." Thereupon he was assigned duties in Headquarters' Office of Operations, with collateral duties of assisting in the preparation of certain law enforcement education material, and of assisting the Engineer-in-Chief in the preparation of permanent land records for property held by the government for Coast Guard use. He served also as a representative of the Treasury Department and as a delegate of the United States at the International Whaling Conference convened at London, England, on July 17, 1939.

A transfer in May 1941 sent him to the Bethlehem Steel Co. at Baltimore, Maryland, for duties in connection with the outfitting of the new Coast Guard vessel AMERICAN SAILOR which was destined to be used for training maritime personnel, which was the responsibility of the Coast Guard at that time. After placing the ship into commission, he commanded it from her assigned station at Port Hueneme, California, where, in addition, he commanded the Maritime Service Training Station (assuming charge in February 1942).

From September 1942 (when the AMERICAN SAILOR with the Maritime Service was transferred to the War Shipping Administration) until February 1943 during World War II, he served as commanding officer of the Cutter HAIDA, stationed at Juneau, Alaska, for convoy escort duty. He was then assigned to the Merchant Marine Inspection Office of the Third Coast Guard District in New York City. His duties there included those of examining officer and hearing officer.

Transferred overseas in July 1943, he became Senior Coast Guard Officer in charge of the U. S. Coast Guard Merchant Marine

Hearing Unit in London, England. His duties there included that of administering and enforcing laws and regulations relating to the functions of Coast Guard vessels and personnel, and as examining and hearing officer administering laws and regulations governing investigations of accidents and casualties involving United States vessels and personnel with the U. S. Naval Forces in Europe.

Later he received the Bronze Star Medal "for meritorious service as Senior Coast Guard Officer on the Staff of the Commander, United States Naval Forces in Europe" during and after the Normandy Invasion, when he assisted in organizing Coast Guard Forces preparing for the invasion and contributed to the efficiency of the merchant marine ships sailing invasion routes.

Meanwhile the French Government awarded him the Croix de Guerre "for exceptional services" rendered in the liberation of France.

In May 1945, he was assigned to duty at Headquarters as Chief, Supply Division. The following month he was designated Chief, Program Planning Division, while in August he became Chief, Budgets and Requirements and Assistant Chief, Planning and Control.

On March 9, 1950, with the advice of the President and consent of the Senate, he was appointed Assistant Commandant of the Coast Guard with the rank of Rear Admiral for a four-year term. Effective May 1, 1951, with a reorganization of the Coast Guard, he assumed the additional duties of Chief of Staff.

He was appointed Commandant of the Coast Guard with the rank of Vice Admiral on May 13, 1954, to succeed Vice Admiral Merlin O'Neill upon his retirement. He took his oath of office on June 1, 1954.

On April 22, 1958, the Senate confirmed a second four-year term for Admiral Richmond as Commandant, effective on June 1, 1958.

Effective as of June 1, 1960, he was appointed to the rank of full Admiral by the President with confirmation from the Senate under authority provided by Act of May 14, 1960, Public Law 86-474, which pertains to a reorganization of top commands, amending Title 14, U. S. Code Section 41 and 44. (Whereas previously only two Commandants had ever attained the rank of full Admiral while in office, the new Act provides that all Commandants shall hereon serve in the rank of full Admiral.)

He was active in international affairs, particularly in the maritime field. In January of 1959 he was a principal delegate to the First Assembly of the Intergovernmental Maritime Consultative Organization, and has represented the United States on four other occasions as head of the United States representation to the Maritime Safety Committee of IMCO. He was head of the United States delegation to the Safety of life at Sea Convention in London in 1960, for which services he was presented the Distinguished Service Medal. In 1961 he was delegate to the Second Assembly meeting of IMCO.

In addition to the above, he was president of the 1960 Sixth International Lighthouse Conference, and president of the Executive Committee of the International Association of Lighthouse Authorities.

He was also chairman of the National Committee for Prevention of Pollution of Seas by oil, and was designated to head the United States delegation to the 1962 conference.

Admiral Richmond was installed in the GW Letterman Hall of Fame which was inaugurated at George Washington University in November 1959. He won his letter in football.

Admiral Richmond retired effective as of June 1, 1962. He turned over his official duties as Commandant of the U. S. Coast Guard to his successor, ADM Edwin J. Roland, USCG, in formal change-of-command ceremonies held aboard the Coast Guard Cutter CAMPBELL on the Potomac River, Washington, D.C., May 31.

Admiral Richmond received a Gold Star in lieu of a Second Distinguished Service Medal for "exceptionally meritorious service" performed as Commandant from June 1, 1954 to May 31, 1962.

Admiral and Mrs. Richmond, the former Gretchen C. Campbell, live at 4105 La Junta Drive, Piedmont Mesa, Claremont, California. They have two sons, John Mason, and Alfred Carroll, Jr.

REV. AUGUST 1966

DECLARATION OF TRUST

The undersigned does hereby appoint and designate as his (her) Trustee herein, the Secretary-Treasurer and Publisher of the United States Naval Institute to perform and discharge the following duties, powers, and privileges in connection with the possession and use of a certain taped interview between the undersigned and the Oral History Department of the United States Naval Institute.

1. Classification of Transcript.

( )a. If classified OPEN, the transcript(s) may be read or the recording(s) audited by the qualified personnel upon presentation of proper credentials, as determined by the Secretary-Treasurer of the U.S. Naval Institute.

(X)b. If classified PERMISSION REQUIRED TO CITE OR QUOTE, the user will be required to obtain permission in writing from the interviewee prior to quoting or citing from either the transcript(s) or the recording(s).

( )c. If classified PERMISSION REQUIRED, permission must be obtained in writing from the interviewee before the transcribed interview(s) can be examined or the tape recording(s) audited.

( )d. If classified CLOSED, the transcribed interview(s) and the tape recording(s) will be sealed until a time specified by the interviewee. This may be until the death of the interviewee or for any specified number of years.

2. It is expressly understood that in giving this authorization, I am in no way precluded from placing such restrictions as I may desire upon use of the interview at any time during my lifetime, nor does this authorization in any way affect my rights to the copyright of my literary expressions that may be contained in the interview.

Witness my hand and seal this 17th day of August 1976

Alfred C. Richmond

I hereby accept and consent to the foregoing Declaration of Trust and the powers therein conferred upon me as Trustee:

R.T.E. Bowler Jr

Richmond #1 - 1

Interview #1 with Admiral Alfred C. Richmond, U. S. Coast Guard
(Retired)

Place: His residence in Claremont, California

Date: Monday morning, 17 November 1975

Subject: Biography

By: John T. Mason, Jr.

Q: Well, Admiral, for some weeks now I've been looking forward to this series with you, a kind of a talking biography. Would you begin in the proper way by telling me the date and place of your birth and something about your family background?

Adm. R.: I was born in Waterloo, Iowa, January 18, 1902, and lived there until I was about nine years old. My mother, who was from Virginia, right outside of Washington, Fairfax County, had married and moved out there. I guess we went back East when I was about three and again when I was six. About that time my mother and father were separated. We lived on there for about three years and then moved to Washington, D. C.. That would have been about 1911 and I lived there and out in Fairfax County until I went into the service.

Q: You were the only child?

Richmond #1 - 2

Adm. R.: I was the only surviving child. I did have a sister but she died before I was born.

Q: I see. Well, tell me about your early schooling, then.

Adm. R.: I started school in Waterloo and then when we came East, my mother eventually remarried, we lived over near the Capitol and I went to school there for a short time, elementary school. Then we moved out to McLean, Virginia, and I still commuted in the Old Dominion Railroad, which ran out there then, to go to the school in Southeast. I've even forgotten the name of it now. A year or so later we moved back into town, near Washington Circle, on K Street, and I went to both the old Weightman School through eighth grade, and I think it was the Grant School, which was down about 23rd and G or something like that.

Then we were going to move back to Virginia. At that time there was a rule that if you lived in Virginia and came in to high school in Washington, you had to pay a little bit of tuition. Anyway, I had gotten the idea that I would like to go away to prep school - or, rather, go away to school, so I wrote away to a number of them and finally decided on Massanutten Academy in Woodstock, Virginia.

Q: What made you decide on Massanutten?

Richmond #1 - 3

Adm. R.: As I recall, I think it was probably that the headmaster impressed my mother as being a good leader. He was known as Colonel Benchoff - to we undergraduates as "Baldy" Benchoff. I remember he came to see us. In those days, of course, automobiles were a rarity. I had a wagon and I remember he caught me going around Washington Circle. Nowadays you'd live about thirty seconds doing that, but going round Washington Circle, you know, with one knee in the wagon, pedaling the wagon with the other foot.

Q: It's a very complicated circle nowadays.

Adm. R.: Oh, I'll say it is compared with then, but then all you saw were horses and buggies.

It was a small school and furthermore it offered me a chance to work my way through or to earn a little bit of my tuition. That was why I decided on Massanutten. We could afford it and I could earn a little something and be away at school.

Q: Was it military in nature?

Adm. R.: Not at that time, no. The last year I was there, of course, the war had come on, or rather we had gotten in the war. The war was on when I went there, but I mean we weren't in it at that time. The last year they started having military training. At first, as I recall it, we did not have uniforms. We had to get some white ducks or something like that. Then we finally got gray uniforms. We had just about one company. There were less than 100 students. It was quite an experience being up there. It was only 100 miles, as you know, from Washington. We used to have to go up on the old Southern Railway from Washington. I suppose the tracks are still there, through Winchester. It was a five-hour trip. I think the train stopped at every crossroad, every three or four miles. Those were the days when traveling was a bit rough.

Q: What about the course of study there?

Adm. R.: It was regular high school. By that I mean there was nothing specialized. We took the usual things that kids took, general high school at that time, mathematics, English, grammar, Latin. I can't think of anything special about the school, other than that I had a good time. The first year I earned part of my tuition by sweeping out one of the dormitories. Then after that, my second and third year, I waited on tables, but we only waited every other week, and you could always get a standby. The food was always good and plenty of it but the waiters always got an extra portion, anyway, and, of course, we were growing boys. You could always get somebody who wasn't working their way through to stand by for you, if you wanted to -

Q: Did you get paid by the hour or what?

Adm. R.: No, no. It sounds odd today but I think the total tuition for the year, board and room and everything was $400, and I think I got $150 or $170 knocked off of that for my labors, such as they were.

The school was kind of interesting at that time. We had two classes of boys, really, fairly young and fairly unsophisticated small kids like myself and older fellows that probably should have been in college and usually quite wealthy whose families apparently owned mines over in West Virginia and let the kids grow up and get beyond the stage where they could conveniently go to a high school. In other words, they were too big, then they'd decide, well, maybe they needed an education after all, so they'd pack them off to Massanutten. So, as I say, we had some great big boys and then we got down to the rank and file like myself.

Q: Did you go in for athletics?

Adm. R.: Yes. I aspired to play football and I might say at the outset about that some people can boast of having played on good teams and even probably been all-star and all-American. I think I have the record of having played -

undisputed record - successively on the world's worst football team bar none. You see, the school was small, and I don't think we ever had more than 100 students at the beginning of the year, then some would drop out. Some were day students, too. As a young fellow, I had to turn out for football because they needed so much cannon fodder to step on and get the practice in, but I think the second or third year I was there the war was on and a lot of these big fellows had been weeded out, so we were down to a point at one time where, to scrimmage, we had to turn one side of the line against the other, which gets kind of rough. But we had a lot of fun.

One of the things that they had there was a training table. This goes back to the days when you had training tables and if you smoked or anything like that, off the team you went. We had our training table and we were quite serious about our football. We won some games. We lost some. And I played a little baseball, but football was the main sport there at the time.

We had some foreign students, too, I remember. Of course, they didn't go in for sports much. We had kind of a small gym there and we used to work out. There was a Cuban boy who was quite a gymnast. He tried to teach me to be a gymnast but that was pretty unsuccessful, really.

I don't remember too much about any of the games. I do remember playing Randolph-Macon Academy one time. I was playing an end and the boy inside of me - well, the other side of the line was a strong line and Randolph-Macon knew this, so they ran every play around our end. This boy and I more or less tossed up to see who would be on the bottom of the pile in the mud because it was a rainy day and the field was muddy. I never ate so much mud in all my life as on that particular day. As I say, you learn by adversity.

Q: I guess you did. Well, you graduated at a fairly early age?

Adm. R.: Yes. I was only sixteen when I graduated from the Academy. As I say, by that time we were in World War I and the school was pretty well depleted. It had gone military, of course. The headmaster, Baldy Benchoff, now Colonel Benchoff, called me in and told me he thought I was foolish to try to go on to college right away. He said I was too young. He said I'd get through all right, but he just felt that I needed more experience, so he suggested that I wait a year or so before I went to college.

Q: I suppose at that early age you were undeveloped socially but able to meet the intellectual requirements?

Adm. R.: I think that was his idea and we all respected him. Some of us were scared to death of him - well, we really weren't, but he was a strict disciplinarian.

As you go through life you learn a lot of lessons. For example, I've often wondered what became of a fellow that was there. Before it became military - after it became military you'd work off demerits, they had the merit system - you had to learn four lines of poetry on Saturday. This was the punishment that you had, and I suppose that from time to time we all got demerits, and the prime book was the <u>Lincoln Anthology of Poetry</u>. We had one boy there - I think his name was Smith - who came from Baltimore and his father was a junk-dealer, owned a big junk yard in Baltimore. Later I suppose this boy inherited his father's junk yard. Smith got so many demerits that finally he got to the point where he'd learned so much poetry that they had to move out of this book, this anthology of poetry, which was about an inch and a half thick, and get him another book. He had learned that whole book of poetry. I have often wondered how it would be to deal with a junk dealer spouting poetry.

Q: Maybe he liked it!

Adm. R.: I don't think he did to start with, but I think pretty soon he did. As I said, I've often wondered what it must have been later in life to go into a junk yard and meet a guy who could recite practically any piece of poetry that was ever written! I don't think much of the poetry I learned

Richmond #1 - 9

stuck with me, so maybe his didn't either.

After I graduated I came back to Washington. It was summer and I planned to look around for a job and I got a job as a plumber's helper for the Frank J. Cornell Company. I worked on that temporary building that was known as the Army and Navy Munitions Building, right down on the south side of Constitution Avenue, between 17th and 21st streets.

Q: That was going up at that time, was it?

Adm. R.: That was going up. I suppose you know that that land is all fill land. At that time they were trenching to put the pipes in, going down 20 or 30 feet. You looked down those trenches and it was just like a layer cake, a layer of ashes, a layer of something else. I didn't work very hard. My main job was running up to the toolhouse to get packing or something.

Q: You were a plumber's helper then?

Adm. R.: I was a plumber's helper, yes. I didn't do any plumbing, as such. I was probably more an errand boy, but I was coining money because I was working ten hours a day and got double pay for overtime and that sort of thing. I probably would have ended up being a wealthy man if I'd stayed with the plumbing business, but the following Saturday my trunk arrived from Massanutten and I was unpacking and we had a guest in the house. She was a yeomanette who worked at the Naval Observatory and she pointed out that they needed people who knew how to use logarithmic tables and so forth up there. Before the war they'd only hire college graduates but now the college graduates were all off to war they couldn't get anybody. They needed them for computers and why didn't I apply. My mother thought that would be good for my intellectual capabilities or something, so the following Monday I went up and applied for a job. I worked for about half of what I was making - or less - of what I would have made if I'd stayed as a plumber's helper. But, as it turned out, it probably was the best thing.

I enjoyed my time up at the Observatory. In my first job I worked with a Miss Lamson, who was head of the computing division. As I say, as you go through life you learn certain things that a lot of people don't realize. For example, I found that heads of offices, generally speaking, look out for their staff and so forth. But if you really want a head of office who will fight for their personnel and at the same time they themselves will give the personnel the devil if they don't do right, you want a woman boss. Miss Lamson was that way.

Q: You mean a woman's more likely to be compassionate?

Adm. R.: No, not compassionate. She was more like a mother hen with her chicks. Let somebody come in and say something went wrong and your so and so did this, why, then she's up, spreading her wings, and tearing into that person. And they won't hesitate to go right to the top.

Diverting for a moment, did you ever run into Mrs. Shipley of the Passport Office?

Q: Yes.

Adm. R.: I recall an occasion during the war where a naval officer who was in the intelligence group watching merchant seaman wanted to take some passports or do something about passports - I was there with him in the Passport Division when he tried to get this straightened out. She said she would call Admiral King before she got through with him, and she ended up by calling Admiral King. In other words, a man would never have thought of doing that. That's why I say if you want someone who will really fight for their division, get a woman in charge of it. It was before the women's movement really took over that I came to this conclusion.

Well, as I say, I worked in the computing division and the following fall I went to George Washington and registered, but I only lasted a month or so. That was the year that the 'flu epidemic was so strong. They closed the school for three or four weeks and I found that working all day and going to night school was not for me, especially because of course we didn't have cars in those days.

Q: Getting across town was difficult?

Adm. R.: Yes, and it was just too much, so I dropped out. I was in the computing division about a year. I was transferred finally out of the computing division down to the time service.

Meantime, my mother had gotten interested and I gave her a course of sprouts on the use of tables and she was employed. They still needed computers, so she was employed up there in the computing division with Miss Lamson. And it was decided that the thing for me to do if I wanted to get an education was to drop out of the Observatory - no, to go on a temporary absence from the Observatory and go to George Washington in the daytime during the winter, the fall and spring semesters.

The computing division had what they called mean place work, which is the reduction of a star transit observation to a mean position. This could be farmed out and I could work on it at home, if I wanted to, and I could have made really good money doing it if I'd only had the ambition to work. But it was more fun to go to dances so, unless I needed money for spending money or something, I didn't. Then I'd dash off maybe $50 or so and turn it in, collect my check, and -

Q: That was certainly a convenient way to earn some pin money?

Adm. R.: Yes, and that was essentially what I was doing. Then in the summertime I'd go back up to the Observatory and work in the time service. During that period I had several trips. If you remember, in those days, they used to send chronometers and torpedo boat watches around to the ships. Part of our job in the time service was to check and have the chronometers, as they were sent in, repaired and check them to see that they were accurate. I made trips to Philadelphia. This was before I went back to George Washington. I also went to Norfolk and other places. I always went up and down the East Coast. I never had any long trips, but for a young fellow it was a lot of fun.

The other job that time service did in those days was to send the time signal at noon and at ten o'clock at night. They were sent out through Arlington and Annapolis. First, it was primarily Annapolis, then they built Arlington.

Q: This went out to the fleet, did it?

Adm. R.: All over the world. Down in the basement we had sidereal clocks and the transmitting clocks were right there in the time service. When visitors would come in they'd see the transmitting clocks. What you had to do was figure out your differential between the sidereal time - the sidereal clocks were the accurate ones. They were in a vacuum at even temperature. What you had to do was to start roughly a half-hour before the time of transmittal and you'd either speed up or slow down the transmitting clocks, which were in the time service and looked like large grandfather clocks, with a simpler case than that. They had a magnet under the pendulum which we would speed up or slow down to coincide with the proper time from the sidereal time. That was one reason they let me come back in the summertime, because by my coming back, having been in there, that gave the other boys an opportunity to have their leave. You see, someone had to come up every night -

Q: They had to be watched constantly?

Adm. R.: Well, not so much watched but someone had to be there to send that signal, and some of us got so that, even though we were supposed to do it with the magnet - the magnet would only do it so fast - but we got our ear so trained that we could grab that pendulum with our fingers and cut it down to three or four thousandths of a second and then let the magnet finish it off, instead of waiting twenty or twenty-five minutes to let the magnet gradually slow down. Those were little tricks of the trade that you learned.

As I say I went to George Washington and entered as a civil engineering student.

Q: What was your intention?

Richmond #1 - 15

Adm. R.: At that time I was thinking in terms of civil engineering, particularly bridge construction. I don't know why, as I look back, but that seemed to appeal to me.

That was the first year George Washington wanted to bring in football again. They had had a team years before.

Q: Was Dr. Marvin there then?

Adm. R.: I don't believe so. I don't think he had come in yet. I forget who was president at the time. I guess undergraduates don't think much about who's president. I remember the head of the engineering school. That was Dean Hodgkins.

Brian Morse was our coach. He had coached at Western High School and he was a sports writer for the Times-Herald. The reason I'm telling this story is that, as I said before, you learn little things as you go along and one of the things I learned about this was it's not what the story is, it's how you tell the story. To begin with, there were only about twenty of us who came out and stuck. Now, to get games, as you know, you've got to schedule for two or three years, so the net result was that they built up the first year schedule with any college that had an open date. We weren't better than probably a second-rate, or if you want to be charitable, first-rate high school. They had to schedule us with anybody they could and probably the easiest team we played was Western Maryland. I think we lost every game, I'm not sure, but we played such teams as West Virginia, Wesleyan, Fordham. West Virginia itself was a powerhouse because they had an all-American fullback that year by the name of Rogers.

Also, out of this twenty, we tried to field a freshman team. Well, we didn't have enough really to do either well, so every week some night school student would come down and say, in effect, that he'd been an old Rocky Mountain halfback or something. So we'd take him out and give him a course of sprouts and the signals - signals were much simpler in those days - and then the following week we'd put him in the game and he might last a quarter, if we were lucky, after which he'd be carried out on a stretcher or limp off, and the iron men would continue.

But we had a lot of fun. They'd set up a training table in an apartment hotel up on G Street, I think it was, about 18th and G. I think it was the old Monmouth Hotel. It's gone now, I'm sure. We were the first ones that ever had night football and the reason for it was this. Where the Jefferson Memorial on the Tidal Basin is today, in those days there was a bath house. That was a bathing beach, right there, for the people of Washington. You'd go down there in the summertime and hire yourself a locker or a little room and go swimming in the Tidal Basin. And right back of that was a playing field that Brian had negotiated with the City authorities for our playing field.

This was all right in September. One doesn't mind too much in September in Washington taking cold showers. But two things happened. One was these showers got colder and colder - this was where we changed our clothes, you see, to play, and the days got shorter. Also we were dependent on some of these boys who were attending night school and a lot of them were working, so we'd get them between work hours. Maybe they'd knock off at 4:30 or 5:00 and then get down there. So then Brian got the bright idea that, after all, maybe we could have lights. So he went to the city authorities and they let him put up some poles and on every pole he put an incandescent bulb. I don't know what it cost, but they were not these big battery lights you have now. All it had was a 150-watt lamp in the thing. This was really worse than nothing because all you could see would be just that one light. You couldn't see beyond it.

Then Brian got the idea that we'd be better off if we had white footballs. Of course, nowadays, you have white leather but in those days you didn't. So he painted the footballs with whitewash. The net result of this was that after about a day's playing with them they looked more like basketballs. Somebody would call the signal and you'd drift down the field then you'd look up and you'd see a light, then just jet darkness beyond that. So you would stand there and the trick was not to catch the ball. The trick was to be quick enough to get out of the way when this white baloon came floating at you, so you didn't get hit in the face. That was the way we trained down there, and it was really something.

About November, few of us were taking showers. We were probably a little high when we got up to the training table!

I might say that I was second-string quarterback at that time. A fellow named McAllister was first-string. Sometimes I'd play on the first team and sometimes I wouldn't. If we had conflicts of dates -

Did you ever know Earl Chesney?

Q: Yes.

Adm. R.: Well, Earl Chesney was one of the boys who played on this team. Is Earl still around?

Q: No, Earl died.

Adm. R.: That's what I thought. Let me back up. Remember, football equipment in those days wasn't what it is today. As a matter of fact, I was very proud of the helmet I wore, which somebody had given me.

Q: It wasn't uniform then?

Adm. R.: Well, we had uniforms.

Q: No, I mean the equipment was not uniform?

Adm. R.: No, and of course the face mask had not been heard of in those days. My helmet, the one I played in, most of the time, was nothing in the world but a kid-glove type of thing just fitted over your head. All it would do was just keep you from being cut with a cleat. There was no padding in it. It was like a heavy leather glove, that's all.

We went over to West Virginia Wesleyan. This leads up to my story of how to tell a story. For some reason McAllister couldn't make the trip so I was the quarterback. In the first place, we had to go over the mountains to Buchanan, West Virginia. I don't know what it is today but West Virginia was sort of a powerhouse in football in those days. They were playing big teams. Going over the mountains on the old B & O it was so rough in the pullmans that we finally - the train would stop and you'd be thrown about, so most of the boys put their helmets on in the bunks to keep from having their brains battered about.

On the first kick-off the kid went for a touchdown for West Virginia. Incidentally, in those days you didn't have six referees, umpires, and linesmen on the field. You were lucky if you had two, a referee and an umpire. And somewhere along about, I think, the third quarter and we were getting desperate - the score then was something like 50 or 60 to 0 - I called a pass and I dropped back and down the field I saw John Lawler. I'm sure he's retired now but he was running an engineering concern in or around Washington up to a few years ago because I saw John just before I retired. He was a big, tall, lanky guy. I heaved the pass and the funniest thing I've ever seen on a football field happened. We were of course, eleven men on each team plus the referee and the umpire, and everybody was so aghast at this happening that the only person on the field who had sense enough to move was John. And here's John running about 60 yards down the field for a touchdown. As I say, eleven men on the other side, ten men on our side, plus the referee and umpire just standing aghast and looking at John run for the touchdown.

Well, to make the story short, the final score was 101 to 7, believe it or not! Now comes the climax to this story. Of course, we had expected to get beaten but we'd hoped it wouldn't be quite that bad. We got back to Washington and then it's not what the facts are, it's how you tell the story, because the Times-Herald had a headline, "George Washington Scores on West Virginia Wesleyan," and you had to read all the way down to the last line before you found out that the score was 101 to 7! Big headlines, you know - well it wasn't across the top but at the head of the column.

That taught me a lesson in how to tell a thing.

We had a lot of funny games. I remember the freshman team went out to play Gallaudet and I had a tackle, a big heavy fellow. All of a sudden I looked over at him and he was pale and trembling. I called time out. I couldn't figure till I got him off to one side what had happened. What had happened was that this fellow was a pretty dirty player and he was roughing up one of these boys from the Gallaudet team on the other side, and finally this opposing guard or tackle, I forget which it was, straightened up. The point was he was deaf but not dumb, and this guy hadn't realized this. So the Gallaudet player says, "Look, you so and so, if you don't cut this out I'm going to knock the hell out of you," or words to that effect. This so shocked the guy that he wasn't any good for the rest of the game and we took him out!

I think another funny one we had was when the freshman team went down to play the Naval Operating Base at Norfolk and the varsity, as such, went over to West Virginia to play West Virginia. The manager of the freshman team and the manager of the varsity had decided to bet on who would get beaten the worst, and the one that did the best would get a free dinner off the other one.

So we went down on the night boat. In those days the old Northland and the Southland used to run down to Norfolk. When we got there there was nothing to do so we took a trip round town. We got some taxis and drove around till the afternoon, when we were to play. The taxidriver said, "Oh, you boys don't have anything to worry about. The high school went out and beat them last week." So we were pretty cocky. Our freshman team averaged about 150 pounds. I only weighed 145 pounds at that time.

So we trot out on the field and out on the field comes the

Naval Operating Base team. You never saw such giants! Of course, they were small compared with professional footballers today. But I think their whole squad averaged about 190 pounds or something like that, and their main player was an Indian who had played with Thorpe. His name was Joe Wheelock. Our only hope was to run around them because, you know, 150 pounds against maybe 190, was kind of like running up against a stone wall. You'd just get bounced. Our line couldn't open up anything. But there is one thing about playing before a bunch of sailors or, I suppose, a bunch of Army men or Air Force either, as far as that's concerned, if the game isn't close they're for the underdog and it was pretty obvious right from the outset that we were the underdogs. The home team could do anything but nobody bothered cheering for them, but if we made an inch we were cheered on. I remember on one occasion I did get around the end. I was running full blast and here comes this big Joe Wheelock. He wasn't running, he was loping. And he must have hit me about ten feet inside the sideline and we lit about ten feet outside the sideline. I wasn't hurt but that was our single threat, I think, of the afternoon, and I had the whole stand cheering for me. We got beaten down there about 60 some to 0. So we slunk back to Washington thinking we were poor. But West Virginia had beaten the varsity I think about 80 or 90 to 0.

Q: Let's go back to the engineering school now.

Adm. R.: Okay. What did I learn in engineering?

Q: Yes.

Adm. R.: Not much. I only went two years and the first year I had a little surveying, calculus and regular pre-engineering. Even in those days the first year didn't vary too much from a liberal arts course. Probably a little stronger on math. I frankly couldn't tell you exactly what I had that first year, what specific subjects. I worked at the Observatory that summer and the second year they moved the early football practice and started out at the University of Maryland. This goes back to the days when Maryland had Curley Byrd. It was a long way out there and I didn't want to stay out there, and there was an opening as business manager of The Hatchet so I didn't play football the second year I was there.

I don't remember too much about the school except that we had a lot of fun. I joined a fraternity, Kappa Alpha, and about all I remember of that now is that, like all the fraternity houses around there in those days, we'd rent a house and be there about two months and then because we couldn't pay the rent and they didn't want us any longer we moved. I think during the time I was in Kappa Alpha we moved about six times.

Q: They were pretty rowdy?

Adm. R.: It wasn't that we were so rowdy, but it was a kind of hit or miss thing.

The summer after my second year at George Washington - as I told you I was working summers at the Observatory and my mother was in the computing division and we were both paid from a fund known as the Miscellaneous Fund of the Navy appropriations. For some reason the House cut the money out so it looked like Mother would have no employment and she was partly subsidizing me to go to George Washington - in fact, wholly subsidizing my tuition, I guess and I was taking care of my expense money. With both my mother and me off the payroll I wouldn't have any expense money or tuition.

About that time the Coast Guard advertised for applicants to take the cadet exam. For some reason, I don't know why, born in the Midwest, I had always thought I'd like to go to Annapolis. I had even tried to get an appointment but had had no success. We had no political affiliations. Now a lot of congressmen give competitive examinations for their appointments but not then.

Q: I think almost universally they do now.

Adm. R.: But in those days it was purely a "who do you know" type of thing. I did, I think, finally end up with a sixth alternate but that proved to be nothing at all. There was very little chance of getting an appointment, and I happened to note this advertisement in the paper, so I decided to take the examination, although frankly I didn't know what the Coast Guard was and nobody else that I knew seemed to know what it was about.

I went down and applied and was told I could take it. But about the time I was to report for the examination, the Senate restored the money and I decided that I wasn't going to take the examination.

Q: Restored the Miscellaneous Fund?

Adm. R.: Yes. In other words, what my mother and I were paid from was restored and, not knowing what the Coast Guard was, I felt why should I. I mentioned this to Miss Lamson, for whom my mother still worked and whom I saw occasionally, and she said she thought I was making a mistake and I ought to go and take the examination. She said, "You don't have to accept, even if you pass, but it's good experience. Some day you may have to take an examination in something you're really interested in." I respected her advice so I went and took the examination and was appointed.

I went to the Academy in July of that summer, that would have been 1922, with the idea that if I didn't like it I'd resign and come home to go back to college the 1st of October for my third year at George Washington. I hung up my suit forty years later, so -

Q: So you liked it when you got there?

Adm. R.: Well, I got interested and I found that it offered a great deal. It appealed to me, yes.

Q: How many students were there?

Adm. R.: The Academy then was at old Fort Trumball, an old Army fort, right across from Groton, almost directly across from the Groton Monument. It was old stone buildings and some temporary buildings. There were no students at the Academy when we arrived. There was an engineer officer in charge and one other officer. In my class, as I recall, there were thirty of us appointed that year. There was one boy who'd been at the Academy and then resigned and he'd been re-appointed. He'd been through a year of it so they put him in charge. I think he hoped to become a second classman. Then, it was a three-year course, and they had engineers and line. I guess there were five engineers and fifty who were there to be line officers.

Q: You intended to be a line officer?

Adm. R.: I was going to be a line officer, yes.

Q: In spite of your previous training?

Adm. R.: Well, you were supposed to be a graduate engineer before you took the engineering exam. Furthermore, that was mechanical and I'd been only in civil engineering.

Q: How many did you say were in your group?

Adm. R.: We apparently entered with 51 and we graduated 21. We had 30 casualties.

Q: Was that a normal kind of attrition?

Adm. R.: Yes. Coast Guard Academy attrition always had been very high.

Q: Why is that?

Adm. R.: Well, even in recent years, I'm speaking now of when I was Commandant, we had arguments with Congress over our attrition rate. They claimed it was too high, although I've never been quite sure it was as high as it was elsewhere. I'm diverting here a little bit, but, for example my older son went to VPI and I went down when he graduated, to give out commissions, and so forth to the ROTC, and I was talking to the dean of the engineering school. When I asked him what their attrition rate was, he said it all depends on how you ask the question. "Do you mean in an entering class, how many graduate in four years?" I said yes so he said, "Well, very frankly then, our attrition rate is very high. The thing you've got to remember is this. A great many boys will enter engineering and, after a year, find they don't like it and go over to, we'll say, agriculture or something else. The figures will show that they graduated as of that class. Also, we get a lot of boys who don't graduate in four, they go five and six years. When you hear these high attrition figures, you've always got to analyze them."

So I've often wondered whether our attrition rate was high primarily for an engineering school. You see, for quite a while, we were the only service school that was accredited by the ECCD. We finally lost that. But there are a number of reasons, I suppose.

Taking my own class, I just saw a name here I'd forgotten for years. He was an Indian from a reservation and he lasted exactly twelve hours. He came in one day and was gone the next, and I think sent his resignation in by postcard!

Q: Sometimes, then, it was inadequate background?

Adm. R.: Probably, or they didn't like it, and then some of them got in trouble, disciplinary trouble.

Q: What was the course like? Was it a pretty strict course?

Adm. R.: Yes, you had to keep your nose to the grindstone, and still do. They didn't have the electives in those days and you had to make the grade.

Q: Was it in a way similar to what the Naval Academy course was, learning by rote and that kind of thing?

Adm. R.: Yes, a great deal of that. I think very similar. You either made the grade or out you went. We used to figure in later years, say when the entering class was 200, that probably the graduating class, after four years - we'd gone to a four-year class by that time, would be maybe 80. In other words, probably 60 percent attrition. Whether they're doing better now or not, I don't know. Admiral Siler could tell you.

When I took the exam I don't think we had the numbers taking the exam, but when you consider that now we were only picking 200 or 250 out of maybe 6,000 applicants and therefore theoretically were getting the cream of the crop, it does seem like a pretty high attrition. But there are so many factors. Some of the boys come and they just don't like the life or, as I say, they get into trouble, and I suppose illness in some cases, some wanted to get married so they quit. There are a number of reasons. I don't know what the attrition rate is at the Naval Academy, but it might have been higher at the Coast Guard Academy.

Q: Congress, in questioning the high attrition rate in later years, was concerned because of spending money?

Adm. R.: Yes, naturally. The attrition rate at the Academy didn't worry me as much out of the Academy as it did out of the service, particularly following the war and especially our being an accredited school. At one time there was an ad run in The New York Times for Coast Guard graduates who wanted employment.

Q: In private - ?

Adm. R.: In private business. We had a lot of trouble - I'm speaking now of later years - with boys who made no pretense, they were just there for an education and to do their obligated service.

Q: What was the obligation?

Adm. R.: It was three years for a number of years.

Q: In your time, when you were there?

Adm. R.: Well, it was three years up to, I think, the sixties and then it went up to four years. I don't know what the figure is now but I should imagine with pay scales what they are, I suppose it's well over $100,000 a piece. I know I always used the figure that it cost us $60,000 or $70,000 to educate a boy through the Academy, and to me it wasn't worth it if you were only going to get three or four years. You'd do much better to train them as reserve officers and then induct them into the service if they liked it.

Q: Yes. You had a summer cruise, too, didn't you?

Adm. R.: Yes. The first summer I went to the Academy, as I say, we were the only cadets there, the upper classmen were on leave or on the summer cruise and there were only seven of them. They came back and we made a cruise over to Gardiner's Bay, just a sort of indoctrination cruise, mainly beat work, learning the rigging, and that sort of thing. Then we came back for our first scholastic year at the Academy. Then the summer of 1923, by that time, of course, we were second classmen and we made a cruise up the coast to Provincetown, over to Halifax, down to Bermuda, and back through Cape May, and back to the Academy. Then we had our leave, and I guess the incoming class went on a short Gardiner's Bay cruise.

In the summer of 1924 we went to England, to London, went up the Thames to Gravesend and were given liberty in London. Then we went to Le Havre and up to Paris, where we had liberty. From there to Lisbon, Portugal, from there to Madeira.

Q: Funchal?

Adm. R.: Funchal, that's right. From there we sailed south, dropped down to catch the Trades and sailed most of the way back to Bermuda, and from Bermuda back up to New London.

Q: This was largely by sail?

Adm. R.: Largely. We were twenty-one days going from New London to England, most of it under sail, because we had the prevailing winds with us, and coming back we were mostly under sail. I don't recall that we sailed too much from Bermuda up to New London. Time was running out and I think we steamed most of the way, but I think we did set the sails some.

As you know, the <u>Alexander Hamilton</u> was a barkentine, square on the fore, with fore and aft main and mizzen. It was good experience.

Q: It was the practical application of what you'd been learning in courses?

Adm. R.: That's right, navigation and so forth. We were first classmen and we had a lot of interesting things, some of them funny and some of them not so funny. I always remember on that last cruise in Bermuda one night. We had just arrived in Bermuda. I don't know whether you've ever been in Hamilton Harbor, but they have these big floating mooring buoys. Captain Harold Dale Hinckley was our skipper. He was also superintendent of the Academy. Harold was somewhat of an autocrat, a nice fellow, and he later was my skipper on another ship, and I liked him, but he sort of rode herd on the cadets and on this particular occasion Frankie Kenner was boat officer. We used to have a boat officer and an engineer in the boat and a bowman. Lyndon Spencer, now Vice Admiral Spencer, was the deck officer. The skipper had gone ashore, so about eight o'clock - nobody theoretically should be coming back to the ship at eight o'clock - Spencer told Frankie Kenner, the boat officer and a classmate of mine, to go up to the drug store when he got in on the 8 o'clock trip. He tied up to the dock, went up to the drug store to get Spencer a quart of icecream and while he was gone who should come down but Harold Dale Hinckley, the skipper, and he jumps in the boat and says, "Shove off, take me back to the ship."

Becky Jordan was the engineer, another classmate, and he said, "Sir, I can't. The boat officer isn't here."

"Where is he?"

"He went up to the drug store." Apparently he didn't say he had gone up there for Spencer.

"I don't care. Shove off, anyway. I'll act as coxswain."

So Harold was standing up in the boat, holding the tiller. They shoved the bow out and they went about fifteen feet, apparently, but what they'd forgotten to do was let go the stern painter! So, of course, the motor's going full blast, and Harold was thrown back on to the after thwart, on his stern, and that didn't help matters any. Then they jammed the stern line to such an extent that they couldn't untie it, so they had to cut it which, of course, was the last thing you were supposed to do.

Then, on the way back, Herb Baker, who was the bowman, was standing up in the bow - it's dark by this time - and he's not paying as much attention as he should, and they end up running bow-on into one of these big mooring buoys, cracking up the boat some. When they came alongside and Harold came up the gangway, you could have heard him halfway to the United States. He immediately said, "Who is the boat officer?"

Spencer, instead of saying he was responsible, said Cadet Kenner. This was the first night we were in Bermuda.

"Well, he's restricted for the whole time we're in Bermuda."

Spencer said, "Shall we send the boat back for him?"

"No," which broke Spencer's heart because here's Kenner standing on the dock - in those days you got your icecream in those containers, packed icecream, not like it is today - and he could see his icecream getting softer and softer. But nobody would go back until the next boat, which I think was nine or nine-thirty. So the boat went in and here comes

Kenner back up over the side with this dripping icecream. It was all milk by that time.

The payoff was that we were there about five days and the night before we were to leave they allowed the cadets to give a party for the girls in Bermuda, on the ship. Kenner was a twin. I don't know whether you've ever heard of the Kenner twins or not. They saw Bill whom they'd met ashore, then when they came aboard they met Frank and they said, "I don't remember seeing you ashore." Well, then the story came out, so they all descended on Harold, all the girls. Maybe we sicked them on to him. Incidentally, he was quite a ladies' man. I mean he liked the ladies. The girls pleaded with him and finally he relented. So the next day Frankie did get to go ashore. I'll always remember Bermuda for that.

Reverting for just a minute to taking the Coast Guard examination, the Kenner twins were from Washington, D. C., Frank and Bill Kenner. They both became admirals in the Coast Guard. Bill is still alive but Frank died a number of years ago. They were the first ones I ever met in the Coast Guard. I took the exam with them. Of course, the exam in those days was a lot different than it is now. It was one of those broad, sweeping exams. For example, you had geography, you had mathematics, you had English. Later, we went to the educational testing. Now, I guess they use the college boards.

Q: Much more scientific!

Adm. R.: Oh, yes. But in those days there was one called General Information, which asked all these fool questions like "How many home runs did Babe Ruth hit in such and such a year?" And in geography "How would you get from Murmansk to Timbuktu or something by ship? I'm exaggerating, obviously, but that type of thing.

The Kenners and I hit it off pretty well. In those days you carried your lunch and we used to go down with our lunch to the Army Medical Museum between morning and afternoon sessions and regale ourselves with how hardy our stomachs were, eating our lunches amidst all the specimens down there.

Of course, the Academy was quite a lot different in those days. It was small. We had one instructor there - I'm telling this on the understanding that, as you say, I can restrict it - Gordon T. McLean. He was a nice guy. I always liked him. He was known as "Don't Know" McLean because he had a stock statement. If you ever asked him a question his answer was "I don't know, but until I do you'll do it as I say." And he had some phobias. There was always an officer eating with the cadets and when he was eating with us he got himself a book called The Royal Air Force Manual. It was how to be an officer and so forth, and every time "Don't Know" had the duty of eating in the mess at dinner we would have to listen to extracts from The Royal Air Force Manual. One of the things that they said in there was that a left-handed person at a mess table was an abomination, and it is to a certain extent. We had about three guys in our group who were left-handed and "Don't Know" insisted on their eating right-handed. Why those guys didn't go crazy, I don't know, because they'd eaten left-handed all their lives and to be suddenly forced into right-handed eating was kind of rough on them.

This goes back to the days when you parted your hair in the middle, or some people did, and he had an idea that anybody who parted his hair in the middle was a sissy. Therefore, no cadet was allowed to part his hair in the middle.

Q: He was pretty meticulous!

Adm. R.: Oh, yes, and I'll give you some more. The only bad feature for him was that Lyndon Spencer, who had hair at that time, he's now bald, parted his hair in the middle. That made it pretty rough on "Don't Know." Nevertheless, he stuck with his guns. There were three of us, Leamey, who's now passed on, someone else, and myself. We never would part our hair in the middle but we would move it around, you know, get it close to the middle, and "Don't Know" used to get so mad at us. In fact, finally, when he handed out the company officers he made a speech and the gist of it was that if Cadets Leamey, Swan (I believe), and Richmond had been more attentive and done what they were supposed to do about their hair, they'd probably have been platoon leaders instead of squad leaders.

Another thing. In marching, you know, when you halt you're supposed to have your feet at a certain angle - and he had made a long stick with a V on it and he had a stick that was the right length between ranks. We'd be out drilling and he'd come out and give an in-place halt. I've always sworn that if you had your foot six inches off the ground when that half came, that's where you left your foot. That's exaggerating a little bit. As you've probably gathered, I'm sometimes given to hyperbole. But, basically, we in-place halted and then an upper classman, an engineer cadet would run down the line to see if we were the right distance and if you had your feet at the right angle. Anybody who didn't have his feet at the right angle had a rough time.

But, as I say, it was fun. One of the wildest things that happened while I was there - and this I was pretty lucky on, too. Cadets didn't get as much then as they do now by any means. I've forgotten what we got, but I think it was $80 a month or something like that, and your mess bill was reasonably high.

Q: Most of your money went for mess?

Adm. R.: Yes. Anyway, everybody was complaining about not having enough money. Jimmy Pine was the exec and "Don't Know" was commandant of cadets and they sent down word to us that if we weren't getting enough money we should make up a budget.

I was getting by and I wasn't too much worried, anyway, but I thought there was something suspicious about this. This was too easy. There were three of us who didn't make up a budget. We decided there was nothing doing.

Q: You were satisfied with your $80?

Adm. R.: Well, we weren't satisfied but we weren't going to be sucked into anything. The net result of these budgets was that the government would have had to pay the cadets about $150 a month for them to live within their budget. In other words, it wasn't a budget for $80, it was a budget for $150. As I say, it really wasn't a budget, they were supposed to estimate what they thought they needed.

You can guess what happened. They said, okay, since you can't manage your money properly, we will keep the money - oh, I think the boys who had made out these budgets were allowed $3 or $4 for candy and shaving cream and so forth - and anything you need, whether it was to get a taxicab because you had to get a taxicab to bring girls to the dances and things like that, because you couldn't walk them down through Spar Yard Alley - Fort Trumball was down where Little Italy is - you'll have to get a requisition.

Three or four months after this all happened - at eight o'clock in the morning they read out the pap sheets - one morning they read out "F. T. Kenner, 20 demerits for unauthorized assumption of funds. W. W. Kenner, 20 demerits for unauthorized assumption of funds." Well, the Kenners sort of blinked. They didn't know what it was all about. As soon as the formation broke up, we all crowded around and asked them, "What did you do, steal some money, or what? What happened." They didn't know. In those days, we had no barber on the place and you had to go down town, so what had happened was that they needed a haircut. They had gotten the required requisitions and they'd gone down to the barbershop we all went to and, at the end of getting their hair cut the barber said to them, "Do you want some foufou on your hair?" And the boys said, "Yes." In those days, you know, they used to sprinkle cologne or something on, so he rubbed it in their hair. I think the hair cut requisition was for 35¢ and the foufou was 10¢, more than the requisition. This is what they got those 20 demerits for, and those demerits stuck. They never got those demerits off. That was the unauthorized assumption of funds! People won't believe some of the stories.

Q: Rather incredible, isn't it?

Adm. R.: The thing that probably really hurt us the worst financially - you see, when you came into the Academy you were supposed to have enough money to buy your uniforms, and our class was really hit because our first set of uniforms were straight-up hats, choker collars, and buttoned-down fronts.

Then, while I was there, they changed the uniform to the open coat, more flared hats, and so forth. The cadet uniforms were gotten through an outfit known as the Baltimore Uniform Company. It seems to me there was one other change that was made. Some of the uniforms didn't fit too well anyway. I guess Baltimore Uniform was a sweat-shop type of operation. But we were resentful, so when we graduated - Rosenberg or Rosenthal or whatever his name was who owned the place, a nice old Jewish gentleman, would come up and offer you all kinds of things if you bought from him - and we were loaded for him. He came up to sell us our officer uniforms and we just jumped on him. One classmate felt so sorry for him he finally did buy from him. We didn't have the money, but what we wanted was to get ours from the best uniform company in the country. At that time, it was Rice and Duvall. All of us paid about twice as much as we would have at the other place simply because we felt that, as cadets, we'd been ribbed.

Q: You had to borrow the money to do it, I suppose?

Adm. R.: Well, they gave us credit, but we were in hock for about a year after we graduated. But we got good uniforms, I'll say that.

One of the things at the Academy that I was most proud of was that we were the first class since 1912 to put out a yearbook. I ended up being editor in chief.

Richmond #1 - 42

Q: Your work on the <u>Hatchet</u>, apparently, had had some influence.

Adm. R.: No, I don't think that. You might like to look this over before you leave because I think the artwork and everything that was done in it is quite good, considering it was a small group that was working.

Going back to the cruise, it does seem to me that on that cruise, that coastwise cruise, we went to Washington for some reason. That would be the 1923 cruise.

Q: You mean she came up the Chesapeake Bay?

Adm. R.: Yes, and why we went to Washington that year I really don't know.

Q: From the dates in this biography, you were only there two years?

Adm. R.: Yes, a little over two years. Just about that time the rum war started and they expanded the Coast Guard, so we graduated in September of 1924, right after we came back from the cruise. We had no scholastic work that I recall that year.

Q: And that was because they needed your services?

Adm. R.: Presumably. They were bringing out the 75-footers to go after the rummies.

Incidentally, I notice here in the three cruises I made we cruised a total of, by our figures, 12,750 miles.

We graduated in September but it was a kind of funny situation for my class. We hadn't all gone in at the same time, in July 1922. We'd all gone in but one classmate, Roy Raney, who had been in the Navy. Whether he hadn't been discharged from the Navy when he came or whether he came later, I'm not sure. Anyway, he was appointed a cadet about four days or six days after the rest of us. Then we had one classmate, Perkins, who, because he was under age, had to be an enlisted man. He didn't become of age until October 18th.

Q: What was the minimum age?

Adm. R.: The minimum age for a cadet then was 18, but you could be an enlisted man if you were under 18.

Now, we graduated in September and presumably were not going to get our commissions - oh, and you had to be a cadet at least two years, so presumably we had to wait, if we were all to be commissioned at the same time, until Perkins' two years from the time he became of age. This sounds very complicated but I think you see the point. So, we all got our assignments and Richards and myself were sent to Washington and given leave till the 1st of October, still as cadets because we couldn't be commissioned.

Richards and I reported in and Admiral Ballard said "Why are you in cadet uniform?"

"Well, because we can't be commissioned."

"Why can't you two be commissioned?"

There was no reason why because we had served our two years. We had come in in July. The class commissions were broken. Richards and I were commissioned as of October 1st, Raney and everybody below him to Perkins were commissioned as of October 6th or 7th, which completed his two years as a cadet, then about October 18th Perkins and everybody below were commissioned. So, on the record, although we graduated as a class, all in September, our commission dates were spread into three groups.

Q: The regular course was a three-year course but because of circumstances -

Adm. R.: Because of circumstances we got out in two years.

Q: And what about that third year of study which normally you would have gotten?

Adm. R.: We were supposed to be bright enough to absorb it by active-duty service, I guess. Maybe they were mistaken! But

Richmond #1 - 45

anyway they needed officers and we were sent out. From then on I had two years at Headquarters.

Q: What kind of duties did you have there?

Adm. R.: I was assigned in the commandant's office as junior aide. Admiral Billard was commandant at the time. He had succeeded Admiral Reynolds, who had been commandant when I entered the Academy. Admiral Billard, I think, had been commandant for at least a year, maybe a year and a half, when I went there.

At that time Coast Guard Headquarters was in an old building that was at the corner, the northwest corner, of 14th and E Streets, across from what is now the Commerce Building. I always understood it had been a stable at one time and had been made into an office building. It was a two-story building. At that time Headquarters only had about 60 civilians, military, and everybody else. You've also got to understand that the Coast Guard at that time had come out of the war with the Lifesaving Service and it was still pretty much of a divided organization, in that it was like Boston, you know, the Lowells speak only to Cabots, and the Cabots speak only to God. The military were the old Revenue Cutter Service and ran almost independently. This isn't to say there was any friction, it was just that the man in charge who had come over from the Lifesaving Service was a Mr. Maxim, who I later become very fond of, a wonderful gentleman. If a surfman had a problem he was the one who handled it, under, obviously, the direction of the commandant.

It was a pretty tight little organization. There was a pay office, an operations and personnel office, a law office, as such, which I'll describe later. Down on the first floor they had the personnel records, which brings me back to my theory about women in charge. The lady in charge was a Mrs. Morgan, and you practically had to get permission to enter these files surreptitiously. She ran that place with an iron hand. It was properly handled and she was very nice, but she could be a martinet, if there ever was one.

In our office the aide was - I guess he was a commander at the time - Steve Yeandle. Steve was noted particularly for his reddish hair and red beard, which led to stories in the service later. When he was on a destroyer, for example, the destroyer had a goat and came back one time with its beard painted with red lead.

Q: That brings a question. Beards were permitted in the service?

Adm. R.: Oh, yes. One of the most handsome officers was old Captain Read and he had a full beard, a full set. Steve's was the van Dyke type. Steve did the politicking on the Hill, primarily and that sort of thing, being aide. I was junior aide and that meant being sort of an odd man for anything that came along.

We didn't have any girls in the office then. The Admiral's yeoman was a little English fellow, naturalized obviously, named "Kewpie" Allen, and when "Kewpie" wasn't working on anything else he worked on his stamp collection. Then we had a civilian in there by the name of Chick Clark. Chick had been with the Coast Guard for years. He and I worked together. He had a large family, so he used to moonlight by driving a taxi at night. Of course, in those days the commandant did not have a car at his disposal. He had to have his own private car. As I recall, Admiral Billard had an old car and Chick used to drive Mrs. Billard and the Admiral on occasion. Steve had an old Studebaker and by that time I had bought a car. I had an old Hupmobile. Steve owned a cabin up the river, above Chain Bridge, and sometimes he couldn't get his car out after he'd been up there, either because the car was stuck or because he was so chicken, and Chick and I would have to take my Hupmobile and go out there.

You were asking what my jobs were. I had this Hupmobile rigged up with block and tackle and all the wrecking equipment necessary. In those days you didn't have snow tires and so forth, so we'd go out and salvage the Studebaker and bring it back for Steve.

I've told others and I think I mentioned to you that in one of the back offices operations and personnel had four desks. Operations was under a Captain Crisp. These four desks were shoved right together so that they made one big expanse. Opposite him sat, as I recall it, Warner Keith Thompson, then a lieutenant commander or a commander, who was Assistant Operations Officer. Next to Crisp sat Captain Benny Chiswell, who was Officer Personnel, and opposite him sat Frank Gorman, who was Enlisted Personnel Officer. As I say, it was a very tight, efficient organization. Operations knew what Personnel was doing, and Personnel knew what Operations was doing.

Every Friday evening, Benny Chiswell would bring the little blue register which we had in those days in to see Admiral Billard and they would decide the fates of those who were going to be transferred in the next week. Enlisted personnel was handled back there. In off moments they regaled themselves, particularly Frank Gorman and Warner Keith Thompson, both these gentlemen are deceased now so I don't think I belittle them any, they both liked to gamble. Back of Chiswell sat a chief warrant officer by the name of Wantke and across from him sat Twine, who was the Operations yeoman for dictation. You could see the bulletin board over on the Post building, diagonally across the street from CG Headquarters, which was then right next to the National Theater. They used to have a board up there that in the summertime had the baseball games playing, electronically. Then in the fall and spring they posted the races, and since both Warner Keith and Gorman liked to play the races one of Wantke's jobs was to race up to the front window in the hall next to the commandant's office to see the result of each race as it came up and rush back and tell them so that they could place their bets with a bookmaker for the next race. It never interfered with the efficiency of the operation.

Q: Incidentally, what was the total personnel of the Coast Guard at that time?

Adm. R.: I once figured it up that when I graduated from the Academy I was 155 - I believe I'm right but it could have been as much as 170 - from the top. So we had probably less than 200 officers in the service and about 3,000 men. There were very few civilians. When I say 3,000 men, I think I'm including the surfmen. Of course, at that time there were a lot more lifeboat stations than there are now. I think we had about 250 lifeboat stations.

As I say, I was a sort of jack of all trades.

Q: It was certainly a vantage point, wasn't it, to get a picture of the whole operation?

Adm. R.: Well, yes. As I look back, I wonder now. You might be interested in this story.

I guess I'd been at headquarters two or three months when

Admiral Billard called me in one morning and said:

"Richmond, Commander Nash died last night."

"Yes, Sir, I heard that."

"There are just Mrs. Nash and her sister in the house and until the funeral I think they ought to have a man in the house."

I said, "Yes, Sir."

"I'm going to call Mrs. Nash and offer your services."

"Yes, Sir, that's all right."

"You get in uniform and go out there at five o'clock tonight."

Commander Nash who was retired had died the day before that. So, at five o'clock I show up at this typical row house in Washington, out in northwest Washington. I'd never met the Nashes, so I introduced myself, and they said come in. I went in, and it was a typical house, you know, with the living room the front room, dining room or sitting room next, and kitchen at back. We sit there and at seven o'clock people were supposed to come in. I'm in uniform with one stripe on, very proud of my one stripe.

They came in to pay their respects and it was pretty obvious right from the beginning that this is going to be an embarrassing situation because the names Richmond and Nash don't quite jive and these people would wonder what I was doing there, whether I'm an illegitimate offspring or something. But they were very polite. Then I learned another thing about funerals, or about these sad occasions when people come around. There's a certain triteness and sameness in what they all have to say. I guess no one ever passed on without your finding that they really were the best person in the world. They can't all be best but that particular family is the best.

Q: A lot of that, don't you think, is induced by embarrassment?

Adm. R.: I think it is, yes, because by about 10:30 I was kind of wishing somebody would come in and say, in effect, "I remember when Nash and I raided the bar in such and such a place." Finally you begin to wonder whether this guy was as good as they're saying.

We were in this middle room and the corpse was laid out in the parlor. Eleven o'clock is deadline, so we throw everybody out and lock up. Then comes the payoff. Mrs. Nash said:

"I haven't told you this before, but we only have two bedrooms available upstairs. The commander and I slept in one and my sister has the other, so we have no place for you to sleep except on this love seat in the living room. I'll bring you some blankets and a pillow."

Well, I don't know whether you've ever tried to sleep on a short settee like a love seat. You debate whether to hang your knees and feet over one end or your neck over the other. Finally about two o'clock in the morning I was sorely tempted to go in and take Commander Nash out of the casket and climb in myself. But I forebore. I thought that would be a little disrespectful, so I stuck it out until morning, and I have to confess I did not go to the cemetery to see Commander Nash buried the next day. I'd had all I wanted of Commander Nash.

There's another angle on that I might mention. At that time we had no regulations for the consignment of corpes to Arlington Cemetery, so the net result was that whenever you had a death from out in the field and then sent to Arlington for burial, they'd arrive at Union Station in Washington and you'd have to go through all kinds of flipflops to get a permit from the District of Columbia to move them to National Cemetery. I found out, however, that if consigned to Arlington they'd still arrive in Washington but you wouldn't have to go through all this. It would just be a matter of transshipment.

So Chick Clark and I got our heads together - this was a little bit after this Nash affair and I'd had several burials in the meantime - and dubbed ourselves "Flags, Funerals, and Ceremonies." And I wrote the first regulation in the Coast Guard - that is, to be incorporated in our regulations - for the handling of the remains to get them across Washington, D. C.. Not that it was any elaborate job, it was mainly a matter of instruction what to do and how to do it so that we wouldn't have all this rigamorole of going to the District Building and getting permits to move the body across town and all that kind of monkey business.

I had another experience along this line the next year. We moved a ship out of the lakes - I think it was the old Tuscarora - down the St. Lawrence, around Nova Scotia. It was a small ship and couldn't carry too many provisions, so they decided to stop off at/Shelby, Nova Scotia, to get some fresh provisions. Apparently, as I recall the story now, you couldn't get in to Shelby, they had no dock, so you had to anchor off and it was fairly shoal. So they sent a boat crew in under a boatswain and I suppose half a dozen men. They got in and they got the provisions and started back and decided to sail, which was a mistake because it got caught in a gust of wind. The boat capsized and five of them were drowned. The undertaker in Shelby was to take care of the bodies.

I think two of the bodies were sent to their homes for burial and three of them came to Arlington, and this was a lesson in the well-known fact that somebody doesn't pass the word. The morning of the day when the burial was to be held in Arlington, why, all hell broke loose. Congressmen started calling and so forth and so on. What had happened was that - I think it was the boatswain - I could be wrong about that - had been shipped home to I think Cleveland and his burial was to have taken place the day before. Anyway after he got there his wife decided at the last minute that she wanted to take one last look at the beloved, so they opened up this wooden packing case and instead of being in a silk-lined casket, here's the boatswain laid out in excelsior, no casket. Also, apparently from the stories that came in later, your beard grows after death to a degree - I think he'd been embalmed but he had one or two days' growth of beard. He didn't look the best in the world, as I understand it.

With that, she went into a deep faint. Then people complained to their congressmen. I think this happened at another place, but that's the one I remember distinctly.

Admiral Billard gave me the job of going over to Arlington Cemetery and getting the superintendent and going into the vault where the bodies were laid out and seeing that everything was all right. What had happened apparently was that Shelby being a small place, they ran out of caskets. Later we learned they told the people on the Tampa, which had been sent up there - about being short of caskets, that's when I learned that you can't depend on someone passing the word - and we were supposed to have known this but we didn't know it.

Q: But the caskets were proper ones in Arlington?

Adm. R.: In Arlington, yes. We got through that one all right. I think there were two caskets missing and it was just unfortunate that that woman had that experience. Of course, there were apologies all around and it was straightened out, but you learn fast when you have to go through some of these things.

I hadn't been at Headquarters more than about three months when Admiral Billard called me in and said - our legal officer then was Judge Harrington, a nice old gentleman, and he had a couple of assistants, and of course legal work in those days in the Coast Guard was mainly the courts and a few contracts and that was about it, deck courts, they called them in those days. Decks and generals were about all you had and most of them were deck.

"Judge Harrington is going on leave for about three weeks, so I'm going to make you legal officer."

"Yes, Sir." Two years at the Academy and now I'm suddenly legal officer! I went in to see Harrington and I said:

"Judge, I hear you're going on leave."

"Yes, I'm going on leave."

The judge was a nice guy but he was getting pretty old and he was always drooling. I said:

"What do I do?"

"Oh, the boys will show you. All you do is review the courts. That's about all you'll have to do."

"Yes, but I don't know anything about review."

"Well, I tell you," he said - of course he was being facetious - but I still remember it, "when you look at these deck courts, if the boy's got a good Irish name, let him off.

If he hasn't got an Irish name, stick him."

That was my introduction to being the chief legal officer. I got by for three weeks.

I have one story that you might enjoy because it was one of the wildest affairs that we ever had, from my standpoint, in Washington.

About that time we had had a serial made called "Casey of the Coast Guard." I don't know whether you remember "The Perils of Pauline," but it was one of those kind of things. I think it was forty reels, two reels a week, and it was made by the Pathe company. As consideration for making this, they had taken out the spicier parts and boiled it all down to seven reels, which were in our vault. It was a horrible thing, I guess, but that was the temper of the times. As you can guess, forty reels, even with the lead-ins and the lead-outs that they have made, Casey was a pretty busy Coast Guard officer. If he wasn't jumping from a submarine to an aeroplane or vice versa or something like that, he really just didn't have a chance to do anything else but keep going.

Q: Was this run in theaters?

Adm. R.: Oh, yes, it was a regular serial, just like "The Perils of Pauline" or any of the rest of them. But, as I say, for the Coast Guard they made it seven reels - they boiled it down to seven reels for our records. That would be a a classic if someone could get hold of it. I don't remember the actor's name but I do remember the actress was a Helen Ferguson, I suppose long since gone. I don't know why I happen to remember that.

Anyway, about that time, down to Headquarters came a little guy by the name of Boggs to see Steve Yeandle. I'm hazy on just what he was representing. I have a feeling that he was in the Interior Department. Why in the Interior, I don't know. It might have been Commerce. Boggs had it in for the Wardman Park Theater and he was putting on a series of educational programs to educate the people on their various governmental departments. He had suddenly discovered the Coast Guard. Incidentally, in my forty years in the Coast Guard I've always been running into people who were imbued with the idea that nobody knew anything about the Coast Guard and it was up to them to enlighten them. I mean either they wanted to have a movie about it or a book or something, and I grant that within limits they were right, but sooner or later I'm hoping the Coast Guard will get discovered.

Boggs approached Steve on the idea wouldn't it be a good idea for them to put on a joint show featuring the Coast Guard. Yes, Steve thought this was a good idea. So they decided that they would put on as a feature the seven reels of "Casey of the Coast Guard". Everytime the news reels that they used to have in those days had anything on the Coast Guard, whether it was rescue or something like that, they'd send us clippings and we had them down in the vault. That was another one of my jobs, to look at these things and see if they were any good. So they decided that I would put together one reel of Coast Guard activities - no sound, it was just a matter of splicing them. I did that. We didn't have any band in those days and that was another of my jobs later - as I say, as you go through life you get all kinds of incidental information from these jobs that you get. Anyhow, they decided that they would have the Navy band. This was fine, but here's another case of somebody who doesn't pass the word.

Apparently, shortly thereafter this fellow Boggs, who was kind of an officious little guy - little people seem to kind of run to that, calls up the Navy Yard, or the Naval Gun Factory, gets the admiral on the phone who hasn't heard anything about this. I'm only guessing at what was said but I presume, having met Boggs, that the gist of it to this admiral was "have your band out there at such and such a time." And since the admiral hadn't heard about this at all, you can just imagine what he told Boggs over the phone. The first we heard about it was when this hit the fan. Boggs calls up Yeandle and says, in effect, the admiral says we can go jump in the lake. Well, Yeandle lets out a scream and says:

"Richmond, you go down and see what you can do about getting the band."

Having heard the details of what had happened, I said - well, I only have one stripe on my arm and going down and talking to a rear admiral - I'm not going to get any place. So I went in to see Admiral Billard and said:

"There's been a hitch. Somebody's got this messed up. We aren't going to get any place unless you make the request. Will you write a letter?" I think the admiral's name at the Gun Factory was Andrews. So Admiral Billard wrote a very nice letter, in which he explained the circumstances, that we'd like to have the courtesy of the band and so forth, and gave me the letter.

Q: Which is what should have been done in the first place?

Adm. R.: Yes. Actually, I think Yeandle would have done that but this guy Boggs, you know, you get these free-wheeling promoters and that's what he was really.

I took the letter down to the Gun Factory and get into the chief of staff's office, "You can't see the admiral. I'll take the letter in." I didn't tell him but, remembering my school "Message to Garcia" and all, I thought no, this has got to go through. So I cooled my heels down in the Gun Factory there for three days. I just sat there and said:

"No, I'm delivering this personally." They wouldn't throw me out. They were polite enough not to do that, but they'd glower at me. "The admiral says he can't see you." So I sat there and on the third day, late in the afternoon, I guess they decided that they'd better give up. Either they were going to have a permanent resident there or I was going to see the admiral. They let me in to see the admiral, who was very nice. I delivered the letter and told him that Admiral Billard had asked me to deliver that to him personally. He said they would think about it.

Then the thing started really to go haywire. In the first place, Boggs for some reason or other was touting the diplomatic corps. Of course Steve was touting the Hill. Well, there were only 500 seats in that theater, so they decided they'd divide them equally, 250 to each one. Then Steve got to thinking. After all, even in those days there were over 300 congressmen and senators on the Hill, I guess pretty close to 400 all together. Then, of course, everybody at Headquarters. So Steve decided that after all maybe we'd better have some more tickets. So he sent down to the print shop and printed up some more tickets.

Q: More tickets than you had seats?

Adm. R.: Oh, definitely. He only had 250 seats. And the worst of these darned tickets was that when we printed them - I didn't have too much to do with it, I can't claim credit for it - but they didn't just say admission for one, they said come and bring your friends or words to that effect.

Now we get ready for the big affair.

Richmond #1 - 61

Q: Had the band been granted?

Adm. R.: Yes, we'd heard we were going to have the band. Then we decided we'd bring the <u>Apache</u>, which was then stationed in Baltimore, around and use the crew to decorate the hall with signal flags and so on. That was the only bright spot of this catastrophe. Apparently Harry Wardman, who built the Wardman Park, was an Englishman and he had served in the armed forces of His Majesty, I think as a Marine, because most of his employees at that time were ex-Marines or, If not Marines, ex-Navy men. I don't think there were any Army in the group.

Well, when I took this group of boys out there, enlisted men, nothing was too good for them. I think they put them in the bridal suite to change their clothing into their work clothes, and those boys left Washington after this affair thinking the Capitol and the public buildings down there were just small fry as compared with Wardman Park. They had two dining rooms, one where they'd feed chauffeurs and that sort of thing. They did feed them in there but gave them the menu and said pick out anything you want. Well, you know, to turn a bunch of sailors who'd been eating in a general mess loose - no wonder. You'd send a guy on an errand and he'd come back in a half hour with a big steak sandwich and a glass of, not milk, but half and half. Those boys really lived high on the hog there for a couple of days.

Anyway, we get ready for the big night. There were two outside aisles and then two aisles down the center and there used to be a long pair of steps coming down to the lobby of the theatre from the hotel lobby, and then there's a kind of drop down to where the seats are when you go in. We'd roped off about thirteen rows of seats to be held for the senior officers of the Coast Guard and guests. We'd passed the word that this was going to get crowded. So most of the people on the in arrived about six for an eight o'clock show and by seven o'clock practically every seat in the place was filled up.

Ogden Mills was then Under Secretary or Assistant Secretary of the Treasury and he'd been invited but he was having a big dinner party and he had thirteen guests. He was to arrive and some of the roped-off seats were for his party. Our boys were acting as ushers. Steve was head usher and I was his assistant. Then our boys all dressed in their nice uniforms were the ushers.

Well, when the band arrived - the Navy had gone from feast to famine but we went from famine to feast - because I think they not only sent the Navy band, I think they'd gone out and gathered every sailor in the yard that could blow a horn or anything and sent them out. It was good music. I don't mean to criticize the music, but it was now that we're in this thing we're going to do it right. So the result was we had to bring in extra seats. We had the orchestra spread all the way across the front, across both front entrances, where you go up to the stage. You had to fight your way through the band to get up to the stage. So right away we're in violation of the fire laws because you're not supposed to block those entrances.

Now the crowd begins to arrive, and by seven or seven-fifteen a senator would come up and say I'm Senator So and So, and I'd have to say, "I'm sorry, Senator, there are no seats left. I'm awful sorry, but you're a little late."

About eight o'clock we got the show off with a bang. Admiral Billard made a few introductory remarks on the stage about this thing. By this time we were putting chairs down all the aisles. We had all the aisles blocked. There was a solid mass of people all the way across. If the fire marshal had come in there that night we'd still be in Leavenworth, the whole bunch of us, but fortunately they didn't.

Boggs had a sister and how she got into the program I never quite knew, but she made a few remarks after Admiral Billard's, I suppose to introduce Boggs' part, from the stage. Things were going pretty well up to that point. Then they put on my reel. Everything was beautiful on that, except that in my haste to get this thing together I had made a stupid mistake. There was one shot of a breeches buoy and instead of having the breeches buoy coming from the ship to shore, I'd put it in backwards so it went out to the ship.

Fortunately, it was a short shot and if anyone noticed it I never heard about it!

Everything was filled up except the seats we were holding for the Under Secretary of the Treasury and his guests, and I looked down and the ropes had gone. I said:

"What in the name of God happened?"

He said: "Well, that lady who was on the stage came down and she saw those empty seats and people standing so she said 'Take the ropes off.'" I could understand the boy. After all, if she was on the stage, she must know what she's doing.

So I figured, well, if there ever was a time to abandon ship, this is it! Ogden Mills hasn't arrived yet and the show had already started. I figured it was time for me to go home. I'm going up those long steps about three at a time on my way for Virginia. I get right to the top and here is the Under Secretary of the Treasury with his guests, all eager to see "Casey of the Coast Guard." He said:

"I'm sorry we're late but I'm sure we'll enjoy seeing the feature. Will you take us to our seats?"

There aren't any seats at this point, you see. I will say for him he was a pretty good sport. I stuttered a little bit and decided I'd better go back and see Commander Yeandle. He was the top usher not me. I get hold of Yeandle and he says, "What are we going to do?"

I said, "Well, there's a little room along here in the back," on those three or four steps you go down, "I'll get some more chairs." So he agreed. He was very nice. They sat back there on these temporary chairs. They knew they were late and they didn't know about the other fiasco.

By that time I figured nothing else could happen and I thought I'd wait it out. I had two guests there of my own. Did you ever know Admiral Nagmin in the Navy, he was in command of the Squalus, the one that was sunk off Portland. He wasn't an admiral then. He married Frances Davis and Captain Mex Keith married Hazel Davis. I had known them at George Washington and when I came home from the Academy we used to double date with midshipmen and all that sort of thing, and I had invited them. I remember Hazel coming out and saying:

"We didn't know an ensign in the Coast Guard had to go through so much until we saw this film tonight."

I said: "Sister, you don't know half of what an ensign in the Coast Guard has to go through!"

So much for "Casey of the Coast Guard."

Q: But it did publicize the Coast Guard?

Adm. R.: Oh, yes, it publicized the Coast Guard.

Q: To Washington officialdom.

Adm. R.: Oh, yes, diplomatic and those who got in. That was a terrible movie.

Richmond #1 - 66

Q: Tell me about the special duty that you had, not that those you've described weren't special, but I mean the other duty that had to do with -

Adm. R.: About that time we were getting into trying to suppress the rum business and the way it was operating was that these schooners - Newfoundland schooners - would come down and they'd anchor just outside the 12-mile limit. Twelve miles hadn't become official yet, but they stayed out twelve miles, just off the Jersey coast there, from New York down. For the people running the rum it was just like going to the grocery store. They'd go out at night and shop up and down from ship to ship, I suppose. It wasn't the organized thing that it became later. If you had a good speed boat, you'd just go out and take your chances, buy up a load and bring it in.

Q: Were these private citizens who did this?

Adm. R.: Yes, but, as I say, later it became organized because they needed more money and they built special boats to bring it down and they had special faster boats to go out. But in the beginning it was just as I say, I think just sort of hit or miss. There may have been some groupings of gangsters that had several boats, but the tie-in was not necessarily back to the source. That's the point I'm trying to make. It was an individual schooner bringing the liquor down to sell it, as a farmer might bring in a load of produce to sell. It wasn't a case of owning it right on through until it was distributed.

The Coast Guard decided that the best way to lick this thing was to set up a picket line. So they collected all of the ships that they could get -

Q: All the Coast Guard ships?

Adm. R.: All the Coast Guard ships - and, in effect, we cruised to stay with these ships twelve miles off the coast there, on the theory that if you're coming out to buy liquor you're not going to buy liquor if there's a Coast Guard ship standing right by. Captain Willy Wheeler was to be the fleet commander and Admiral Billard decided that Captain Wheeler needed an aide, both to code messages and take care of the peper work and that sort of thing. So I was assigned to be the aide, so Willy and I went up and went aboard the Tampa and cruised out there. I spent forty or forty-one days, I've forgotten which, out there, off the Jersey Coast within sight of the lights of New York.

Q: Was this a seasonal thing?

Adm. R.: I've even forgotten now what time of the year it was.

It must have been in the spring of 1925 but I'm not sure about that.

Q: From May to July?

Adm. R.: Of 1925?

Q: Yes.

Adm. R.: I guessed it right then.

Q: I mean the rum-runners, was this a seasonal thing?

Adm. R.: No, no, they had been there year round. I suppose if the weather got real bad they'd stay off the coast and come back. It was a question of supply and demand and as long as the demand was there, they were under this prohibition thing, why, they were in there.

As I say, I spent forty-one days off the New Jersey coast. We could see the lights of New York in the sky. Of course, the ship had to go in and we went over to the old Gresham, I think it was, for three or four days while the ship went to fuel and then back to the Tampa.

Most of the schooners had up-anchored, decided they couldn't sell their stock and gone on home.

Q: You had the legal right to apprehend the people who came

from the shore?

Adm. R.: Oh, yes. We couldn't touch the schooners. They were selling, so they closed shop and went home.

Q: But the people who came from shore and loaded up you could apprehend?

Adm. R.: Oh, yes, but they didn't come. Knowing we were out there and they stood a chance of being caught, and we were supplemented by smaller boats. If they got free they could run away from almost anything we had, but the point was that we could move right up alongside if they came close. We had practically ships for ship. That was about what it amounted to. Sometimes you might have to handle two ships. It was really quite successful.

Q: What percentage of them would you apprehend?

Adm. R.: We didn't apprehend any because with us out there, as I say, we were sort of a picket line. There may have been one or two that dared us but, generally speaking, I think they figured they'd outwait us. We'd quit and then the ships would come back. Our ships would be needed some place else and they'd outwait us, so they just stopped running it for the forty-odd days we were there. Then the schooners departed.

They had the same thing up in Boston, as far as the schooners were concerned. It wasn't quite as pronounced a line.

Then they sent for Captain Wheeler to come in for a conference because, as I say, the schooners were departing and it looked like it was successful. They left the Gresham as flagship. Captain Ben Brockway was the skipper of the Gresham. He became fleet commander in Willy's absence and he thought he needed an aide. Well, Ben Brockway needed an aide like I needed a hole in the head, and I knew what was going to happen because they were shorthanded. So Willy said:

"I think I ought to send you over to the Gresham while I go in for this conference."

I said that was all right, so I arrived at 11:45 p.m. and here's Ben Brockway and Ray Hall, who was the exec, and their first words to me when I said "Reporting aboard, Sir," were:

"Okay, you've got the midwatch."

So I had time just to throw my stuff in.

They didn't think much of this. They thought the whole thing was a lot of horseplay, anyway, so they were out to ride me. We had a day or so there, then all of a sudden there was a distress case down off Bermuda, so the Gresham took off for this.

By this time, as a result of this conference, they'd decided to move all the ships up off Boston and Willy would take command up there. So Willy wanted his aide back and the air began to get filled with the question "Where's Richmond?" You'd have thought I was really important. After all, I was only an ensign.

Meantime, I was having a good time. After he found that I wasn't rising to the bait of being ribbed a little bit, Ben Brockway was telling me how I should make my fortune in Kennicott Copper and so forth and so on. We discussed stocks. I didn't have any money and I didn't have any stocks, but he had some and he was giving me advice as to how I should make my fortune in the stock market. I don't think he ever did, so I don't know that the advice was too good, but it passed the time away. Meantime we were cruising down off Bermuda, looking for this ship, but Ben wouldn't answer the messages and no one knew where the Gresham was. He was just stubborn enough not to say. Then they would kid themselves about faking orders that I had been transferred to the Gresham and so forth.

We finally got back after a week or so and went up off Boston and continued the patrol up there.

Q: Did they think it was being more effective up there?

Adm. R.: No, but we wanted to chase them away up there, and that really was the end of Rum Row, as such. That is what it was called.

Q: Whose idea was this, anyway?

Adm. R.: I can't tell you. It was dreamed up at Headquarters as a way. I suppose Admiral Billard and Captain Crisp probably between them thought this was maybe one way of breaking it up. And it did. It broke it up.

Q: Was it publicized? Did it get in the press?

Adm. R.: I can't answer you truthfully. I don't know. This much I know. Up to that time, there'd be articles in the paper about if you want liquor all you've got to do is go out in your boat 12 miles and buy it from the ships, just like you go to the grocery store. They didn't put it that way, but that's what it amounted to. I suppose people who wanted to have a nice binge, if they had a yacht they'd just go out and buy some for local consumption, for home consumption.

But it did change the whole aspect of the rum war, because then it became a syndicate deal and they began to build these special boats, heavily powered, very low silhouette, and, I suppose, terrible living conditions. They were carriers, that was all.

Q: And they originated in Canada, did they?

Adm. R.: Yes. They'd come out of St. Pierre and Miquelon

and Nova Scotia. Also, the syndicate got speed boats and they had communications and would work on rendezvous. That's when we went into the destroyers.

Q: You had to have faster boats?

Adm. R.: Well, the destroyers were not really adequate. I don't know just how many years it took to swing over from Rum Row per se to this method of bringing them down by these specially built boats. Most of them were 50, 60, 75, or 80 feet long, low silhouette, just a small cabin -

Q: Then, you say, it was an organized effort?

Adm. R.: It was organized.

Q: The Mafia, I suppose, got into it?

Adm. R.: I can't say that. I don't know. I would presume yes, that probably somewhere along the line they did.

Gradually they worked to the point where, as I say, they'd come down, have a given date when they were going to meet, and the boats would run out, make their rendezvous, pick up their cargo, and run in.

We'd got the 75-footers and we'd gotten the smaller boats, too. But it was never a fair game. We made a number of seizures, but I'm talking now about 1926 and 1927. I wasn't in it at that time so I can't really give you the facts. I could give you the names of people who were in it and know more about it.

Q: When these boats made their rendezvous, loaded up, and came back, where did they dock?

Adm. R.: Oh, there are plenty of little coves and things they'd come in. It had gotten organized to the point where - you see, a lot of people said, "Why can't you catch them? You can build just as fast boats." But here's the difference. They had certain rendezvous dates. They might make one trip a week or two trips a week, or maybe only one every two weeks. Well, a high-powered motor you can keep tuned up for that, but you can't keep a high-powered motor out there every night, banging it around, and, of course, with fog and other conditions and so forth, and not being absolutely sure where these people were coming from. Even assuming you had exactly the same type of motor as the other fellow and the same speed, you're not tuned up to his pitch. In other words, this was a dash out, load, and dash back.

Q: You don't have the initiative.

Adm. R.: That's right, it's essentially that. We were working behind the eight ball but we did make quite a number of seizures. Remember too, it was not a popular law, let's face it. Up in Boston at that time, even if you made a seizure, it was very, very difficult to get a conviction of any kind. I'll just give you this story.

A number of years later, I was in the district attorney's office up there once - I forget just why, and this guy wandered in. He'd been a professional bank robber and he'd been "sent up" a number of times. I remember the conversation.

The assistant district attorney I was talking to turned to him and said: "Hey, what are you doing around." He was all dressed up and he said; "I'm doing pretty good."

"What are you doing now? What banks are you after?"

"Oh, I'm out of that business."

So the attorney said: "What are you doing?"

"I'm running rum now." This, to a U. S. attorney. And the guy said: "Why?"

"Well, if I get picked up and they give me six months. What the hell's six months to a guy like me?"

This was the attitude. You do six months and you're right back in the business. If you held up a bank you got five to ten years, anyway.

Q: When this liquor was seized, what was done with it?

Adm. R.: It had to be condemned through the courts. Frankly, I don't know just what was done with it. Some was destroyed and I think some of it was used for medicinal purposes.

Q: This was an across-the-board selection of liquor? I mean it wasn't confined to rum?

Adm. R.: Oh, no, no. Rum was just a generic term. I'd say most of it was probably whiskey.

It doesn't seem to me we were off Boston more than about three weeks. That didn't last very long. Then, as I say, I kind of lost track of what was being done up north. Rum Row, as such, never really got constituted as a line up there. But to be absolutely accurate you'd have to verify somewhere else, they did start using the schooners and tried to come down with the schooners and rendezvous. In other words, it began to get into a big operations and probably was reasonably successful, but we became more successful. After all, a schooner doesn't move too fast. It's pretty easy to keep your eye on a schooner. By that time we had a few planes in the service, and ships cruising out there could see a schooner coming. It was a little more difficult to make a rendezvous. So gradually they were forced out of the schooner business. I think they'd decided the line was no good, so they tried this other thing, but that wasn't a success. Oh, it dragged on for a year or so and sometimes they'd be successful, but sometimes they'd have to go around in circles for quite a while before they could slip through undetected and maybe make a rendezvous, all of which complicated their problem. That, in turn, led to the building of the sophisticated "rummy," as I called it, that brought the stuff down.

Meantime, as I say, I'd gone back to Headquarters.

Q: In 1926 you got sent to the Academy.

Adm. R.: Yes, and that summer was the sesquicentennial. Admiral, then Commander Waesche was in charge up there and I went up as his aide, then that fall I went to the Academy.

Q: Was this something you asked for or was it a routine assignment?

Adm. R.: I think I did suggest to Admiral Billard that I thought I'd better get away from Headquarters, but I really don't know how it came about. Both Richards and I went back to the Academy. It might have been that Hinckley asked for Richards and me to come back as instructors. I know I got word that I was supposed to teach math. I remember up at the Sesquicentennial, they brought the <u>Alexander Hamilton</u> up and I went aboard and met Bill Derby for the first time, now deceased. I guess he was a commander at the time and he was the assistant superintendent. He said:

"Oh, Richmond, you're coming to the Academy?" I said yes, so he said, "I suppose you know what you're going to teach?"

I said: "Yes, Sir, I think so."

He said: "You're going to teach English," whereupon I fell through the deck practically because the one thing I didn't want to teach was English. The first year up there I did teach English and math, then I unloaded the English on somebody else.

Q: This was a two-year assignment you had, was it?

Adm. R.: There was never any specific assignment. I was there two years. We were building the Lake-class cutters, and I did ask to get away from the Academy. I figured four years ashore right after graduation was too much.

Q: Did you, as is the case in the Navy, have to watch and be sure that you were getting an appropriate amount of sea duty?

Adm. R.: To a degree, although I don't think we were particularly conscious about it at that time. No, I just felt that I was missing out on what I had really thought was the best part of the service.

Q: Is there anything significant about those two years that

you were there?

Adm. R.: At the Academy, no. Lots of funny things happened and I enjoyed instructing.

Q: Was it a three-year course now?

Adm. R.: It was still a three-year course, yes. Probably the most significant thing to me in that period, at least it sticks out in my memory - I don't remember the classes so much. I taught mathematics and English and I also had signals and coached the basketball team, not because I was a basketball player but because somebody had to do it. I might just comment for a moment.

I remember one time we got up to Newport to play the Newport Torpedo Station, and who should trot out on the basketball floor, playing for them up there, but my old friend Joe Wheelock, the one I mentioned down at the Norfolk Naval Operating Base. I mentioned to him that he had once smeared me all over the football field. In typical Indian fashion, he just kind of grinned.

One afterthought on that football team. I told you about the fellow who told us the high-school team had beaten them and we thought we could beat them. But what he didn't tell us was that the high school had beaten the electricians' team. They had about fifteen teams, every rating had a team. And what the Naval Operating Base would do was go round to each of these teams and take the best players they could find. What we played was the Naval Operating Base. What the high school had beaten was the electricians' team.

The cadet cruises were interesting then. Of course, I was now an officer and instructor -

Q: And the instructors went along on these cruises?

Adm. R.: Yes. There would usually be a cadre staff from the ship - some of them would take leave or something like that.

The first year we started out on the Hamilton and we got up off of Nova Scotia some place when the Hamilton dropped her wheel and they were afraid to sail her with no auxiliary power. So the Hamilton was towed back I think by the Tampa, then the Mojave was assigned to complete the cruise, so we transferred from the Hamilton to the Mojave and made the cruise on that ship.

We went to England, down the coast to Gibraltar and Casablanca, and my recollection is that we probably stopped at Madeira on the way back. Of course, the cruise was shortened some by the loss of time in switching vessels. We lost two or three weeks. On the other hand, there was no sailing, it was all under power.

Q: What hat did you wear? Did you have formal instruction

on board?

Adm. R.: It was more practical navigation and practical seamanship. Formal education aboard a ship is a snare and a delusion, as far as I'm concerned. First, it's very difficult to schedule classes because of required watch-standing and that sort of thing. Second, the space isn't available, especially on a cutter, to hold a class, unless you do it in the open on deck which is not the best place to be operating in wind and weather conditions. Then, if you're below decks and do have the space, as you know, at least in the old days, the air, even with air-conditioning, isn't as good and I found, especially if the ship was rolling that the students got drowsy. It's just not the best conditions. So I've never been much for subjective training on board ship. Vocational yes, but subjective, no. To me, it doesn't work out. I've always been leery of these so-called university cruises and things like that. From the standpoint of seeing the world and practical learning, yes.

We had a rather odd situation that year because they did not want to strip the Mojave down of all her officers and crew, so we had the Academy complement of officers who'd been on the Hamilton plus the Mojave officers. So we had more watch officers than any ship I've ever been on. We all took our different watches.

One interesting experience that year was that when we got to London they took us almost up to the Tower of London.

They locked us in to St. Catherine's Dock, which is just outside of the Tower of London, just below it. I don't know whether you know how they do on most of the English rivers. On most English rivers the docks are not on the riverside. You go into locked areas, warehouse areas. I always remember that cruise for one experience we had.

We had a doctor aboard, Dr. Stroop, who was from Arkansas and quite a vehement southerner from the standpoint of southern rights and all that sort of thing. Doc Stroop, Bill Kossler and myself had been uptown and I suppose we had eaten - and I know Doc had drunk a little bit too much, and we were, as I say, in the dock and that night about one o'clock in the morning we were all awakened by screams. Incidentally, the wardroom on those ships was forward, up in the bow, and Doc had the stateroom right across the passageway from me. We were awakened by these screams and everybody came out into the wardroom and dashed to the Doctor's stateroom. Doc claimed that he was dying and he was doubled up with pain.

I ran up on deck and told the cadet quartermaster to run up to the gate and ask them to call for a doctor, because we didn't know what to do for Dr. Stroop. Meantime, we all stood around and did what we could. He was really doubled up. I think he had a little touch of ptomaine poisoning or something like that. A half hour or so later, the cadet quartermaster came down, stuck his head in and said:

"Sir, the doctor's here."

I said, "Well, bring him down. Can't you see the man's dying, at least he says he is."

He said, "No, I think you'd better come up on deck, Sir, first."

I went up on deck and, at the gangway, was a tall, jet-black gentleman with a typical doctor's case, a Prince Albert coat, pin-striped trousers - this is now about 2:30 in the morning - and, with a clipped Jamaican accent, I guess, or West Indies accent, he tells me he's here to see the patient.

Well, I did a double take and explained to him that maybe I'd better go back and see the patient first, because Doc being from Arkansas. So I went down and said:

"Doc, the doctor's here."

"Oh, bring him down. Don't you see I'm dying. I can't stand this much longer."

"Well," I said, "I'll tell you, Doc, there's one problem. The doctor's here. The doctor's black."

You've heard of shock treatment, well this was shock treatment. That's where I learned the value of shock treatment. He sat up in bed and with a good deal of profanity said:

"No so-and-so black so-and-so is going to attend to me."

I said, "Now, look, Doc, you're dying. You just said so."

"Well, I'll die first."

To make a long story short, I went back and, you know, try to explain to some guy that you've broken out of bed at

2:30 in the morning why he can't see the patient! Finally, I paid him handsomely and we compromised on me describing the symptoms and he prescribing the medicine that Doc was to take and which I had gotten Doc to agree he would take, and we sent the fellow off. I've often thought there probably were not at that time more than half a dozen, if that many, colored doctors in the city of London and why at one or two o'clock in the morning we had to choose one for a southern doctor was beyond me, but that was one of the experiences on that cruise.

We had a number of interesting experiences on that cruise. One particularly was going in to Casablanca. Not many people know this - Morocco at that time, of course, was under the French, and apparently when it was opened up before the turn of the century, the 1860s and 1870s stick in my mind, various business interests of the other countries wnated to do business with the Moroccans themselves. However, the Moroccans, even though the French were in control of the government, were still under a tribal system. The Sultan owned everything technically. If you were in a tribe anything you owned belonged to the sheik of that tribe, and everything the sheik owned belonged to the Sultan, so, in effect, if the Sultan decided that he wanted x sheep the word went out and it went down the line, the sheik passed the word down, "You don't have ten sheep in your flock any more, you only have nine, because one of them is coming to me," and so on up.

Obviously, a business concern whether it was U. S. or anyone else could not do business on the basis that a guy might be wealthy today but bankrupt tomorrow. I don't think the United States ever got in it too much but what they did was to establish proteges. In effect, a wealthy businessman would be appointed a protege, which to all intents and purposes took him out from the sheik system or the tribal system and made him a quasi U. S. citizen, German or whatever, of course French, too, to a degree. This was a very-sought-after privilege. If you had money and you'd like to keep it, the thing to do was to get to be a protege. So when our ships went in there our fellow Moroccan citizens would give big dinners. In Casablanca we probably had only two or three proteges and they'd give two dinners for the cadets, one for each watch, and one for the officers. It was quite an experience to go through a Moroccan dinner because of the various customs and the way they ate and so forth.

Bill Kossler and I decided we would go to Marrakesh. In those days Marrakesh was a large city but actually, as I remember, there were only about 2,000 Europeans in a city of 100,000.

Q: It was still rather inaccessible, too, wasn't it?

Adm. R.: No, we took a bus out. It's about 120 miles from Casablanca, as I remember. That was a very interesting experience because there was only one decent hotel and even that was pretty fly-bitten. I remember sitting in the market place in front of the hotel, it was a sort of French type with tables outside, and looking across the market place at all the berbers and natives on the other side of the street staring at us. We were staring at them. I suppose we were as much a curiosity to them as they were to us. Actually, it was not safe at that time to go much south of Marrakesh. Unless you had a military escort, you didn't go any farther south.

We took a guide with us. We didn't do this on our own. We hired a Morroccan to take us up there, so he arranged to take us to call on the protege who actually in Marrakesh acted as the American consul.

Q: An honorary American consul?

Adm. R.: In other words, he would take care of any U. S. interests up there. He couldn't speak English. We went down this little mud-wall-lined street and into what looked like just a door going out of an alley, but once you got inside there was a beautiful patio. Opening onto the patio was sort of a porch with Moorish arches and all. We met the old gentleman and tried to converse with him. He spoke French and we had a smattering of French. Of course, our guide acted as interpreter. He had a little ditty box I guess somebody had given him and he had all his letters in there. People who'd been there and been entertained by him that had/written to him. I always remember this place. I'd say the room was 40 or 50 feet long and 15 feet deep. We sat there on these divans and had tea served, and tried to converse.

Apparently he had a penchant for these 400-day clocks, the ones with the bell on them. He must have had at least 100 of these clocks on little shelves all around the wall, some of them quite ornate, some of them –

Q: They were of German origin?

Adm. R.: Well, I think German, French, and Swiss all made them. I don't think one of them was running but he had them all sitting there, 100 or so of them at least. That was his idea of decorating his place.

We had some interesting experiences there and down in the Medina. I think they have a different name for the Medina now. But it got us away from the ship.

So much for that cruise. I don't remember anything else particularly on that.

Then the following year we made a cruise. The <u>Alexander Hamilton</u> had been repaired, of course, by that time. She couldn't carry all the cadets so we took some of them on the destroyer <u>Shaw</u>, which was one of the old raised-bow 1,000-tonners. I was assigned to the <u>Shaw</u>, but the unfortunate part of it was you couldn't slow the Shaw down economically to much less than about 14 or 15 knots, whereas the Alexander Hamilton could under the best of conditions make a snappy 8 knots. And again returning to the fact that Harold Dale Hinckley was, if nothing else, always a stickler for protocol, we could have gone to Europe and had a glorious time but not according to Harold Dale because if anyone arrived in England before him and he made the mistake of going on the Hamilton, he wouldn't go on the Shaw - that was the flagship, so there was nothing for us to do but go in to Ponta Delgada where we spent about ten days.

Q: That's a charming place.

Adm. R.: Well, it might be, but ten days of it get pretty boring.

Q: You could go to some of the other islands.

Adm. R.: No, we were supposed to stay at Ponta Delgada and we did. We tried various forms of amusement but, at that time at least, you could see the whole town in about a half-hour or so. You could only walk so far when you went ashore. We were anchored out in the harbor. Our main occupation was playing ping pong on the wardroom table. Gradually, we got down to one remaining ping pong ball. It was so hot that we'd have the ports open and every now and then a lucky shot would go out the port. Then you'd see this wild scramble out of the wardroom, out onto the boat boom, and into the motor launch, and this chase down the harbor after this little ping pong ball dancing on the harbor waves.

Pretty soon, the residents of Ponta Delgada got wise that something was going on. They never did discover what it was. There'd be 50 or 100 people standing down there to see this wild scramble rescue operation of the ping pong ball. We were too far out for them to see what we were chasing. I don't think in the whole time we were there they ever understood what this crazy going-on was.

I remember going to a show there. They had a pretty nice little theater, but it was a Portuguese show and it was pretty grim.

Q: Did you go up to the twin lakes?

Adm. R.: No, we didn't get out there. You see, transportation wasn't what it is today. I learned another lesson there, though.

While we were there the Portuguese training ship came in and, of course, calls had to be exchanged. Captain Finley was our skipper and I learned then that if two people can't understand each other, I mean they speak different languages, they go on the mistaken idea that if they speak slowly and yell loud enough they will understand each other. They never do, but they still work on that principle.

After the Alexander Hamilton had gotten far enough beyond the Azores so that they felt they would arrive before us, we were allowed to proceed. Then everything went fine. We started steaming up the Thames and, of course, we had to take pilots, but then everything went wrong because, although the orders were that one of us was going to St. Catherine's Dock and one was to go into a dock farther down, we were supposed to steam up in column, the Shaw behind the Hamilton, but unfortunately at the speed the Hamilton was making the Shaw wouldn't maneuver and the pilot refused to obey commands. He was protecting the ship and so we had to steam on past them with the net result that we ended up in St. Catherine's Dock, at the dock where the Hamilton was supposed to be which didn't endear us to old Captain Hinckley.

We went back to Casablanca that year. I don't recall all the places we went to but I think we went to France. It was kind of a messed-up cruise because I can't think of two more opposite types of ships.

Q: Unmatched speeds?

Adm. R.: Yes, unmatched speeds. Then we had to be with them at times because we had to transfer cadets. Some of the cadets on the Hamilton came over to us and we had so many back and

Richmond #1 - 91

forth.

That's about all I remember distinctly of my experience at the Academy and, as I say, after two years I felt that I ought to get some sea duty. We were building the new ships and so I went to the Pontchartrain.

Q: But in preparation for that you had a special course?

Adm. R.: Oh, yes, I did go down to the Sperry Gyroscope school. When I went in the service the gyro compass was sort of a novelty. We were just beginning to put them on, and since the Pontchartrain was going to be equipped with this new wonder of navigation - I guess it had been out about twenty years at that time. Some of the older ships didn't have it yet.

Q: How long a period would you spend in a specialized school like that?

Adm. R.: That, I think, was only a two or three-week school.

Q: Did the Coast Guard have a series of schools that they sent their men to?

Adm. R.: Not so much at that time, no. Later, yes. Aside from the Academy we had - well, we used Navy schools a lot and we had Groton where we trained all kinds of rates, particularly after we had the Lighthouse Service. I guess we got that just before the war.

Q: Then there was an interchange and you used Navy facilities.

Adm. R.: Yes. Our aviators we went to Pensacola, you know, for training.

Q: Tell me about the Pontchartrain, she being a new type.

Adm. R.: We built ten of that Lake-class cutter and I think the Pontchartrain was the second or third that came out.

Q: What were her distinguishing characteristics, this class?

Adm. R.: As I recall it, she was 255 feet long. They were larger than anything we'd had up to that time. In over-all style, you might say in contour line, they didn't vary too much from the earlier ones like the Tampa, Modoc, and Mojave. They did not have the wardrooms forward, they had the wardrooms aft. You went down a companion way and you had a kind of an orlop passageway and staterooms over the wardroom. You went down steps to the cabins, aft of the staterooms.

Q: Tell me about the design of a Coast Guard cutter. I mean, who's responsible for it?

Adm. R.: At that time we had a construction man by the name of Honeywell who'd been with us for years. He was a civilian. I guess he did have a uniform but like I mentioned about the professors of astronomy he had a sort of relative rank. Honeywell, in other words, never went to sea. He was a naval architect. He had a small staff. I really wasn't too close to how the ships were designed.

Q: Where was he located?

Adm. R.: At Headquarters in Washington. He had the Construction Corps, if you want to call it that, but that was the design section. Then he would consult with the engineer. As I said earlier, when I first went into the service we had engineers and line and I think it was 1925 or 1926 that we finally did away with the engineers and combined it all into one corps. The theory was that the engineers could never assume command.

Q: Was there any difficulty in amalgamating the engineers and the line officers?

Adm. R.: No, there really wasn't any particular difficulty. There were one or two engineers who felt discriminated against when they were not given command even though senior to the line exec - that caused a little friction, but I think it was more a personality matter. Generally speaking, it was a very smooth take-over. The line officers themselves, of course, never aspired to get down in the engine room particularly, and some engineers actually were given command.

Q: I asked that because in the Navy they had quite a difficulty.

Adm. R.: Well, as I say, I don't remember any. I know of one case, in fact I was a party to it and almost got caught in it, but the fellow who caused the trouble was a sort of a peculiar individual. He probably never should have had command even if he'd been trained as a line officer. I've always said the Coast Guard made a mistake. What they should have done with him was to get 40 acres and build him a laboratory down in one corner of them, and one of two things would have happened. Either he would have come up with something wonderful or he would have blown himself up. Either answer would probably have been advantageous.

Q: That causes me to ask another question. Does the Coast Guard have a research and development section?

Adm. R.: I think they do now. Whether they call it research and development, I don't know. They certainly are doing a lot of experimental work, particularly - this is secondhand information I get from reading in the papers and that sort of thing - in port-control systems and also in oil clean-ups and things like that. So I'm sure they're doing some work. When I left the service we had no particular appropriation for a research and development group. I'm not sure that they do now, but I am sure that a certain amount of money is put aside for experimental work.

I don't know whether you could really classify it as research and development in the true sense, as I understand the terms, but they certainly are alive to trying to find new and better ways of doing certain jobs.

Q: I suppose the unit that was headed by this one man on ships' characteristics and that sort of thing has grown, too?

Adm. R.: Yes, I think so. As I say, I don't really know who's doing that. It's really part of engineering now, as such. It would be difficult for me to really answer just how they're working it now. Whether they're going out when they build new ships and having outside architects give them the preliminary, it's really difficult for me to say because I just haven't been that close to it. I know this much. If they have anything at all it's in construction. Of course, there was quite a little work being done in addition to the cutters in lifeboats.

The Coast Guard has always been quite active in developing different motor lifeboats, surf boats, and that sort of thing for out life-saving stations. And, of course, we worked quite closely with the British Royal Lifeboat Association, exchanging ideas. Later, when I became commandant, I remember that the Germans had developed a very special boat operating off Kiel. I made a special trip to see it and I was quite impressed with the capabilities of this boat and the way they operated. And I think some of our designs have been incorporated in some of the British boats. I suppose we've also taken liberally from some of their better ideas.

Q: In other words, there was a free exchange of ideas?

Adm. R.: More or less, yes. After all, you're in the business of saving lives and anything that makes it easier or better is a help. It's not like getting a better gun.

Q: No, and having an advantage over the other fellow.

Adm. R.: Here's a field where we're all working for a common good so why not exchange ideas. But, by the same token, what is good for one place - like that German boat I mentioned, it probably would not have been of value -

Q: At Cape May, for instance?

Adm. R.: It might not because they have a different situation. They had certain problems that they had to meet and they had met them. But, at the same time, some of the ideas we did incorporate.

Q: I suppose within our own service you had different requirements. The Great Lakes, for instance, differed from the Atlantic Ocean?

Adm. R.: In many ways, yes.

Let's see. We hadn't gotten on to the Pontchartrain yet, had we?

Q: Yes, you were.

Adm. R.: I went to Mobile with her. Unfortunately, the ships that had preceded us in Mobile, smaller ships, one of them had an officer complement that gave the Coast Guard a rather unsavory reputation.

Q: Why, because of the personnel on shore?

Adm. R.: Well, because of the actions of the officers involved. You know, in a southern town it doesn't take much to start a little gossip, and one of the commanding officers had been a pretty heavy drinker and indiscreet and one thing and another. So the Coast Guard was not in too good repute, and they built us up a little bit, gave us a nice new cutter, and so forth. We were very fortunate in that we had hardly arrived when the vice president and his assistant in charge of new business of one of the big banks there, Merchants National Bank, came down, of course, for new business. Through them we were given entree to some of the masked balls.

We arrived in December, as I recall it, or the latter part of November, and that's when they start their masked balls.

Q: Pre-lenten?

Adm. R.: Pre-lenten, for the mardi gras. Mobile has a mardi gras that in some ways I think antedates New Orleans, Of course, it's nothing in comparison in size, but they put on quite a show. We had a number of single officers and we got entree to many of the parties. You have to know somebody down there to get to the parties because they have a rule - in the first place, you don't know who are members of these societies to get invited, but unless you do have an invitation from a member, you don't go. It doesn't make any difference who you are. It isn't a case of a committee saying, "You're President of the United States, please come to our party," or something like that. Somebody has to individually invite you.

So it was pretty nice and we had an enjoyable time. As far as duties were concerned, the <u>Pontchartrain</u> cruised all round to the different ports. My skipper was Harold Dale Hinckley again, who was quite a sportsman. As navigator, one of my jobs was to know where the good fishing banks for red snapper were, so every time we'd go into a new port I'd go down and visit among the fishermen and get information about how you would line up a fishing bank from landmarks on the shore.

We'd go to various celebrations, like the Gasparilla. We made some seizures, did a certain amount of boarding for safety features on fishing boats and on private boats. I can't remember anything very distinctive about our service down there. We made one seizure of a Mexican tug that was running liquor, but by and large there wasn't too much liquor-running down there at that time because, very frankly, the local populace drank their own local corn liquor and there was no demand for the sophisticated liquors - at least, not much demand.

Q: I take it the speakeasy system wasn't as highly developed down there?

Adm. R.: No, it really wasn't. As I say, everybody knew some boy who was putting away a little moonshine up in the boondocks and you could get all you needed, that is provided you could stand corn liquor.

A few schooners came up, as I indicated. There was the famous "I'mahlone." case. It was prosecuted on the doctrine of hot pursuit. He was finally seized quite a way out after having been picked up inside the limit and fled. But it wasn't organized to the extent it was being organized up off the East Coast or off the Florida coast. The Florida coast was really rough because, of course, there they were catering to I suppose you might say the vacation crowd particularly. Many of the people working in the Florida liquor industry were so-called Florida crackers and to them life meant very little. In fact, we had a boatswain shot down there and the man who shot him was finally convicted and had to be hung at the Coast Guard station at Fort Lauderdale - or was hung there - because that was the only nearby federal land on which the penalty could be carried out. I wasn't over there. The Pontchartrain led a reasonably uneventful life.

Q: Would you say a little about this doctrine of hot pursuit?

Adm. R.: Well, as you know, in terms of seizure of a vessel on the high seas the theory is that if the perpetrator of a crime - on the high seas or any place else - is known but you can't pick him up in the area, as long as the pursuit is not broken off and you're chasing him you can pick him up even though he's technically out of your jurisdiction. This is on land and this has been extended to the high seas.

I think I'm right in saying that by this time we'd gotten the customs laws amended - they were supposed to be outside the 12-mile limit, or if they got inside the 12-mile limit, they were vulnerable. I'll take that back. It wasn't necessarily 12. The law, as I recall it, was an hour's steaming distance, but I think they finally agreed that that was 12 miles or an hour's steaming distance.

Q: That could vary with the boat.

Adm. R.: That's right. Whether it came back to an average of 12 or whether everybody agreed that 12 was about right for normal speeds, my memory is a little hazy.

Generally, I enjoyed the whole time in Mobile.

Q: One other question about the safety boarding. When you discovered on a given ship that you boarded that the facilities were not adequate and not up to the standards required by law, what did you do?

Adm. R.: A report would be made and they'd be called before what was then the Bureau of Inspection and Navigation and they either had to make good or be penalized for this. Most people, I think, say, they were shy life preservers or something like that would get their life preservers -

Q: And did the Coast Guard follow through on this?

Adm. R.: No, we rarely did because, in the first place, you might board somebody today and they move on or you move on and you might never see them again. Reports were filed wherever their home port was. It went through their home port and was supposed to be checked out. We spent a whole day boarding lots of times. We used to do this on the West Coast, too, with the fishing fleets and that sort of thing.

Of course, nowadays when they board it's mostly pleasure craft. There weren't too many pleasure craft around in those days. When you boarded it was more of a check-up and more of a threat. I myself wondered many times just how effective it was. It was just to see whether they were seaworthy and had their proper papers. I suppose sometimes, back in the olden days, it was more a question of checking their crews, if they were fishing vessels, and that sort of thing.

Q: In that time, no thought was given to searching for drugs?

Adm. R.: No. As I say, I can't recall a single instance of even considering drugs particularly.

Q: What about ships smuggling things in that they would have to pay a heavy duty on?

Adm. R.: Of course, basically, as you know, every Coast Guard officer was, and I suppose still is, a customs officer, so we were always supposed to be on the alert for that. But during my experience I never ran into any smuggling.

Going back to your question about drugs, the first thought I ever had about drugs was a number of years later, when I came to the West Coast. When I was cruising, particularly out of Seattle, there were stories that the old Blue Funnel Line coming in had a system of jettisoning. One sailor or someone would jettison a package of something on a float and a boat would pick it up. For a while there was a certain amount of trailing the Blue Funnel Line, but if they dropped it they dropped it when we didn't see.

Q: Who owned the Blue Funnel Line?

Adm. R.: It's a British concern, it was a British concern, I don't think it's in existence any more, and I don't know. That was the only trafficking in drugs and we used to sometimes pick up the Blue Funnel Line off the straits and follow them in to Seattle. But, as I say, I never saw any evidence of boats hanging around to pick up anything nor did we ever see anything thrown overboard.

Q: You were on the Pontchartrain for two years and then you were transferred to the Wainwright?

Richmond #1 - 104

Adm. R.: Yes. I went to the Wainwright, a destroyer.

Q: And she was stationed in Boston?

Adm. R.: The Wainwright worked out of Boston, the Boston division. By the time I got back up there, this rum war had changed a great deal and the coast from New York to probably about Block Island was divided into three areas. From there on up round the capes there were about three other areas. We worked a five and ten schedule. You'd go out for five days and you'd go into your areas and the job was to keep these low-lying rummies that I mentioned earlier from slipping in and making rendezvous. Of course, they never made the transfer in the daylight, or rarely, I would guess. I forget now how wide these areas were but probably 20 to 40 miles in width, and we'd start in the morning and, starting on the inside, make almost a retire-and-search curve, zigzagging back and forth, hoping to pick anybody up coming in. On the parallel sides would be other ships doing the same thing.

If you picked them up, they would realize that their chances of making a rendezvous were off. Sometimes you didn't pick them up, they'd get by you. After all, there is a limit to how much you can cover.

Q: I take it they had good communications?

Adm. R.: Oh, yes. As I say, by this time this had all passed to the syndicate, you see, and they had plenty of money. They were making money.

Q: What about interception on the part of the Coast Guard, of messages?

Adm. R.: Yes, they did some. I had a classmate who worked in that, but we never had much. No, I'll take that back. We would get occasional messages. We'd hear that such and such a ship was standing in and so forth and we'd try to intercept them. But, generally speaking, we didn't get too much that way. Anyway, you'd pick this fellow up and sometimes they'd continue right on in and you'd stick with them until they got in. It was a very interesting experience because you'd get into their rendezvous area, which could be anywhere, they never came inside the 12-mile limit, they'd come to 15 or 20 miles off a point and lay around there, and you'd slug around with them. We were in destroyers now.

When darkness came, usually about nine o'clock - they might hang out, say, about 20 miles because they figure if they could get away they'd have another three or four miles to run in to their rendezvous points - they never got inside the 12. And maybe about 8:30 or 9:00, after it got dark, they'd douse their running lights and start cutting circles and laying down smokescreens - then you'd start chasing. They had the advantage of a smaller turning circle. You had to be right on your toes for maneuvering because every now and then you'd be turning right and they'd be turning left and they'd show up under your bow. We weren't trying to run them down or anything like that so we'd have to go full speed astern. It really got to be quite a game.

Q: There must have been instances of collision?

Adm. R.: No. As far as I know, we never collided. There might have been on other ships, but I never heard of any. They knew what we were doing. They were very fast handlers, but you rev a destroyer up to 20 or 25 knots and start cutting circles and you're really having problems. We'd have the searchlights going to try to hold them all this time. This could go on for an hour or an hour and a half, around 10:30, if they hadn't shaken you by using smokescreens and evasive tactics, they'd turn the lights on and sit do-do in the water, and that's the way it would last until midnight, after the watch changed. Then, as soon as the watch changed, all this monkey business would start again.

Q: Why was that?

Adm. R.: Because they had a new guy on and he might be softer than the guy who'd been on earlier and it was later at night. It seemed to me it never ran quite as long, maybe forty-five mintues of fun and games. Then, if they hadn't shaken you, why they'd turn the lights on or head back out to sea, and you could rest for the night. Mainly, I think, because by that time, if you'd held them that long, they'd missed their rendezvous so they might as well go and steam on out. Then, a couple of days later, they'd be back again.

Q: I would think there'd be collisions with the rendezvous because they didn't have radar and the lights were out and this was done at night?

Adm. R.: You mean between the boats coming out and them?

Q: Yes.

Adm. R.: Oh, no, because they weren't maneuvering at that time. They'd just proceed to a given spot, you see, and lie there and the other boats, I presume, would feel their way in. Of course, I never was in on an actual contact, so I don't know.

I was quite interesting and a lot of fun in a way. Kind of hairy at times.

Q: Almost a hopeless assignment, wasn't it?

Adm. R.: It was. Mainly I think it was hopeless because

even when you seized them you weren't sure there's be any great reward. It wasn't really considered a criminal act. That's the point. Sure, it was against the law and people criticized the Coast Guard but, as I said, it didn't make any difference to us. It wasn't that we were against liquor. The point was if they'd been bringing in broomsticks and broomsticks were against the law, it would have been the same game. That's all it was.

I know of one case when a classmate of mine was on the ship. There was a really bad storm. I forget all the details now but, in effect, this rummy was disabled. Our ship knew he was disabled and stood by him. This was one of the Nova Scotia rummies. We stood by while he was in distress and offered to take him in but he said no. They sent another boat in and towed him out finally. But I mean they exchanged pleasantries. They stood by him for twenty-four or thirty-six hours in the storm in case they capsized and had to abandon.

Q: The skipper changed his hat!

Adm. R.: No, but, after all, these were human beings and just because they were trying to break the law was no reason to let them drown unnecessarily. Later, I think, this fellow sent him -

Q: A case of rum!

Adm. R.: No, but he sent him some gift and a very nice letter thanking him for standing by in this trouble and saying he'd see him again sometime. The next time he came in, he probably tried to run right by him, but it was a gentleman's game, if you can call it that. We hadn't passed the law and we were neither for nor against it. It was just to be carried out. And, as I say, I think that was true of most of the people in the country at the time.

Q: And that was the job of the Wainwright in that area?

Adm. R.: Well, of all the destroyers. You see, the destroyers were divided into divisions. and we were working out of Boston. I guess I was on the Wainwright about six months.

Q: A very short time, actually, from July to November 1930.

Adm. R.: Then I was sent down to Philadelphia, to the Herndon. The first destroyers we got were the old 750s, with raised bow, and the Wainwright was a 1,000-ton raised-bow.

Q: These were Navy?

Adm. R.: All Navy destroyers from World War I. Then we got I think about five or maybe more of the first flush-deckers, whatever size they were. Parenthetically, just going back for a moment, I don't know whether you even knew the fate of the old Pontchartrain?

Q: No.

Adm. R.: She was one of the cutters that were transferred by Roosevelt in World War II to the British, and she was one of the ships that broke the boom at Oran. I think there's a new Pontchartrain now.

Q: How did the Herndon differ?

Adm. R.: She was a flush-decker, and they were a little bit larger. I don't know whether they were 1,200 or 1,500 tons as against the 1,000 tons.

Q: How was this effected? The Navy built the ships?

Adm. R.: They were in the back channels. They were World War I destroyers, all of them.

Q: The Herndon was?

Adm. R.: Yes - well, she might have been built right after the war but she'd been decommissioned. We took her out of the back channel. She was already out when I got there. We changed them a little bit but not much. I had two interesting experiences there.

You mentioned this question about the engineers and the line officers. This one engineer I spoke about had been on the destroyer in Boston, not my destroyer, another destroyer. He was a nice guy except he was a bit nuts. He was quite mad about the fact they had not given him a command. Actually, what had happened was that they had gone down to the races off Newport.

Q: The yacht races?

Adm. R.: The Shamrock, yes, and the skipper of the ship was transferred over to the flagship to act as chief of staff and a classmate of mine, who was the executive officer, was junior to the engineer officer on the ship. That made this engineer officer mad because he wasn't put in command. There was quite a fiasco over that and it ended up with what I called the Battle of the Napkin Rings, which we need not go into here because I wasn't a party to it. There was almost a casualty but not quite.

So after he got back to Boston he was crying on my shoulder, and I frankly think that the regulations were a little bit hazy in that they said the senior man will command. He was senior, but on the other hand they hadn't given him command. He was to be the engineer on the Herndon, so he wrote a letter and asked me what I thought of it. Well, it was a good letter, and I said, "I think you ought to send it in. It's something that ought to be straightened out."

So he sent it in and the net result of this was that he made them all mad at Headquarters, so they transferred him from the Herndon and assigned me as engineer officer of the Herndon! I only mention this because, in the first place, I'd had no engineering duty and I didn't aspire to be an engineer and I didn't aspire to learn. As a matter of fact, some of my class had been sent for a year as student engineers on the destroyers, but I hadn't had this. What made it even worse - I always remember going down to these two enginerooms and, of course, it was nothing but red lead and so forth down there, and this boy I was speaking of had been there long enough to take every piece of machinery, including the fans that were on the bulkheads apart. Of course, we didn't know about atomic bombs in those days, but it looked to me, as I looked at this scene - everything, the covers were off the turbines and there wasn't a motor that wasn't ripped off. I took one look and I started to say something. I always remember that guy standing there looking at it with a gleam in his eye like you might stand before a famous painting. He turned to me and I didn't have the heart to say anything. He looked at me and he said:

"Isn't it beautiful?"

Well, if I ever saw a God-awful-looking mess!

Richmond #1 - 113

I wouldn't have known where to start. A jigsaw puzzle would have been easy. So I went down to Washington a couple of days later and I said:

"Look, I'm perfectly willing to take this job but it would be cheaper in the long run to put me through four years of an engineering college than it would be to let me experiment on a half-million-dollar job."

So, about a week later, they assigned an engineer officer and I went back to being exec on the ship.

We had another interesting experience - not interesting but terrible, as it turned out. The Navy Yard was doing the re-conditioning and we were living aboard. They'd gotten the quarters fixed up but they hadn't finished the engineroom and they hadn't scaled the decks and what not. In order to save money, we were living aboard, running our galley, and about that time one or two of our boys came down with what they said at first was scarlet fever. I don't think it was. It was scarlatina, I imagine. They carted them off to the hospital and then the Navy made one of those beautiful decisions that I always think stand out as being high marks of military service. They decided that they'd have to quarantine the ship, but on the other hand they wanted to keep the work going. So what they would do was - we didn't have a full crew on, I have to say that, but we had all our officers - during the daytime when the Navy Yard workmen were aboard everybody, crew and officers, had to stay off the deck and below decks. In other words, there'd be no contact, which was stupid, because if you've got a contagious disease it's going to be floating around everywhere.

Q: At that time, perhaps their understanding of how to spread a disease -

Adm. R.: I don't know whether it was understanding or not. I think the idea was they had to make a pretense of quarantining, at the same time they wanted to get the work done, and they didn't want to wait. So from eight in the morning, when they started, till four or four thirty, the officers all sat in the wardroom. You talk about fun! All you've got to do is sit in the wardroom of a destroyer with an air gun going on the deck above you, chipping. That's really something. Eight hours of it. That's pretty rough.

There wasn't anything to do. There was really no paper work. We weren't even commissioned yet. So we played bridge. I guess there were just four of us at the time. I'll always remember those bridge games. We'd sit there and play bridge by the hour.

We had a pharmacist's mate aboard who was always very meticulous. If you came in with a cut finger, he'd have to put his white coat on before he could treat it. His name was Chambers, and every half-hour Chambers would come in with a spray. I don't know what this was supposed to do, but whatever disease was floating around he was going to keep it from us. Well, it got to the point where you'd be sitting there and say, "I bid one spade," you'd open your mouth to say it and Chambers would pump spray in, then he'd move on around to Admiral O'Neal. You can mention this to him when you interview him because he'll remember. He'd give Admiral O'Neal a spray.

Q: You had to open your mouth?

Adm. R.: Oh, yes, you'd open your mouth and - he had one of those syringes - he'd give it a spray, then he'd move on to the next one, all four of us. Every half-hour we got our spray. Whatever he did, at least we never came down with anything. We almost went nuts but that wasn't Chambers' fault!

Finally after about two or three weeks of this they let us out of quarantine, and eventually we got out of the Philadelphia Navy Yard. We didn't have much of a sick bay. We really had no sick bay, but the medical locker was one of the prettiest medical lockers you've ever seen on any ship because Chambers had gone and gotten these old-fashioned, small medicine bottles. I often suspected that there was just colored water in most of them, but he had them all arranged in a synthetic arrangement of colors. That was our pride and joy on inspection, to take a look at the medicine cabinet, with these racks of these beautiful medicines up there. As I say, I don't know what was in there, and I'm not sure he did, but they looked nice anyway.

We got out of there and we went to Boston.

Q: You were assigned to Boston, too?

Adm. R.: We went back to Boston.

Q: On the same kind of duty?

Adm. R.: The same duty, for I don't know how long.

Q: Until May of 1932.

Adm. R.: Yes, and then I think I went to the rifle team from that.

The thing that happened there was our collision. I was on the Herndon when she collided.

Q: Tell me about that.

Adm. R.: We were cruising down off of Long Island in a fog and, of course, that was when the rummies could really give us fits, so you had to cruise pretty actively. I think it was the Mystic Coal Company, the old Burroughs. We'd just finished lunch when we heard this signal and we all jumped up and started to try to get out. We heard our engines going astern. I remember getting to the top of the companionway just as the bow of the Burroughs came right alongside of me. I always remember looking up about 30 feet and here's the bow lookout of the Burroughs looking down on me. I don't know what he thought. They backed out and then they lost us in the fog. That's how thick it was.

Q: But you did collide?

Adm. R.: Oh, they started in just about the wardroom. They hit the wardroom, cut right through the skin of the ship into the pantry, which was on the port side, and right on into the forward engineroom. The bow of the ship stopped on the saddle of one of the boilers. Another six inches and it would have gone into the boiler and that would have really caused trouble. When they backed out, in the pantry to the wardroom, the steward and two boys were sitting there eating their rice and fish or whatever they were eating, and I often thought it might have been a horrible sensation because they couldn't get out. Just like sitting in this room - and the pantry was probably only eight feet square, you know - and just to have the outside skin taken away by this ship and then when she backed away, here you are, sitting right on the front porch looking out to sea!

I'm not sure, but I think the doors had jammed a little bit so they had the devil of a time getting out.

You learn by your experiences and that taught me one thing. For years I've always kicked at collision drill at quarters, putting that crazy mat over, and thinking this would never work and so forth and so on. I was right because, after all, we had a hole 40 feet long skinned off the side of the ship and just open to the ocean. I was right about that, but it did teach me one thing about the value of drills. Of course, it is true it was in the middle of the day, but in two or three minutes every man was at his station. There wasn't any confusion, and fortunately nobody was hurt. One guy did have a bum back. In fact, I believe it was Chambers himself because he slipped going up a ladder and somebody stepped on him. But it was minor, nothing serious.

Of course, we got all the bulkheads battened down and water-tight doors.

Q: The Burroughs was what, a coaler?

Adm. R.: A collier, ferrying coal for Mystic Coal Company, I think.

Q: Was she damaged?

Adm. R.: No, apparently not. It was just like a knife slicing off a piece of cheese. The further along it got, the deeper it got. She started in thin, right about the wardroom, and took off maybe two feet of the pantry after that. I forget what was aft of that, I think the office, and she took off about three feet of that. It was about five feet deep by the time it got into the boiler room.

Q: What is the procedure in the Coast Guard? Is there a court of inquiry?

Adm. R.: Yes, they had a court after this. Actually, it wasn't anybody's fault, as I recall it.

Q: The skipper was not held accountable?

Adm. R.: No. As I say, the thing loomed up all of a sudden. In the wardroom we heard their signal once and we heard our engines going astern, and that was all. The officer of the deck hadn't heard it. Of course, we'd been sounding our signal, so it was just a case of two ships being in the wrong place at the right time.

It seems to me we had some trouble getting out signals at first. I guess we killed our power. I think that was it. The Burroughs sent out a signal that we had collided, but for a while we were lost. Nobody knew where we were. Nobody could find us. The Burroughs couldn't find us again. As a matter of fact, in Washington they heard about this. Admiral Spencer, the one I mentioned was at the Academy, was in Washington and he knew my mother. He called her and said if she saw anything in the papers or heard anything, don't pay any attention because he was sure it wasn't bad. They thought, as a matter of fact, that the ship had gone down.

About four o'clock in the afternoon the fog started to lift and it was the darnedest sight I've ever seen. We were right in the middle of what must have been ten ships in a circle all around us, looking for us and maneuvering in. But when the fog lifted, we were right in the center of them. They took us in to New London. All the staterooms were flooded. I lost everything I had in the way of clothes - all the staterooms below were flooded. The captain had a stateroom right under the bridge.

They got us in to New London on Saturday, I think it was, Saturday morning, and here again you learn by experience. We were down by the bow. I think Captain Crapster was the Destroyer Force commander at the time. Of course, everybody came down to see the wrecked ship with her stern up in the air and bow down. They wanted to look down below to see the damage, so before we could stop the visiting party they opened up the chain locker and so on. We had this all battened down. We said no, no, let's not open this or that up. Oh, yes, let's open it up. So, okay, we opened it up. Of course, we had a certain amount of buoyancy, being sealed down, but the minute we opened up the hatch covers, why out came all the buoyancy and the next thing we knew the bow was sitting on the bottom. Of course, the stern was still up.

Q: After you'd been towed in!

Adm. R.: Yes, we'd been towed in. The bow's sitting on the bottom. Fortunately, we were in shoal water, so the bow is under water but the bottom stopped it from sinking further. It couldn't go any lower. I don't know what would have happened if we'd been out in deep water.

Then, of course, you see it's Saturday and the whistle blows. It's time for everybody to go home. So all the shore-based personnel shove off and here we are with our ship and "just make the best of it, boys," in our fairly wet clothes. We started the pumps and managed to pump out some and get her half-way afloat.

I had kind of a scare. I was trying to get the ammunition out of the forward ammunition hold. We had one of these underwater pumps. Of course, the doors to the ammunition holds were closed - you go down into a well, you know, to pump the water and we weren't watching them. By this time, it's about midnight Saturday and we'd been up about twenty-four hours, so I guess none of us were paying too much attention and it sucked dry, and those underwater pumps if they come out of water they arc. Boy, we got the darnedest arc out of there you've ever seen, and we thought for a minute we were all going to kingdom come. Actually, all it was was an arc but, believe me, we got that one cut off pretty fast.

Q: You mentioned the ammunition. What sort of guns did you carry on a Coast Guard destroyer?

Adm. R.: On those destroyers, we had the regular guns. What were they? Four-inch, I think, as I recall. I started to say 5-inch, but I don't think they were.

Q: What would a gun like that be used for?

Adm. R.: Well, it was the regular Navy armament we carried. And, of course, at that time we had started sending the destroyers south to Guantanamo. I never made that trip because I got off before that, but we would send them down to go through gunnery practice, and we used to fire target practice. This brings up another story.

Q: Let me pursue that just a second. When would you use, under what circumstances would you use, 4-inch guns?

Adm. R.: Well, if we were operating as part of the Navy. You see, we were supposed to be able to operate the guns and fire them.

Q: But not in strictly Coast Guard service?

Adm. R.: No. Well, there were shots fired at some of these rummies to stop them, they'd fire a shot across the bow, but we never used anything of that caliber. We'd use the 20-caliber or something like that.

Q: So this was just in case of a conflict when the Navy took you over?

Adm. R.: Yes, well the guns were there and it's the old story, you might as well be able to use them. The Pontchartrain had two 5-inch. The guns were put on there as part of the Navy's equipment.

So, as I say, our destroyers used to go down to Guantanamo and fire target practice, and then we'd fire off the coast.

I started to tell you this story, and I've always liked this one because it seems to me it's the proper answer for most everything.

One division would observe for another division. I wasn't present on this, so I'm only repeating the story as it was told to me, but I know what happened. The commanding officer of the Boston Division was a very ardent ordnance specialist. He really liked it, and he was also a very intense, able, sincere officer. The commanding officer of the New York Division was an equally able officer but a sort of devil-may-care type, nothing ever worried him. They were going to fire off of Gloucester. The Boston Division were to be the observers and the New York Division was to do the firing. The commander took his Boston Division out, put them in line, and in order to get this thing off to a big start, waited for the New York Division, which was due to arrive. So, here's the Boston Division holding their line, and up over the horizon comes the New York Division. They come steaming along, right in front of the line. They pass the flagship or the division commander and no signals, no nothing, and head right straight for Gloucester. By this time, they're getting pretty well along the line, so signal flags begin to go out and so forth, and the gist of the message was:

"What are you plans?", assuming that the New York Division was all set. Back from the New York Division, finally a signal comes up:

"We have no plans," and they steamed right on in to Gloucester!

So that's always been my pet statement. Someone says, what are your plans, and my answer is I have no plans.

There was an aftermath of that Herndon story. They finally moved us back up - this one's on the GAO - to Boston and we went into Boston Navy Yard for overhaul. Well, as I told you, the wardroom was completely flooded out and the forward engineroom was. I had lost everything I had, clothes and everything, to sea water. I made a claim and eventually I was reimbursed reasonably well. But when we got to Boston I was still wearing the same clothes I'd had on on the day of the collision, which was just the week before. I found out, though, that merchants sometimes can be pretty decent. I went up and got credit and told them they'd get paid sometime. So I got some clothes together.

The ship was finally hauled out and we couldn't live on her so we got authority from headquarters to live ashore, so three of us got an apartment up on Beacon Hill for the two months and a half and drew quarters allowance. Three years later - in fact, this was the GAO's wedding present to me - I had just gotten married and I got a letter from headquarters, the gist of which was that I was to reimburse the federal government - I don't know what the quarters were at the time, but it was around $300, which wasn't hay in those days - for the two months or so that I'd been ashore. I was to reimburse the federal government and, if I wanted to, I could spread it out over a number of months. But the point was I had to reimburse them.

Now, the gist of this famous decision by GAO was this. To begin with, you were never allowed to draw quarters while you were on sea duty. Now, here's the ship up in a dry dock, no quarters to live in, that's immaterial. That meant nothing.

Q: The status of the ship hadn't been changed?

Adm. R.: They had never told us to decommission the ship, so our commission pennant was still flying, even though she was in dry dock, therefore the ship was in commission, therefore I was on sea duty, therefore I would reimburse the government for my quarters. I paid them back. Frankly, I suspect if it had been enough and we'd gone to court of claims we could have beaten it. There were two other officers and myself hooked the same way. I guess I'd drawn as much as anybody, probably about $600 for the lot of us, so what was the use of arguing for $600. We paid it back. Except it didn't endear government reasoning to my wife, I can tell you.

Q: When did you marry?

Adm. R.: In 1934. This was several years later. I think what some of these people get now as compared with some of those rules. As we go along I'll have other stories about some of the wild things - not wild things, but the decisions, monetary and other.

Q: Was the Coast Guard affected by that 15 percent cut?

Adm. R.: In 1932?

Q: Yes.

Adm. R.: Very much so. Well, the same as everybody else. I have a story on that but it doesn't belong here. A young officer was getting married and I convinced him that he was a brave man - he was an ensign. He came in the wardroom one day, all exuberant, he was getting married in three weeks. I didn't mean to be funny at all, but this kid was kind of a sap anyway. We'd just gotten a message in typical governmental language. In those days you got $20 a room and an ensign who was married was allowed two rooms, which would be $40. What they did was to cut it by one dollar, so you only got $19. In other words, he'd lose $2. Then you were allowed 60¢ a day for rations, and they cut that 10¢ to 50¢. The message was perfectly clear, except it said "cut one dollar, repeat one dollar" and so forth. You know, the typical government language.

So he came in and we were all sitting around the wardroom table having coffee when he came in. I looked at him and said:

"You certainly are a brave man to get married with this cut facing you."

He said: "What do you mean?" And I said:

"Well, here," and I picked up the message and read it to him, "it says you're only going to get $1 a piece for each room, that's $2. Your base pay is $125 and you're only going to get 10¢ a day, that's $3." I guess he was allowed two rations. "You're going to be living on $136."

"Oh," he said, "that isn't so. Let me see the message."

By that time, his hand was shaking so he couldn't read the message, anyway. He left there convinced that this was it.

Of course, the minute this thing started, everybody around the table picked it up and started pouring it on. How was he going to make out and so forth. But it backfired in a way because I was to be one of the ushers at his wedding. Well, this crazy gook goes up town and he runs into the son of the district commander. Of course, the district commander, being a captain, got about six rooms or so, so he starts commiserating with the son about how much his dad was going to lose on this $1 deal. Instead of getting $120 he was only going to get $6. The son then runs to mama and mama gets on the phone to dad and says "how awful, our pay's going to be practically cut in half," or words to that effect. So dad says that isn't so at all. It was just, as you said, the 15 percent or whatever it was.

At the rehearsal, the wife of the district commander descends on me - oh, I might say this boy had left, he had hired an apartment, this was in Seattle, and we were making up all kinds of plans about how we could take some of his furniture off his hands to help him out, we might even take the apartment over for him. I was single at the time. Anyway, the district commander's wife descends on me about how this was horrible to take advantage of a poor boy who was getting married and so forth. She gave me the devil. So, finally, I thought of a switch and I said:

"Now, look, Mrs. Alger, you've got it all wrong. You see, what we've really done is to give that boy about a $54-a-month wedding present."

She said, "How do you mean?"

"Well," I said, "because after he learned about this, he adjusted his living down to the base of $130 or so and we had him all convinced that he could live on that. Now, he's going to get about $160."

She finally bought this story!

Q: In 1932 you were transferred to the Coast Guard Headquarters?

Adm. R.: Yes. I was at the Headquarters for a very short period. Actually, I really went to the Rifle Team. At that time we were making quite a bid to build up a competitive rifle team and the man who had been in charge of it for several years was Bill Kossler, whom I knew very well. I was to succeed him.

Q: Had you demonstrated your prowess in that area?

Adm. R.: No, I wasn't a particularly good shot, but being

captain of the team was more of an administrative job, anyway. Bill didn't fire. We used to fire for fun but we were not the competitors at the time.

Alos at that time - I've forgotten now whether it was before or at the end of the season - I had thought possibly of getting into aviation. I went to Headquarters to be assigned to the rifle team which, for administrative purposes, was assigned to Headquarters. We trained up at Camp Ritchie for a while and then moved up to Boston, what's the name of it?

Q: Wakefield?

Adm. R.: Yes, Camp Curtis up at Wakefield, and then we went to Camp Perry.

At that time, they were going to put some fellows in aviation so I went down to Quantico and took the examination with another officer.

Q: This was a volunteer thing, was it?

Adm. R.: Yes, I wanted to go into aviation.

Q: What induced you to think about aviation?

Adm. R.: I don't know. We were expanding, getting some

better planes, and I thought I'd like to learn to fly. I was single and it was no great problem. I passed the flight physical all right, but then they decided that I had had too much special duty already so they wouldn't send me to aviation, which was basically correct, except it made me kind of mad why they hadn't made the decision before I went to all the trouble, as I said, of having drops put in my eyes and being spun round in a chair and other things for a medical aviation test. It wasn't a decision that affected my life very much. I wasn't "sold" on it. I mean I wasn't going to go cry about it.

Q: They hadn't decided prior to that perhaps because it was so new and they hadn't developed real policy?

Adm. R.: I don't know why. I think somebody probably handled my application and said go down and take the flight physical, then when it came up to the head of aviation or head of personnel they probably said, well, he's had too much special duty, anyway.

I was then shipped west, to be exec on the Haida, and we were sailing out of Seattle. That was the fall of 1932. Also 1933 I was in Seattle. It seemed like Captain Hinckley and I followed each other around, or I followed him, because he was now district commander in Seattle. At that time Alaska was part of the Seattle district, it was not a separate district, as it is now.

Q: What was the particular function of the Seattle District?

Adm. R.: The same thing. We had rum problems and rescue work and cruising, and also the Bering Sea Patrol. That wasn't confined only to the Seattle area. All the ships along the West Coast took part in that. Of course, in the early days, the Bering Sea Patrol was a seven-months cruise, but by the time I got out there it had been reduced to where the first group went up in April and stayed till about July and then the next group came up and they came down maybe in October.

Q: What was the nature of that patrol?

Adm. R.: To begin with, the commanding officer was a U. S. commissioner and the executive officer was a deputy marshal, and you carried legal and medical aid to these outlying villages all up and down the coast and out in the Aleutian Islands, and visited the native villages. If any serious crimes had been committed, you picked the perpetrators up and brought them back for trial in federal courts or in the courts back at Sitka or Seward or Juneau. But minor offenses, and that's what they mainly were - you know, somebody assaulted somebody, the commissioner would hear the case and we would handle it. Just perform general services. Remember, Alaska in those days was still pretty primitive. That must have been 1933 and, as a matter of fact, I took census through Kodiak, which is now quite a little town - I wasn't the only one, several of the officers did it - and there were no roads you just wandered into the back yard of one house and the front yard of another house. That kind of thing. You wandered in and out and tried to find out who lived in the village.

Q: That was pretty rugged duty, wasn't it?

Adm. R.: I don't know. I liked Alaska, I always did, and I enjoyed the duty. Some people thought it was difficult duty.

Q: I was thinking of weatherwise?

Adm. R.: Well, it can be horrible and it can be very good. It's like the little girl with the curl, you know. It can be very, very good but when it's not good it's horrid. I used to use the expression and I think it probably still pertains - Alaska was never as bad as most Coast Guard officers who'd never served there would like to have you believe it was, but it wasn't as good as the Alaska Steamship folders said it was - "sail in sheltered seas." That's about the best way I can describe it. It was and I guess still is a magnificent country. The weather's rough but -

Q: Judging from the accounts I've heard of the williwaws!

Adm. R.: Yes, but the williwaws are not bad if you're out in the open, but it's pretty rough to be making a docking and have one of those williwaws catch you because it's just like one of these down drafts on a landing strip. One minute you're being blown off the dock and have to fight to get in, and the next minute, wham, you've switched 180° and you're hitting the dock. That kind of thing.

Q: And the fog, too?

Adm. R.: Yes, the fog and the snow. I won't kid you. It can be rough at times. But, as I say, I've always enjoyed Alaska. Of course, it's changed so much now. There's still lots of beautiful country and lots of open space.

I was very fortunate. I liked Alaska from the very first. I got out there in the fall, probably in October, and except for the fact that I had an appendicitis operation about a month after I got out there which laid me up for a little bit, but the next summer Harold O. Hinckley - in those days the district commander was supposed to cruise his area once a year - decided that the way to cruise his area was to have a hunting and fishing trip. So he chose the Haida and he took with him the then-coach of the Washington Huskies, Jim Phelan, and the collector of customs, a man by the name of Hubbard, and a guy called Skinner of Skinner, Eddy Shipbuilding. We went up the Inside Passage as far as Juneau but, unlike most ships that go up there, we went, for example, to Wrangel - ordinarily you just stop there and go on up - but we went all around the island, hunting and fishing, fishing mainly. They were bear-hunting, with guides, of course, and we were fishing and taking pictures.

So I really got an unusual bird's eye view of southeastern Alaska, from Ketchikan all the way to Juneau, Sitka, and all these various places. It was an interesting way to cut your teeth. That, I guess, was in the spring. Then I made a Bering Sea patrol. I must have made two Bering Sea patrols. I enjoyed my whole time up there.

Q: Were there any incidents of Japanese espionage?

Adm. R.: I suppose there were. I can't say from actual knowledge that there were. Every Alaskan up there in those days was suspicious of the Japs - we didn't take the Japanese seriously down in the United States. I used to facetiously say that the Alaskans instead of telling their children that there was a boogeyman in the closet, probably told them there was a Japanese in the closet or something like that. They claimed all along that the Japanese were moving in. But whether it was a question of espionage or jealousy over the fact that the Japanese were sending these big fishing factory ships into Bristol Bay. There were some clashes with them up there, but I think they were mainly over fishing rights and things of that nature. You'd hear stories about how at Adak - you know, when you go in and visit the village the natives would say, "Well, you know, last fall a Japanese fisherman came and lived with us all year."

You'd ask what he did and "He wandered around." I haven't any doubt that these were planted. In other words, he was supposed to be in distress and, of course, the natives would take care of them. He'd live with them and then he'd take these long walks and I haven't any doubt he was probably out surveying. This was quite a common story and I'm sure that was going on.

Q: You went to the Pribilofs, too?

Adm. R.: Yes, we went to the Pribilofs. That was another thing we had to do, patrol the seal fishery and the halibut fishing off -

Q: Was this to see that the treaties were being observed?

Adm. R.: Right, that there'd be no pelagic sealing. And, of course, we were always on the lookout to see that there was no sea-otter fishing because they're entirely protected.

Q: Did you discover any violations?

Adm. R.: The ships I was on never did. I suppose that from time to time there were violations.

Q: The treaties in that time were not very stringent, were they?

Adm. R.: Yes. By the time I got up there, the seal herds had developed to a point where they knew the herds were safe. Before I left Alaska, maybe this was right after the war, but I heard at one time they had more sealskins than they knew what to do with. They were all supposed to be governmentally taken and then put into a common pool. I guess they were stored in St. Louis or something as stock for the various signatories rather than for pelagic sealing. They did it that way.

I don't know how true this is, but I heard that really they had enough sealskins to make it a reasonably cheap commodity, but, like diamonds, they controlled the output to hold the value up. Whether that's true or not, I don't know. Another thing, of course, was that the bottom had dropped out of sealskins to a degree.

Q: Because money wasn't available to buy them?

Adm. R.: To a degree, but also you don't see sealskin much. There was a time when it was like raccoon coats, you know. If you had a raccoon coat, you were "in."

Another thing we used to trade in up there - I say "we" traded in but I mean was traded in a lot were fox skins, red fox, blue fox, and all the rest. There were quite a lot of foxes on those islands.

It was interesting duty.

Q: It was diversified duty!

Adm. R.: Oh, yes, and it was interesting cruising. The first Bering Sea patrol, I went up to Nome. That was before the fire, the old Nome. We still have a lifeboat station there. In fact, it was the only piece of beach along there, in front of our lifeboat station, that was part of the first beach line and you could still pan a little gold out of it, at that time.

I don't know whether you know the story there. Nome had what they called "the first beach line." The ice had pushed the land down. The first beach line was where gold was first disvoered. You could just go down where the water rolled in and pan your gold. Of course, that had eventually panned out. Then they discovered gold back on the second beach line, which was sort of back of the town. They used to dig a little bit in the tundra and you'd get down to the second beach line and pan it there. I guess that eventually wore out. Then they went back to what they called the third beach line. When I was there they were working the third beach line. But working the third beach line required a lot of money because they had to dig a hole and put in these hydraulic dredges and that sort of thing. They were still getting gold out in sizeable quantities from the third beach line. That was forty years ago. I don't know what's up there now. I guess nothing.

Q: Was there anything comparable to the Atlantic ice patrol in the Bering Strait?

Adm. R.: No, there was no need for it. There wasn't enough shipping and if you went up there you went up there on your own. In fact, the only ship that I recall running up there regularly was, at that time, in Indian Service vessel, the Northwind, but they played the ice pretty well. And, of course, in the summertime the Bering Sea is free of ice and the fact that you have the strait there precludes icebergs coming down. Malaspina Glacier spews out a few icebergs. That's, of course, right at the bend at Yakutat, right where Alaska takes that bend to the west. And, of course, up in Prince William's Sound, off the Columbia Glacier, you get breakouts, but by the time they get out to the gulf, where there might be major shipping, in the first place they're relatively small to begin with and by the time they get out they've practically gone. I don't remember encountering any appreciable icebergs.

Q: All of this was happening based on Seattle?

Adm. R.: I was based on Seattle. As I say, the first summer I made this cruise with Hinckley - the Haida made the cruise, taking Hinckley on his inspection. Then, the following fall, I'd guess in November, we had an interesting experience. If you recall, I forget just when it was, prohibition was repealed. I think that would have been the fall of 1933.

Q: 1933, that's right. The 18th Amendment was repealed.

Adm. R.: Yes. We had done some chasing of rum-runners up off the Washington coast, but not a great deal because, in the first place, the weather was rough, and it was rather an unproductive place to try to run in because of the long distance in to, say, Seattle, or to come in the Columbia River. There are no big cities near the coast, that's what it amounted to.

Q: Did they use the Juan de Fuca Strait?

Adm. R.: Well, even coming in there, there was too much chance of being caught. There was a little bit of it. I remember staying out with one rummy for a while, but with the rough weather and all there was very little going on up there.

But when prohibition was repealed there were quite a few boats down off of Los Angeles, where they used to run in. They had a great big steamer, a supply ship, that used to cruise off Ensenada. There were some schooners, and there were some of these modified rum-boats that I mentioned on the East Coast.

Q: Their source of supply was where?

Adm. R.: Most of them were from this big freighter, for example, that carried it down. To answer your question specifically, some of it came out of Vancouver, some of it came from Tahiti - they'd bring it all the way across and run it in.

Well, when prohibition was declared, apparently these boys who were working off - I'd had nothing to do with this up to this time - some of these boys who were owned by syndicate people decided that, after all, now that liquor was acceptable in the United States, they would like to bring it in, put it in, put it in bond, and then sell it to local dealers like Distillers, I guess, which was pretty sensible, except I think the real catch was that Seagrams, for example, had been laying up for prohibition going out and had their vats filled with liquor which they'd probably been storing for a good many years and they wanted to sell. This is supposition. I can't say it was so. But I've always felt that probably when this proposition of bringing it in, putting it in, putting it in a bonded warehouse, and holding it till it could be sold in competition with home-grown stuff, they put pressure on the federal government one way or another to say, "Hey, you boys have been doing this to us, running it in, for this many years, we're not going to take this. So get going with your liquor."

So here were these boys off the coast of southern California with a very sizeable supply of liquor. Most of these fellows were lying off of Ensenada down here. They weren't off Los Angeles. And then the runner boats would go down, pick up a load, and come back. So it was decided that we would reinstitute more or less the picket-line concept, so that these boys could not possibly get their liquor in, and we weren't going to let them bring it in to bonded warehouses. In other words, this was an insult to the majesty of the government, after trying to run it in that they should bring it in legally. So they collected all the ships on the West Coast, amongst which was the Haida, and we came down and worked out of Los Angeles. We'd go down and spend three or four weeks off of Ensenada. We were down there from, oh, I'd say November until after Christmas. Very, very boring. Anchored. Just lying there day by day. At night you'd sit there and signal over to them, and talk back and forth. They had no place to go. They were waiting for orders where to go with their liquor. They knew they weren't going to run it in. They were hoping to get permission to take it in and put it in bond, but it was pretty obvious with us collected there that probably the government wasn't going to give on this point.

As I say, we just lay down there. We hadn't anything to do, really. Most of the time we were anchored. Some times we'd pull up the hook and cruise a little bit for fun. We would have boat races and anything at all to kill time. Play shuffleboard. We laid out some shuffleboard counts on deck.

One funny thing came out of it. Finally, one of these guys, after he'd been there for a long time, began to run short of water. He wanted to know if we couldn't sell him 30,000 or 40,000 gallons of water. After all, the poor fellow was getting thirsty. Of course, the answer was pretty obvious that we could even give him water, must less sell it to him. But I've always been amused because our ship passed the message to the fleet commander, the fleet commander passed it to the district, the district passed it all the way to headquarters, and finally the answer came back no. I always thought it was kind of stupid. We ought to have told him no right off, or else ask for permission to trade him x gallons of water for x gallons of liquor, but nobody ever took my suggestion seriously.

I was down there, I think, until January. Then I think the big freighter went back to Vancouver. I think he finally got permission to put his stuff in bond in Vancouver. I don't know where it was from. One schooner was from Tahiti. He turned round and went back to Tahiti. Gradually they dispersed and there was no more rum-running. They weren't even trying to run it, so there wasn't anything to do.

That was the end of that, so we steamed merrily back to Seattle.

The following April I got married.

Q: Did you marry a Seattle girl?

Adm. R.: She was actually born in Michigan but I had met her in Seattle. I got married and nine days later I left on the Bering Sea Patrol.

Q: To be based in Alaska?

Adm. R.: No. I came back to Seattle after the end of the Bering Sea Patrol. It was on that trip that we went to Nome and all the way out to the islands. I visited practically every island up there, and came back and had a 45-day leave. I took my wife east on our honeymoon to visit my mother and family.

We came back and I got a new skipper, who was Frank Gorman, the same one I mentioned was enlisted personnel officer back in the old days. Frank relieved Mike Ryan, who had been my skipper. As you know, Frank Gorman had really been the crown prince of the Coast Guard. He was a brilliant man. I've facetiously said many times that drunk he was smarter than most officers sober. Unfortunately, he drank too much. Otherwise, he would probably have ended up by being commandant.

I think it came as a sort of surprise to him when in December the ship was transferred, or ordered to proceed, to Cordova, Alaska, as our station.

Q: Was that a regular Coast Guard station?

Adm. R.: It hadn't been up to then, but for some reason or other they had decided to station a ship there. The only ship we had in Alaska at that time was the Tallapoosa, which had been in Juneau.

The Tallapoosa was there, and they decided to have a ship out to the westward. You see, on the Bering Sea patrol they only had ships at Dutch Harbor. That was our base. We operated out of Dutch Harbor. Of course, there were no ships up there in the wintertime.

There had been a couple of disasters up there. Many of the merchant ships coming across followed the great-circle course and the Japanese current, which brought them a few hundred miles south of Dutch Harbor, and in the winter in some of those gales there had been one or two bad disasters. So I think they figured that they ought to have a larger ship farther out to the westward and, some way or another, they chose Cordova. Seward was a little farther out, but not much. It wouldn't have made any difference, or much difference. So we were transferred to Cordova.

I was there, then, from about January until the following fall. It was an interesting experience.

Q: You were separated from your new bride?

Adm. R.: No, because we knew we could get quarters up there of sorts, so as soon as we got up there we started looking around. There was the Winslow Hotel, I think, and they took two or three rooms and made them into a little apartment. I think it was April when my wife came up and she stayed up.

We had some interesting experiences there.

The first experience we had was going up. Here again, we get into stringent government regulations. Prices in Alaska have always been high, as you probably know, because you've got freight charges. This was before the Matanuska Valley experiment. There were really no green groceries that you can ever get, or couldn't at that time, anyway. We knew that things were going to be expensive, particularly for the enlisted men. It wasn't too bad for the officers. We figured we could ride with it.

So we wrote to headquarters and asked could we sell to the men, who had taken their wives up, from the general mess. And, of course, as was to be expected, this had never been heard of, so the answer came back a flat, emphatic no. I don't know who thought it up - maybe I concocted the idea, but anyway we decided to make a canvas to find out how many men wanted to take their families up. Then I went up to Swanback, this wholesale grocery, and asked them how good the wardroom credit was. They said very good. We bought our own supplies from them. So they gave me a wholesale catalogue and I asked each man who was taking his wife to take a catalogue home and come back and give me a list of what they thought they would need for the next three, four or five months, in the way of canned goods and various things.

What we were going to do was to take this aboard - well, what we did. I made up a composite list of all these things. We put it on the wardroom bill, that is, the wardroom owed the money to Swanback. Then when we got up to Cordova we let the men then take this stuff ashore and they paid us monthly. No profit. It was just whatever it cost, they paid, and we shared.

The net result was when we left Seattle the wardroom was packed tight with canned goods - that was the only place we had to stow it. You could barely get to the mess table, walking through these columns of canned goods.

The wardroom owed something between $3,000 and $4,000 for food for the families that we were underwriting for this period.

I had one interesting experience. I was compiling these lists and one of these orders was for a case of tabasco sauce. Well, to me, a bottle of tabasco sauce is used maybe once in ten years - one in ten years. So I rang the bell for the boy and I said:

"Have the watertender - I think he was a watertender - come up."

He came up and I said: "Look, you don't use a case of tabasco sauce. One bottle."

"I don't know," he said, "my wife made it up. If you say, so, Sir, one bottle."

So I ordered one bottle and we sailed off to Alaska. About six months later, we were down again and went through the same rigamarole, and the same thing happened - a case of tabasco sauce. So I rang again and he came up, but this time he was prepared. He said:

"Oh, no, Sir, you're wrong. My wife likes tabasco sauce. I want a case of it."

So I got a case of it, but I found out the real story. It's unfortunate and that's why I don't want to mention names. His wife drank fairly heavily and I suppose every morning she had a Bloody Mary or something and half a bottle of tabasco sauce in it! I always laughed about that case of tabasco. I was convinced that he didn't mean it.

Well, we sailed up there with all this stuff. The trouble in Alaska even at that time was they didn't use pennies. If something came out to be 16 cents, you didn't pay 16 cents, you paid 20 cents or 25.

Q: Always the higher figure?

Adm. R.: Always the higher, never the under figure.

I was up there about nine months and then transferred back to Washington.

Another story comes back to me. I had one officer who always seemed to be able - he was quite an electronics expert, but a little bit on the odd side, and he would always tell something on himself. He was the chief observer at some target practice for one of our 125-footers. They'd gone down below Port Angeles. I forget what those 125-footers had on them in the way of armament, but it could have been a 3-inch. They fired at an anchored target. So they anchored the target up against a bluff down below Port Angeles, and, of course there was nothing but trees and so forth in the back. He was chief observer. They started firing away at this target and I guess it was going pretty well, when, all of a sudden, the air got full of messages from Port Angeles, "For God's sake stop shooting up the railroad."

He gets in a boat and goes in to Port Angeles. It seems

that back in the woods there was a spur line that ran down to the Indian reservation and they had to replace a rail. The boys had worked merrily on putting this rail down and fortunately the noon whistle blew just about the time they had it halfway down. They grab their lunch pails and go over to one side and sit down. Just as they were sitting down, up through the woods comes a 3-inch shell and catches this rail right in the middle, picks it right up off the tracks and bends it into a perfect U. Whereupon these Pollocks lit out for Port Angeles on the double!

The fellow who managed the railroad gets on the long-distance phone and calls the firing party. The chief observer explains that they won't do it again. "Okay," he said, "just forget it. I'll tell them to put the rail back, but for God's sake stop shooting our railroad to pieces."

They never made an official report but he told me this story. It just shows how sometimes you can be lucky.

I remember another occasion. There used to be an old Alaska Steamship Company vessel, the _Victoria_, that ran - took passengers - out to Juneau and out to Seward and back. They left just after Christmas to go up to Juneau of their regular cruise and somewhere up in Narrows they went aground, and they were hard aground. We were in Port Angeles at the time and we were dispatched to get up there as fast as we could.

You were talking about rough running. No, it wasn't

Seymour Narrows. That's where you're supposed to go through on a slacktide. It's since been blasted out, I think, but in those days that was the scary part of running to Alaska. But it was snowing, and it took us just about twenty-four hours to make the run. They were aground somewhere right below Ketchikan, as I recall it. We had to run at a certain speed in order to hit Seymour Narrows - we ran full out, let's put it that way - on the slack tide to get through there. We had everybody who could stand a watch standing it because you couldn't see beyond the bow of the ship. That was really a hairy experience, and the worth of it was that we got up there and found the ships passengers enjoying a New Year's Eve party. It was still snowing. We arriving up there on New Year's Eve.

An ex-classmate of mine who had gotten out of the Coast Guard but was back in as a temporary officer, was on the ship - he and his wife - going up to go to the Tallapoosa. I took the boat and went over to see what the conditions were before we put a line on them to pull them off and here he was, leaning over the side. Everybody on the ship was having a wonderful time. It was New Year's Eve and they were really celebrating.

Q: So they weren't afraid at all?

Adm. R.: Oh, no. They were high and dry. As I recall it,

the old <u>Victoria</u> had a wrought iron hull so that all she would do was hit the rocks and bounce a little bit. But in this case they had wedged themselves in, and we finally put a line on them the next morning and gave them a heave-ho.

That was a hairy run. It really was. I had several of them while I was on that Alaskan duty. I had to take the ship out of Cordova one night, and Cordova was a nasty place to run out of, too.

Another interesting experience I had up there. The Fisheries always had a representative.

Q: The Bureau of Fisheries?

Adm. R.: Yes. They had a representative because there's a limit on the salmon that they can take and that sort of thing. This fellow's name was Gus Hawkins. He had to fly quite a little bit. He'd been over to Juneau and they were coming back from Juneau and the fog set in and they were flying pretty low along the beach line at Malaspina. Kirkpatrick, the pilot, caught his wing on the tip of a tree and plonked down on the beach, and it was about a week before they were gotten off. That kind of killed Gus' enthusiasm for flying. His secretary was his daughter. This was a seasonal job for him and for her, and she'd fallen in love with some guy there who had gone south, so she decided she's go home. My wife had been a stenographer, so he offered her the job of being his secretary. Every weekend he was supposed to fly to the fish traps to see that they were closed for the period.

After he had this accident, he decided he'd lost his interest in flying and, since there were only two in the office, and she was junior, why, she was elected to fly the fish traps. She asked me if I wanted to go along. She'd sit up in the front seat with the pilot, Kirkpatrick, and we'd go out and fly all round Prince William Sound and we'd come up to a fish trap. She didn't know whether the thing was closed or open. I didn't either, as far as that's concerned. Kirkpatrick would point down and she'd nod. Then this Beechcraft would take off and round we'd go. It was a lot of fun because we had a chance to see Columbia Glacier from the air and all around. It was about six weeks that she had this temporary job.

It was a lot of fun up there in Cordova. It was one of these places where when the ship was coming in the line telephone operator would get on the line and ring all the wives and tell them the ship was on her way in. And when the mail came in, everybody would go down. You'd see the ship come in to the dock and then beat it up to the Post Office. The passenger ship only came in once a week. You'd wait outside till the mail was distributed, and that was a chance to visit. We really enjoyed the time there.

Then, in the fall - I don't know whether I'd applied for it but I think I had - I was ordered back to Washington to go to law school.

Q: What induced you to turn to law?

Adm. R.: I'd always been interested a little bit.

Q: After all, you'd taken a judge's place!

Adm. R.: Oh, that didn't enter into it. I was only in there two or three weeks while he was on leave.

I think they sent out and wanted to know whether anyone was interested and I thought it would be a good opportunity.

Q: They wanted some legal training in the service?

Adm. R.: They'd decided that it was time to train some officers. So Ralph Curry, another officer, and I were the first to be chosen to go to law school and we came back to George Washington.

Interview #2 with Admiral Alfred C. Richmond, U. S. Coast Guard
(Retired)

Place: His residence in Claremont, California

Date: Tuesday morning, 18 November 1975

Subject: Biography

By: John T. Mason, Jr.

Q: Well, Sir, when we concluded yesterday, you were going to tell me about your experience in going to law school in Washington, D. C..

Adm. R.: You asked me why I was interested in law and it occurred to me, after thinking it over, there was another incident that had taken place some years before that had made me rather interested in law. It was while I was serving on the destroyers in Boston. I don't recall now whether I was then on the Wainwright or the Herndon. I think it was while I was on the Wainwright.

We had a very unfortunate incident happen off Gloucester, one of these unusual circumstances that sometimes come up. The Gloucester base, at which our 75-footers were moored during the rum-running days and so forth, had been having quite a bit of trouble with rum-running, especially up the Essex River and those various little rivers there, and the commanding officer, who was then Commander Eugene Coffin, got himself authority to get a small - I believe 14-foot -

outboard motorboat, with the idea that this boat would cruise up the rivers that the 38 and 75-footers couldn't in the shoal water.

On this particular night they dispatched out a warrant officer by the name of Olmstead, who had with him a young man, a seaman, as I recall, whose name I don't remember, and they cruised up north of the cape there at Gloucester into that bay off New Hampshire. About dusk or a little bit later, they located or saw a cabin cruiser anchored off the coast, so they went over and boarded it. There was nobody aboard and there was nothing on it to indicate who owned it or anything. There was a chart on the deck and the particular section in which the boat was anchored was torn out of the chart in the cabin.

It was sort of unusual to find an abandoned cabin cruiser and Olmstead reasoned that maybe this was a marker that had been left there for rum boats to run in on. In afterthought, maybe it was fallacious thinking, yet the whole thing was a little bit unusual, but he said, "we'll stake out here for the night and see what happens and, if nothing, in the morning we'll go in and report the boat and have it towed in."

I've forgotten the name of the lifeboat station just north of there, but they were also at that time cruising to stop the rum-runners and they had their surf boat out on night patrol also. And round about ten or eleven o'clock at night they spotted the cabin cruiser and started to work in without lights.

Olmstead told the fireman - I remember now, it was not a seaman but a fireman - who was with him on this patrol to pass up the machinegun and a flashlight and was lying on the bow of the cabin cruiser when the surfboat got within hailing distance. He hailed them and told them to stop. Now, there's confusion as to what the hail was. Anyway, apparently the surfboat, thinking they had stumbled into some rummies or something, turned to head out. Olmstead called to them again and then opened fire.

One of the bullets caught one of the surfmen and killed him. Of course, the surfboat beat it back, said they'd been fired on by rummies. Olmstead went on in and reported he'd fired on rummies. The confusion was rampant, and the papers picked it up. It obviously led to a court, first a board, and the board recommended that Olmstead, who had fired and one of our own men had died, be court-martialed.

Commander von Paulsen was the prosecutor. I regret to say that the commanding officer of the base was a little evasive on the orders that these boys had had. In other words, he wasn't standing behind Olmstead too clearly. I don't know how I got into it, maybe because of my brief experience at headquarters in the law office, but I was recommended for defense counsel. I was the defense counsel with him before the board of inquiry - or maybe it was a board of investigation. I don't know. We had both in those days.

I had done quite a little bit of what I would like to call pseudo detective work in trying to unravel what had actually happened. Apparently the cabin cruiser was perfectly legitimate. It had broken down out there and the people had taken their skiff and gone ashore and were coming back the next day to get it. There was no connection there, except that they were very evasive as to why they were out there on that particular day. There seemed to be no connection between them and the rummies, nothing that you could definitely trace, anyway.

It was marred on the lifeboat side by the fact that after they had left the station they had tied up at a dock for a while, presumably to get supplies, but the man in charge - I think he was cleared - was married, but the man who was killed had had a couple of girls come down and entertained them. I don't think there was anything out of the ordinary, but it would have looked bad to say that these girls were on the surfboat and all. It was the kind of thing that in the open you didn't like to bring out a lot of things that might smear a reputation and really were quite innocent and had no bearing on the facts of the case.

Also, there was confusion on the boat. Olmstead claimed that what they heard was something to the effect, "let's get the hell out of here" and his fireman backed him up. Of course, there was only one survivor for the lifeboat. It was all conflicting and it was entirely possible that the survivor in the boat really felt that he had heard what he heard. On the water, you know, sounds and voices change, and probably both sides were scared to death as to what they were getting into.

The one thing in our favor was that the bullets had entered the lifeboat from about midships, going forward. The man who was killed was actually in the bow of the boat but the bullets hit him from the rear, indicating that the lifeboat had turned - had partially turned, it had not made a complete turn, or else they'd have got the coxswain of the boat, the senior officer.

The board of investigation recommended that Olmstead be court-martialed, and I think that was where it really went wrong. Headquarters went along with this recommendation on the theory that, well, all right, so we find that he was guilty of violating orders and that's all there will be to it and it would be entirely in the Coast Guard. As a matter of fact, yesterday in my discussion I mentioned having been in the district attorney's office. Now, it comes back to me why I was visiting the district attorney. He assured me that if Olmstead was found guilty - guilty of misfeasance or anything like that, even if the Coast Guard reduced him in rank or gave him what amounted to a slap on the wrist - it would be more or less incumbent on the district attorney's office to step in and prosecute outside the Coast Guard for manslaughter. But I couldn't convince headquarters that this would happen.

So, to make a long story short, he was court-martialed. At this point, I began to get scared that I was not adequate counsel and, through the recommendation of friends, I prevailed. I regret to say I've forgotten the name of the lawyer who replaced me as senior defense counsel, but he was a corporation counsel. That was where he made his money, but I interested him in the case and told him that Olmstead didn't have a whole lot of money to pay. I think that, as a corporation counsel, he thought the chance to try what could be - to appear in a court-martial would put him back in quasi-criminal law, so he considered it a sort of busman's holiday and took the case. He was a very able counsel. The long and the short of it was that we were successful in getting Olmstead acquitted of the court-martial charges.

It was a very sticky case and probably really excited my interest in law, and that was probably why, when the information came out that they were going to send officers to law school, I put my request in.

Q: So this was a great motivation for studying law in Washington. Where did you study?

Adm. R.: George Washington University.

Q: And did you go during the day?

Richmond #2 - 161

Adm. R.: Yes, I was completely relieved of all responsibility at headquarters. Now, the Navy officers that were there, reported in daily, I believe, but we were completely relieved of duty, except in the summertime. In the summertime, we didn't go to school and spent the time at headquarters.

Q: This was sort of comparable to the Navy's sending a man to postgraduate school?

Adm. R.: Yes, it was. As I say, we had just inaugurated about that time our first PG courses. Up to that time, I don't think we had many. I don't remember just when we inaugurated sending officers over to the PG school. I think several years before. Then they decided that they'd expand it into law. Later, we sent officers to MIT and a number of schools.

Q: Where was your PG school?

Adm. R.: We used the Navy's in Annapolis, particularly for engineering and so forth.

Q: So you spent three years there?

Adm. R.: I spent three years there, which was very interesting. I enjoyed it. I found that as you get older, you probably have a better appreciation of what you're studying but I know in my class - most of the other day students were a lot younger than either Curry or I and they were much quicker at picking up things, that is memorywise. We had to really bone for our courses.

One interesting thing we had during that period was that Admiral Waesche, who by that time was commandant - Hamlet had succeeded Billard and Waesche had succeeded Hamlet, had the idea that we would have better federal law enforcement if the commanding officers, who were generally warrant officers or mostly chief petty officers, of our small boats - 75-footers - had a better understanding of the maritime laws, both the inspection laws and enforcement laws primarily, because, as you know, the Coast Guard is the law enforcement agency on the navigable waters of the United States. So it was suggested that we form a team of officers, about three officers, actually, and kind of put together a course. I think it was my second summer. We'd got round to the various bases where we had these boats and take the commanding officers of the boats and personnel from the boats and give them a course of sprouts in the generalities of law enforcement. Obviously, it couldn't be a complete course or anything like that.

Admiral Kerrins, who was a year behind me at the law school - he was in the second group that came in - and Ralph Curr who had gone into law school with me, and I went all round the country for about eight weeks, visiting bases on the

West Coast and on down to Biloxi, then on the East Coast to Florida, New London, and any place we could get to with this course we'd dreamed up. We used our manuals and the various laws that these men might be called upon to enforce. I think it was very successful, and I say that only because - well, in the first place, it was the first time it had been condensed in that way. We spent five days a week. We traveled on weekends. We'd get in on Sunday and start in on Monday. The first thing we did was to give them an examination, which was selected yes and no answers, and the last thing we did, at the end of the week, was to give them a similar examination. In every case, we found that after the exposure of a week it was surprising how much they hadn't known at the beginning of the week and how much we hoped they knew at the end of the week. In many cases, scores would double and triple in a week.

So I think, from the standpoint of law enforcement in the Coast Guard, that was really very productive work that came out of going to law school.

Then, the following year, as soon as I graduated from law school -

Q: You graduated with distinction, did you not? And what degree did you get?

Adm. R.: Juris doctor. I had gone for the juris doctor for

several reasons. One was that at that time we were still in the question of the academic proficiency of the Academy. We were accredited but there was still some question of acceptance, and George Washington had a system where if you went there, say, from high school, if you went four years you got your LLB, or you could go seven years - six years, excuse me, to get a juris doctor degree. But George Washington had a system whereby you got an LLB in four years or, if you wanted to go six years, you got your LLB in the equivalent of three and your juris doctor at the end of six. But, if you came with a BA or equivalent, then at the end of three years you could get a JD degree. Well, of course, I'd only been at the Academy two years, although I had had two years at George Washington but that was immaterial. I could have gotten the LLB at the end of three years, but I went to see the Dean and convinced him that the Academy was an accredited institution equivalent to a four-year college, and we were at four years at that time. In other words, I had the equivalent of a BS degree - well, in fact, we had been granted BS degrees by that time - and my BS degree ought to be accepted for going for a Juris Doctor degree. He permitted me to try for a JD degree, which I did receive.

It wasn't only that I wanted a JD degree but I thought it would help for the prestige of the Academy.

Right after I came out of law school I was assigned to headquarters. That would have been in 1938, and either that summer or the next summer, I'm not sure which - it was the summer of 1938 - the Secretary had gotten for the Coast Guard, as I recall the figure $10 million for construction. At that particular time, they were still trying to prime the pump. Anyway, there was $10 million available for the building of Coast Guard facilities in different places, providing the money would be spent or contracted for by September 15, I think was the date, and this was in early June. So I had no more than graduated and really was preparing for the bar exams, when I was told to report to headquarters, and Admiral Johnson gave me the job - they'd decided on the projects that they wanted to spend this money on, but in order to spend the money they had to have clear title to the land - of seeing that we got clear titles so that the contracts could be let.

You see, the Coast Guard did not at that time pursue - and I'm not sure they do today - the acquisition of property. As a matter of fact, it had to go through the Department of Justice, but before it went through the Department of Justice it had to go GSA, the General Service Administration. Through a lawyer down there, who I remember very well, I had to fight with him continually, who had a persuasive argument, I must admit, although, of course, I was working against time to get this done. Every piece of property that was acquired for the government had to clear him first, even before the Department of Justice started proceeding against it. I used to go down and sit in his office and ask him to expedite these various projects. Some of them I had to visit to get papers straightened out and things like that. He was a Civil Service employee and he had a pile of papers on his desk, projects that he had to clear, probably a foot high, and ours were spread in there at different points. His question always was why should he pull one of my projects, or one of the Coast Guard projects, out ahead of we'll say a customshouse or a post office that was sitting on top. And that's a pretty hard argument to somebody who knows their salary is going to be the same next year as it is this year and nobody's going to fire him, politics, or anything else.

But by hook or crook we did manage eventually to clear most of the projects. Some of these were involved with some of our old surf stations, lifeboat stations, and there was an interesting aspect of that that's probably been lost over the years. In the first place, at that time we still had in the service an old gentleman who had handled this for the Lifesaving Service, a man by the name of Latham, who was one of these people who operate with the idea that as long as he keeps every piece of information in his own pocket nobody's going to get his job. So he was a pretty hard man to work with. I gradually won him over on a few of them.

Back in the old days when the lifesaving stations were set up, long before there was a Coast Guard, many of these stations were built along the coast on, say somebody's farm and the land was acquired on what is known as a determinable fee, a "use and occupation" deed. In other words, you can have the land as long as it's used for lifesaving purposes. Once it's not used for that it reverts to the heirs. Well, I got into trying to make a record of all the pieces of property owned by the Coast Guard. Very frankly, the records were almost nonexistent. If they weren't in Mr. Latham's pocket, they weren't in any files, either, that I could find. I ran into some very, very interesting things.

Remember, many of the early lifeboat stations were simply four-room wooden buildings set up on stilts and a boathouse. I suppose what would happen was that the coast has a way of eroding here and building up somewhere else and district superintendents would come down - I'm guessing now - the ocean was getting a little close to the lifeboat stations, so they'd talk to the old farmer who owned the land and, oh, well, move it 500 yards and it will be all right. About a third of these were described one way but could be a mile down the beach or a mile up the beach. In fact, one of the most interesting ones, although it hadn't been moved far, had drifted from one county into another county - this was up on the lakes. It wasn't even in the same county. Frankly, I think it had only moved about 500 yards but that was so.

Even a site like the Coast Guard yard at Curtis Bay, over in Maryland, had no deed on record. As a matter of fact, I went over to Annapolis - I suppose I could have had it copied, but I copied the thing by longhand just so we would have a record in the meantime.

That was the state of the records at that time.

I worked on regulations and at various jobs during that year.

Q: They were clean-up jobs that had to be done?

Adm. R.: Mainly clean-up jobs and things like that. I was not in the law office. I don't remember all of the various jobs that I did have. One job that I remember was quite interesting.

Admiral O'Neill and a civilian who had come from the Lifesaving Service by the name of John Myers and I were given the job of writing the regulations for the Coast Guard Reserve. Not the present Coast Guard Reserve, but what is now the Coast Guard Auxiliary. Admiral Waesche had gotten the idea that motorboats and things like that needed to be controlled - we were beginning to have increasing problems, cabin cruisers were coming to a point where you didn't have to be a millionaire like J. P. Morgan to own one. They were becoming an increasing problem. Also the Power Squadron was moving in to get a quasi governmental status like the Boy Scouts. Admiral Waesche recognized that if anybody organized the boatmen in a quasi governmental status, the Coast Guard ought to do it. So they put through a bill that created the then Coast Guard Reserve so that yachtsmen could put their boats at the disposal of the Coast Guard.

By that time the TVA had come in and other dams and we were getting problems in the interior. The minute you create a body of water, somebody puts a boat on it, and the minute you put a boat out a storm comes along and somebody gets drowned. So pretty soon you've got problems. We recognized that outside of the Great Lakes - or Admiral Waesche recognized and people at headquarters - I didn't have anything to do with this - but I'm trying to give you the background of the way the thing developed as I saw it - that this was creating problems for the Coast Guard because, outside the Great Lakes, the Mississippi River and the Missouri River where we did for many years and still do, in the case of a flood, send surf boats out for rescue purposes, we had little or no experience and we had no equipment. On Lake Tahoe and places like that boating was gradually beginning to build up, nothing like it became after the war but certainly at that time we were beginning to get problems. It was pretty obvious we'd never have the equipment to cover all these places.

So, as I say, this idea of the auxiliary was conceived - or the reserve, as it was then called - (a) to create groups of yachtsmen who could serve and, although I doubt that this is a matter of record, to kind of kill this apparent effort on the part of the Power Squadron to get quasi governmental status like the Boy Scouts or something like that, to get approbation from Congress.

Truthfully, I think it was a poorly written bill, perhaps because I don't think anyone really had the concept of exactly what they wanted other than the hope that by having these yachtsmen available to send a man or an officer and a couple of men out, hoist a Coast Guard commission pennant, and, in effect, convert this yacht or boat to a vessel under government control.

Admiral O'Neill, John Myers, and I were to write the regulations and that was probably one of the weirdest jobs I ever had in the Coast Guard because, when we stopped to analyze it, what we were creating was a cross between a reserve organization, a Trinity House of England, and a lodge, and a religious organization. There were no guidelines. For example, if you're going to create a military reserve you could go to the Navy and the Army. Probably, when you interview Admiral O'Neill he'll tell you that he almost threw the book at me dozens of times because every time we'd come to a sticky problem I would always say, "Well, how would this apply to J. P. Morgan's yacht, the <u>Corsair</u>?" or something like that. For example, they hadn't spelled out in the bill the status of these people. They thought of it in concepts of single owners. Well, suppose you had a boat with seven owners or four owners. You couldn't raise a single question but what something would pop up.

Of course, the big question and it later developed that it really was a big question was this.

You own a boat. All right, you put it at the disposal of the Coast Guard. It's a boat large enough that you employ a man to keep it up and run it for you when you go down on weekends. You say to the Coast Guard, "You can take it to patrol a regatta." All right, but here's a nice question. Who pays the salary of your mechanic or this guy who's on the boat? And, as it later developed, the big question came up as to who was going, in case you tore the bottom off the boat, to repair the boat. The Coast Guard repairs one way, but if you're a yachtsman you only want your boat repaired at a particular yard which is not subject to competitive bidding and that sort of thing.

Even such questions as to what distinctive pennants these boats would fly as members of the Coast Guard Auxiliary.

But we finally came out with regulations and the Coast Guard Auxiliary was created. I guess we worked two or three months.

In August or September of 1939 Commander Walsh and I were designated and sent to London for an International Whaling Conference.

Q: That was actually in July of 1939.

Adm. R.: Did we go there in July?

Q: Yes.

Adm. R.: I didn't think it was that early.

Q: At least, that's what this biography states, July 17.

Adm. R.: Well, that probably is right. We were over there probably pretty close to a month. The war broke out in September and even while we were there the tensions were growing. We came back, though, before the conflict. I guess we were there three or four weeks at the conference.

That was very interesting and it was another thing that I'd been involved in in the preceding year, working on the drafting of the whaling regulations for the United States. I guess that's really how I got swept into this. We had been a signatory to that whaling business and we had to draft regulations. I learned many things in that. Of course, the State Department was involved.

The United States was never greatly involved in whaling. We had some out here on the West Coast, some whalers who were whaling for cat food and stuff like that. Instead of horse meat they were using whale meat for pet food. Yes, we had been, too. We'd been involved in that we had two whaling ships working, one under the American flag, and we'd had our observers aboard. Commander Walsh had been one of them. He'd been to the Antarctic and down off of Australia after the humpbacks. I think Hogan had been on the other ship. <u>Ulysses</u> was one of the ships. I've forgotten the name of the other one.

Q: I take it that this whaling conference was only one of a series that had been going on?

Adm. R.: There had been agreements before, yes, but they called this conference to reconsider regulations. I had worked on our local regulations and that's how I got into it.

An interesting aspect of that was that whaling was controlled in the Department of Commerce - it has since gone over to Interior - and I always liked the title that it was controlled under. It was the Black Bass and Anglers Division of the Department of Fisheries in Commerce. Just how whaling got in with black bass and anglers I never quite figured out, but maybe they didn't have any other place to put it.

Q: It was a miscellaneous section!

Adm. R.: Yes. I got a good lesson in the writing of government regulations. These regulations had been drafted from earlier regulations - State Department, Commerce, Dr. Remington Kellogg, who was then our whaling expert and a wonderful man. I've often wondered about him but I guess he's long since passed on. We sat in conference one day, I remember - these regulations at that time were probably four or five pages long and in fine print, we argued from nine in the morning to about three-thirty in the afternoon. We were quitting at four-thirty and would come back the next day, if necessary. The whole argument was over page one whether you say "waters of the world, on the world, or in the world." Then from three-thirty to four-thirty we finished up the other four pages of regulations, and I don't know yet what we finally decided on - I don't remember what we finally decided about which preposition we should use!

The other thing I learned at that time was about the State Department. The State Department guy was sort of younger and he said: "One thing about the State Department is that it's only been in the last two years that we've gotten to the point where we write a letter to somebody, giving them hell, and then end up with the expression 'I have the honor to be your obedient servant, the Secretary of State'". I think that form had remained just to about then.

Anyway, getting back to the conference. It was quite interesting. You learn a lot about your compatriots in other countries. Actually, the conference was primarily to establish the quotas. Remember now, this was just before the war. Oddly enough, I found myself more in sympathy with the Germans and the Japanese on their approach. The situation was roughly this.

The United States was even then for restrictions. Today I guess you'd call it ecological or preservation of the species. We were for restriction in a sort of altruistic way. The Germans were for restrictions because they wanted to preserve the supply of fats. The Japs were for restrictions, within limitations, because it was a source of food supply, protein. Whale meat is supposed to be very good if you don't have it three times a day. The Norwegians were for very, very limited restrictions. They were providing most of the ships, the gunners, on the killer boats. So, to them, it was a livelihood and therefore restriction only to the extent that it would continue the industry. The English talked restrictions and piously hoped that there would be restrictions, but at the same time they had money invested, or their industry did, and that had to be protected and if it meant fishing them out in five or six years, take the gold while it's there sort of underlined it.

So, it was a very interesting conference. As I say, I learned quite a little bit. I learned another thing about the English, the British particularly, that stayed with me even when I went to later conferences during the war and after the war. Any time you sit down with the British at a conference and you come out with your shirt on your back and your gold in your teeth, you've gained a moral victory. I hope this is not for publication. But basically - and it's for this reason - let's say you have a conference and you've got four representatives from the United States and four from the British. Individually, your four - we'll say you've got an engineer and a lawyer, four different professions - individually, the four United States men may be in their technical fields equal or superior to the British. However, we go on the principle that if something comes up that the lawyer's supposed to speak on, he speaks and the others keep their mouths shut because it's not their field, or the engineer speaks, depending upon what's up. Okay. The British come to the conference and the chances are, whereas the Americans have probably been home sleeping or looking at television the night before, the British have been up till about three o'clock in the morning, as a team, tossing this thing back and forth. So, what happens is when you get in the conference your lawyer, let's say, may out talk the British lawyer, but if it looks like the British lawyer's getting the worst of it, then somebody from the British team throws in a diversionary tactic or something, and at the end of the day, when you begin to analyze what has happened, the British may not have pushed the ball forward for the full ten yards, but you can be darned sure they gained a couple of yards. As I say, this is a gratuitous observation, but I've been through a number of conferences with them. This is not to say I don't like the British. I think they're wonderful. But basically, as I say - well, in many ways, I think their liberal education makes them more fluent operators in many instances than we are.

Q: They think more clearly, perhaps?

Adm. R.: I really think they do, yes.

Q: And you made the point, they do their homework in a way that we don't.

Adm. R.: That's right. It's a fact. They know exactly where they're going.

Q: Tell me about the results of this conference.

Adm. R.: We came to agreement on sizes of whales that could be taken and the prohibition which had been in existence, anyway, or partially, on taking females with calves. Of course, the prohibition against the Right Whale and others existed before we went. It was really a reaffirmation and cutting-down on sizes, and also the setting of quotas of whales that could be taken. There had been some discussion how to measure in length. If I recall the figure, the Blue Whale, which is I believe the largest, the minimum was 70 feet, and there were some other questions that had to be settled.

Generally speaking, it was a very satisfactory conference. We accomplished our purpose and it probably would have been all right, except that two months after I returned, or a month after I returned, the Germans marched into Czechoslovakia and Poland and that was the end of it.

Q: I suppose it was all held in abeyance until after the war was over?

Adm. R.: Of course, there was no more whaling any place.

Q: Now, you were going to tell me about something else that happened in that year after you got your degree?

Adm. R.: Yes. It could have been and probably was after I came back from the whaling conference - yes, I'm sure it was. I was transferred up to the Treasury Department and worked for the assistant to one of the Assistant Secretaries for a while. That was a sort of a deadly job. He didn't know exactly what I was supposed to do. I was supposed to listen in and advise him on Coast Guard matters. Then Secretary Morgenthau got the idea - the war was on now and he wanted to check the arrival of ships in our ports, so down in the Treasury Department they set up three - ships had to get clearances to come in -

Q: These were merchant ships?

Adm. R.: Merchant ships, yes. They set up teletypes and on the arrival of any ships, the collectors of customs would forward in the name of the ship and we had to give them clearance. This was a twenty-four-hour job, so there were three of us and we stood a continuous watch. Sometimes we'd work twenty-four hours on and forty-eight off and that sort of thing.

That was finally closed out and Admiral Hirschfield and I were transferred back down to Coast Guard headquarters, which was then in the old Liberty Loan Building, and we were given the job of monitoring the commercial radio broadcasts. Frankly, it was a stupid thing because, for some reason or other, Secretary Morgenthau had the idea that if anything happened we'd probably hear it commercially before we got the word officially from any other source.

Q: What sort of thing did he anticipate?

Adm. R.: Remember, the war was on and he wanted to be kept advised of what was going on.

Q: You mean this was a news digest he wanted?

Adm. R.: Not so much a news digest but an idea he had that the news reporters would come out with a scoop in case it didn't come through official sources, whatever, it might be.

Admiral Hirschfield and I alternated on twenty-four-hour duty.

Q: Listening to the radio?

Adm. R.: Listening to the radio, and if you want a stupid, dumb job, because, basically, the news at noon or eight o'clock in the morning and ten o'clock at night is essentially the same. Of course, if anything breaks there might be a little change. And, of course, we were trying to monitor two or three different newscasters. About the only interest in the job was to see how different newscasters would say the same thing in different words.

Q: From a personal point of view that must have been quite interesting!

Adm. R.: It was interesting for a day or so, but pretty soon you could almost write their script.

Q: Didn't the Secretary have a ticker tape?

Adm. R.: Probably he did but, you see, he wouldn't be there twenty-four hours a day. We were supposed to call him if anything broke. It was one of those sort of things. It was stupid, I grant you, but orders are orders.

Well, in the meantime, at or about this time or maybe the year before - it was the year before, it could have happened even while I was still in law school - the Maritime Commission had gotten a bill through - I mean the Maritime Administration - which provided for the training of seamen and officers. They could either do the training themselves or they could delegate it to some other agency.

Admirals Vickery and Land were over there at the time and they and Admiral Waesche were quite friendly. Anyway, the Coast Guard ended up with the maritime training on an assigned basis, with the exception of the cadet training. At that time, as you know, the cadet training - you became a merchant marine cadet and you were put aboard ship. They didn't have King's Point. That was either organized just at this time - well, it was divided into two different bases. We were going to train merchant marine officers from scratch - no, what we were going to do was to take officers and give them, that is men who had licences, refresher courses. We went up to New London, the old Fort Trumbull base there, as I recall it - I never was there, so I'm not sure it was Fort Trumbull, but I think it was, and we had this refresher course for merchant marine officers.

The Maritime Administration got money to build - well, they opened Hoffman Island for training merchant seamen and I believe that to start with that was more of a refresher course for men who'd been at sea and maybe been away for a while and wanted to go back to sea. Although later they did take in raw recruits. This was to be a very good course. Then they built a base at St. Petersburg and attached it to a ship. And they built a station at Hueneme, California, on Coast Guard land.

I was very much interested. I was fed up with headquarters at the time, fed up with these odd jobs, jumping from one to the other, regulations and one thing and another. So I applied for command of the ship that was to service the station at Hueneme.

Admiral Derby - Captain Derby then - was head of the Maritime Service and he said I was accepted for that job. Then I had to take a course of sprouts, you might say, in the Maritime Service. By that time the station at St. Petersburg was operating so I went down there and made a cruise on the American Seaman. This course was to train raw recruits, six months training - three months at the school ashore, getting basic seamanship, and then three months on the ship. That was the theory of the thing.

Q: These men who were being trained were the personnel for the new merchant ships that were being turned out under the Maritime Administration?

Adm. R.: Yes, because we were short of seamen, and it was more or less anticipated that sooner or later there was going to be a need.

Q: And there was to be a flood of new ships.

Adm. R.: Yes, although I don't think they were completely

committed at that time. But it was recognized that the American merchant marine - that had led to this basic act, in the first place - was at a low ebb and had to be built up. This was even before the war. This was not necessarily a war product. It was the fact that there'd been a move to revive the American merchant marine by putting competent personnel into it.

Then I was sent down to Panama, the idea being to find out the needs, to get more familiarity with the merchant marine, the problems of the crews and the officers. I spent a week or ten days in Panama. I stayed in Panama City and every morning I'd get up and go down and the pilots would put me aboard the ships going through the canal, different ships, different types. I rode through the canal every day, practically, talking to the officers, talking to the crews.

Q: What was the attitude you discovered that prevailed among the merchant seamen vis a vis unions and so forth?

Adm. R.: At that time, I recognized no particular problem. Of course, they each had their own union. There was the firemen's union and so forth, and the engineer officers and deck officers had their unions. But on the ships that I rode through on, I found everybody willing to talk. No particular problems. They liked their jobs and were paid well, nothing like they were later. There had been problems on the West Coast particularly, with the longshoremen under Bridges, at the time, and there's been some problems up on the East Coast. Joe Curran had by that time come into prominence.

But right at that particular time things were generally quiet in the merchant marine. And, of course, there was no objection to what we were doing. Presumably these boys, when they were turned out, would be joining a union and we were not in the job of -

Q: You were not involved in that anyway.

Adm. R.: No. That was an interesting experience down there. Then I came back and went over to Bethlehem Steel, where the American Sailor, which was the ship that I was to command, was being outfitted. We were delayed quite a while getting out because Allis Chalmers was on strike and they were making our generators.

Q: They'd been on strike for a couple of years, hadn't they?

Adm. R.: Yes, they had been. Anyway, we were delayed a month or so, but we finally got in commission, made our trial run, got out. The American Sailor, as I recall, had been built by Skinner and Eddy in Seattle. Probably, if we had a fair wind, we could make ten knots in her, at about the best.

We went up to Hoffman Island and picked up our first quota of trainees, about 300, boys who had just been inducted, raw recruits.

Q: That's the number you took at one time?

Adm. R.: Three hundred, yes. I might just make a commentary here.

More and more, as I got into this training of seamen aboard ship and also considering what we mentioned yesterday about training aboard ship, training boys aboard a merchant ship like that is not the ideal answer. Now, there's nothing like experience, but for what we were doing - let me just give you an example.

Theoretically, you're supposed to teach a man to steer. All right. I argued this in headquarters for quite a while. He's supposed to be able to take the helm and handle the ship. All right. Now, there are 300 boys aboard and they're all supposed to be trained. Well, you figure it out. There are twenty-four hours in the day and if you steam for ten days, straight across the ocean, which isn't teaching a man to steer anyway.

Q: You have to zigzag!

Adm. R.: Even if you zigzag, you steam for ten days and you've only done 240 hours and if you left a man on a wheel for an hour - of course, you could break it up in half-hour sections and all that - but if you give them an hour, you only train 240 men. It just isn't logical but we did the best we could. Also, we had some classrooms and they had classroom study and that sort of thing.

Q: That, too, you said yesterday, is not very feasible.

Adm. R.: It isn't the best in the world because you have to rotate your men through watches and they miss a class because they have to be on watch, or they have to knock off to clean up. It's very difficult. Another thing, we used to hold "Abandon ship" drill, boat drill, and even lowering two boats at a time on "Abandon ship" drill, we'd start at eight o'clock in the morning and knock off at five o'clock in the afternoon and we still hadn't gotten all the men into the boats and out. I said "Abandon ship" drill, but I mean "Man overboard" drill. "Abandon ship," of course, we sent as many boats away at once.

Really, the ideal thing if you want to train, and I'll come to this later, is to have a number of smaller boats and smaller groups. Even though they may later serve on a larger ship.

Q: What was the tonnage of the American Sailor?

Adm. R.: Ten thousand, as I recall. It was an ample ship.

We came down and went through the canal in the latter part of July.

In the meantime, the Maritime Administration, the training and all the rest, had been changed over to the War Shipping Adminiration, and this leads to what was later a deplorable or sad situation. I'll explain why the changeover came later.

In the Maritime Administration there were people who were not very happy about the Coast Guard having gotten this job of training. They felt it was a mistake.

Q: What was their reason?

Adm. R.: Well, after all, the way to promotion and pay is to build up your own organization. Parkinson's Law and all that sort of thing.

I guess the fellow who was really in charge of training to start with, academically, was Telfer Knight. I only met Telfer Knight once or twice. I don't think he was happy. I always had a feeling that Telfer was one who could talk both ways. The man who finally scuttled it, though, was one of the commissioners by the name of Macauley. Most of this is hearsay.

M auley, as I understand it, had been or was a Navy captain. He'd been in command of the ship that Roosevelt went to some conference in, or maybe he'd known him as Assistant Secretary of the Navy, I'm not sure. Anyway, to make a long story short, he had an inside track to the White House or so I was told. And he apparently had been one of those who had balked Vickery and Land in the original decision of it coming to the Coast Guard. He was in the War Shipping Administration. Whether the commissioners were all the same in both agencies, I'm not sure. Anyway, the moment we went over to the War Shipping Administration it almost looked, as I understand it - I wasn't in headquarters at this time, as if the handwriting was on the wall, that the Coast Guard was going to lose out in this training. They couldn't give it back to the Maritime, but we heard rumors that War Shipping would take over the training.

I'm not so sure in hindsight that it wasn't good that we did get out of it because some of our wartime efforts would have been diverted to training. Anyway, the reason I brought this up at this time is that we were heading up the coast and we had figured we'd stop at Acapulco and Mazatlan, let the boys have some liberty, and see the country. But somewhere down the Mexican coast, we began to get messages "no matter what you do, no matter what breaks down, no matter what happens, be sure you get to Hueneme by August 4th." August 4th was Coast Guard Day, and McCauley was coming out to dedicate the new base, and the ship had to be there to polish it off, as it were.

So we steamed as fast as we could and we made it. That's why I know it was in August.

Q: And this was August of 1941?

Adm. R.: Yes. In the meantime they'd opened the school, the base there, and the base had been built on a piece of land that originally belonged to the Lighthouse Service and, of course, when the Lighthouse Service had come over to the Coast Guard we had title. But what they didn't know, and this will come out later - the coast at Hueneme, right there where it comes more or less south then turns east, and the light was right on the point. They'd gone out and looked at this land and they had come in to build a harbor, and the idea of this harbor was - it was country up around Oxnard-Ventura, what they call the delta country - the harbor was promoted and built, as I understand it, on the basis that vegetables, fruit, and so forth could be shipped out without having to ship to Los Angeles or any other port. San Pedro, really, is the closest port. It probably was a good concept, except the war came along at that time and changed it. But they channeled in and built a sort of a square basin in there. In doing that, their dredgings had been dumped on the south shore of the Coast Guard land. So, apparently, when they decided to build here, they looked out and they had a beautiful sandy area there, good and solid, and ample room to build on. There was, of course, basic land there, but it had been extended by this fill to a great extent. So that was where the station was. It was a very beautiful station, in the sense that it was ample for the 200 or 300 boys they'd take in at a time. The main building was in the form of a Greek cross, with the mess-hall and kind of open barracks - open-air barracks, I should say.

I had roughly 300 boys on the ship and there were 300 in the station, who had been gathered from the West Coast and were just beginning their training. Captain Toll had command of the Base. I had command of the ship. My boys still had roughly three months to go.

We made short cruises off the coast. In order to popularize this program and lay the groundwork for more recruits and so forth and so on, we made a trip up to Seattle, Portland, down the coast to Oakland, and we took the ship up the river to Sacramento, then came on back. We had it laid on that we would leave in early December and that would be the final trip for our boys before they got their papers as ordinary seamen of firemen.

Q: Was it intended that the boys who were at the Port in training would eventually go on board ship?

Adm. R.: As soon as I got rid of my group, they would come on.

Q: Then another group would come in?

Adm. R.: Yes. It rotated every three months. That was the

plan and it was a good plan basically and we would have turned out some able seamen, I'm sure, because they were doing a good job ashore, or would have been. I know at St. Petersburg they were doing a good job and practically all these boys we had went to sea.

We were all set to make a trip. We were going to go to Honolulu, Tahiti, and get back, as I recall it, just before Christmas, except one thing happened. As a matter of fact, had we carried out our plans, or the reason we didn't carry out our plans was by that time the situation was critical, as you know, and I believe it was on the 1st of November that the Coast Guard was transferred into the Navy. It was about that time, anyway, so everybody knew it was critical. There was quite a demand on the tankers at that time for seamen, so the Bureau of Marine Inspection and Navigation decided that these boys that we had - they had probably four and a half months at that time - could go to sea, that they'd had enough training to go to sea.

Q: You mean all six hundred?

Adm. R.: No, the 300 that I had aboard ship. Inspectors came up and we gave them all examinations the week before Pearl Harbor. If it hadn't been for that and holding up to give these boys their examinations and place them in jobs, we would have been in Honolulu the day the Japs attacked, because that was our schedule. We were going to leave right after Thanksgiving and go over to Honolulu, and then, as I say, go on to Tahiti and get back before Christmas.

We were saved from that only because of this early graduation of the boys on our ship, if you can call it graduation.

Q: Tell me how these boys were recruited. Was it all volunteer?

Adm. R.: All volunteer.

Q: Just through advertisement?

Adm. R.: Through advertisement and I believe our recruiters recruited some.

Q: Coast Guard?

Adm. R.: Coast Guard recruiters were recruiting both for this maritime service - I don't think there were any special recruiters out for the maritime service. I could be wrong about that. I wasn't in that end of the game and my recollection is hazy on how it was done. But they were sent to us, they came. They wore regular Coast Guard uniforms, the only difference was instead of having a shield they had a circle round the shield.

Q: Just to get an idea of how many ships could be manned by the men you were training, approximately how many men are required on board a merchant ship of, say, 6,000 to 8,000 tons?

Adm. R.: I'm not sure myself now, but it seems to me that around forty men. Of course, with the mechanization that's come in now, I don't think it's as high as it was.

Q: I was thinking of that particular era.

Adm. R.: Yes. At that time, I think we figured forty or so. For some reason or other, it seems to me about twenty-eight deck hands, fourteen firemen, and steward personnel. But that's memory and at my age memory gets a little hazy on some of these details.

As I say, we'd gone in the Navy I think on November 1st, which brings me to another perhaps sarcastic comment.

I've always been intrigued by the first message that we got after Pearl Harbor from the Navy Department. The gist of it was that we were to wear uniform at all times, even at home if we had guests - I think it was if you had more than two or three guests you had to wear uniform even in your own home. And I've always thought that, with the war breaking around your ears, I could see these retired admirals on the Uniform Board sitting there and debating should it be two guests or three guests! I always thought that must have been a classic decision, with the bricks falling around your ears, to decide what you should wear.

Right after Pearl Harbor the situation was rampant, out here on the West Coast particularly, because the Japs had struck and everybody was finding a Jap in their closet, practically, and, as you know, all the American-born Japs were picked up and tossed into - well, they don't call them concentration camps, but from some of the stories I guess some of them were pretty grim. There was pandemonium. Lights were out and everybody was seeing airplanes in the sky. My own feeling was that the Jap high command was kind of stupid in some of the things they did, too. You know you can really make some good diversionary tactics with just a small expense in men.

Very frankly, if they'd only thought about it and they said this afterwards, pick out Hueneme Harbor, and they knew about it. Had they sent a submarine over here with about a dozen men and a couple of motorcycles with sidecars, grabbed one of our fishermen, nobody would have stopped them sailing into that harbor, the boys get on their motorcycles and drive down Ventura Boulevard, now the Ventura Freeway, but then the old pike, and go up to the railroad, set off their dynamite, blow both up, they'd have closed off Los Angeles from the north. Then, when they got through with it, with doing all this, all they would have to have done was go to the sheriff and say "So sorry," and they'd have been thrown in jail and lived happily the rest of the war.

The point is in a war everybody is involved in grand strategy and they don't worry about these little things.

As an example, all the lights were out the night after Pearl Harbor. I cracked my car up. I ran into the back end of a car that was running without lights. I was running without lights. I was going down to the ship. I thought I'd better go down to the ship just to see if anything had happened, but nothing did happen.

The first time I tried to get in to Hueneme there was a guard of something called the California Naval Militia - whatever it is I never did find out. I think the next day there was a sheriff's group there or state police, it doesn't really make much difference. The third day there was somebody else, and the fourth day there wasn't anybody and there never was anybody after that!

Q: When they took your men from you, you took the next group of boys?

Adm. R.: Yes.

Q: And the whole system continued?

Adm. R.: Yes. It just speeded up.

Q: Were you not somewhat curtailed as to your - ?

Adm. R.: We haven't gotten into that yet.

The American Sailor, incidentally, was painted a beautiful white. We were told to stay in port except when we had to go to San Pedro to fuel, there was no fuel at Hueneme. So we went down right away and fueled up and then in January we made another trip to San Pedro. Meantime, I was asking when we were to paint the ship, and the word we got back was "The Japs won't shoot you." She was painted white just like a hospital ship, but, hearing what the Japs were doing -

Q: One of their prime targets!

Adm. R.: Yes - I wasn't too happy about this situation. I don't know why, but we made several trips down to San Pedro.

I think it was in January that the Japs caused some excitement. My recollection is that it was the night that Roosevelt was making a speech. They flushed up a submarine at a place between Ventura and Santa Barbara, called Carpinteria, and just took a couple of shots at an oil refinery. Do you recall that?

Q: No.

Adm. R.: Well, they did. They lobbed in a few shots. I think it was the only time the Japs actually bombed, but it just so happened that that night - I think at the same time they appeared off the Oregon coast - or on that particular day, we were down in San Pedro fueling. Incidentally, the Navy captain of the port down there was a fellow by the name of Pete Hines and he got me in and said:

"Look, if you don't get that ship painted, you're not coming back in to San Pedro again, as far as I'm concerned, because even at nighttime you're a sitting duck for them to lob in on us."

"Well," I said, "I've asked and they just say keep it painted white, but I'll try again."

Anyway, we started up the coast, we had a head wind, choppy sea, and, as I say, the air was filled with rumors about the presence of submarines. Everybody was fighting submarines up and down the coast. Whether they were actually there or not, I'm not so sure. I have an idea the guy lobbed his shots and was flying home as fast as he could. Still, people were seeing submarines. Any time a whale came up, that was a submarine. Of course, that was the day to catch head winds and choppy seas. We didn't leave till probably noon and we were making a fast 6 knots up the coast. That was a nasty entrance at Port Hueneme, a narrow channel, and when we got there it was just about dusk. We did have range lights to run in on. We started in and, with this north wind blowing and not having much headway, it caught us and we ended up on the beach, not hard.

There was no tug there. In fact, we were the only sizeable ship in the place. We got out our power boat and with our own power we backed out. By that time, the weather conditions were such that we were afraid that we wouldn't be able to get in, so we decided we'd have to stay out all night, which was one of the hairiest nights I've ever spent in my life.

Mind you, the total armament of the <u>American Sailor</u> was one .45, which the paymaster used to go to get the payroll. So we decided the best thing to do was to go up the coast towards Ventura, about five or six miles, off a place then called Hollywood Beach, and snuggle in as close as we could to the beach, figuring that hopefully the submarine at least would have to surface. So we did that.

Then the debate, figuring he had sonar equipment, was what would be the best thing to do, keep everything running or turn everything off. We decided we'd cut the engines, everything, off, lights, engines, everything, and be absolutely dead in the water. We were anchored. Well, as it turned out, that was a crazy decision because I suppose if anybody had been sounding on us or trying to pick us up from the noise of our engines, it was all right. But, on the other hand, it was fairly rough. I don't know whether you've ever been in a dead ship with the sea fairly rough, but the sea would hit her "bang," and every time you heard "bang" for the first hour you thought that was a torpedo, in view of the circumstances. But nothing happened. We got through the night, more or less, a fairly sleepless night. Everybody on the alert, thinking the worst. Incidentally, he wouldn't have had sonar, but some other type of sounding equipment.

Next morning, we steamed in merrily. What we hadn't realized - well, we realized it but there wasn't anything we could do about it. The next day, five or six of our friends, some fellows from Ventura who knew us and somebody from Hueneme, came down and wanted to know what the hell we were doing out there last night. The thing of it was, it was a full moon, and this white ship, we must have looked like - and, of course, they couldn't figure out why we were anchored, they didn't know about us going aground, off the coast there. We were out a mile or so.

So that was one of my early experiences in the war.

When we got in, I called up headquarters and finally got Admiral Derby and told him:

"Look, I can't go down to San Pedro again." No, I talked to Hank Jewell, who was Derby's exec, and I said:

"Look, Hank, you tell Admiral Derby I'd either like to paint the ship gray or I'd like him to let me put a target amidships so that they'll know where to hit me."

A few hours later I got an answer back, "You can paint the ship gray."

So we got out the paint and painted her gray. Then, about that time, they decided that after all - the Navy was then putting armed gun crews on the merchant ships because now we were in the war - so they decided they'd do the same for the American Sailor, so they transferred us down to the Bethlehem Steel shipyard in Long Beach. I don't remember exactly when it was, but I would say it was probably about February or March. It was after we had the ship painted gray, I know. At about the same time, Captain Toll, who had had the base - I had the ship, the Hueneme base, became district commander in Long Beach, so rather than send the commanding officer, because our cruising was hampered and, in the first place, the ship was down in Long Beach. It might have been as late as April before we got down there.

As I said, we did some cruising back and forth for fuel. I know we made several trips. It may even have been as late as May or June before we got down there because something else happened so I think we were in Hueneme longer than I thought.

We went to Bethlehem and when Toll went to the district I became commanding officer of the base.

Q: What date was that?

Adm. R.: That was in February of 1942. I think the ship was still at Hueneme at that time. I don't know exactly when we were transferred down to Bethlehem to get the guns put on and the rest of the work done that was necessary, and it doesn't make much difference. But what it resulted in was that I had a kind of split command and I was commuting between Long Beach and Wilmington, San Pedro, really, and Santa Paula, and Hueneme. I'd spend about three days down there and three days at home. It was a very peculiar set-up.

Q: It meant then that you had 600 men under your command?

Adm. R.: Yes, I had the men at the station and the men on the ship.

Returning for a moment to the question of training, I had this theory that we weren't training too well, having so many men on one ship. So down in San Pedro, in one of the backwaters, we found three old steam-driven whaling killer boats. They were in terrible condition, but we got the bright idea that we'd take our men, and it would be good experience for them - I forget whether we sold the idea of buying them or how it was, but after we bought them they weren't worth much, they were mainly junk - and fix them up with the idea that if we ever got out of Bethlehem we'd have a fleet. These would carry about twenty men. Of course, they had Scottish boilers and old steam-driven plants, but at least the boys could learn to steer and I figured that they'd learn signaling, and you could train a lot better than you could ashore.

My main problems, then, were not with the ship, however, so much because we were pretty well organized, were at the base because earlier I mentioned how the base had been built. Well, the thing that hadn't been realized was that the beach along there was in a continually eroding situation. It was not like some places where the surf rolls in and rolls out so the sand comes and goes in and out, more or less, but it was a saw-tooth motion. The waves would come in and take the sand out and move down. For years that beach had been reasonably stable all along there because, while the sand was always moving down, there was always plenty up above. But when they put the channel in, apparently, for the harbor at Hueneme, they had gone deep enough to unearth an underground river that poured out there. In other words, they always had a current running out through there. So when the sand came down, instead of building up, it was just being carried out to sea. The sand that had been dredged out of the harbor now begins to erode and begins to approach our building.

I screamed to Washington and they had suggestions, so we put in what was known as a Wakefield bulkhead. Well, that was love's labor lost. I don't know whether you know what a Wakefield bulkhead is.

Q: No, I do not.

Adm. R.: You take 2 x 12s that overlap. You drive one line

then drive another behind it and so forth and so on. We had about 100 feet of Wakefield bulkhead trying to hold this. Somebody suggested that we put in groins, which means that you put a spur out from the beach and that's supposed to catch the sand. But that wouldn't work there. The Army engineers told us it wouldn't work.

As I told you, this building was in the shape of a Greek cross and the top cross was the administrative part and the wing out to the sea was the officers' lounge. We had a pool table in there. When these waves would roll in and hit this Wakefield bulkhead, the whole building would shake. So we gave up playing pool because it was much more fun to put the balls on the table and gamble on which ball would roll in which pocket when the pool table shook. But more and more I was getting worried because sooner or later something was going to happen. The building itself was on the old basic land. I was sure of that because I'd looked at the old maps and chart lines and I had talked to the keeper of the light. He showed me, and really the basic land, you might say the basic spit, was about ten feet outside of this wing, but the rest of it was out beyond. Even then, I suppose, the basic land, which was not too solid, would have gone eventually.

Finally, they decided they'd send somebody out from GSA. This was probably dirty pool, but the guy arrived in Los Angeles in the afternoon and we met him, I was to bring him up - this was much more impressive at night - so I stalled this poor fellow, I told him there was no hurry to get there.

Q: You mean the vibration and shaking were more impressive?

Adm. R.: No, the waves.

I stalled him till about eleven o'clock at night. I took him to dinner in Los Angeles and so forth, then brought him up. Then I took him down to see because when the waves would come in and hit this Wakefield bulkhead they'd go thirty or forty feet in the air and made quite an impressive show, but it was much more impressive at night. They looked twice as high as they probably really were. That convinced him they'd have to do something, but the question was what, because it was going to cost money.

Fortunately, at that time, the Navy was building Point Mugu, the station down there, and they had opened a big quarry back in the mountains, back of Camarilla, or near it, I think - I never saw it. So we were in the process of negotiating with them how we were going to get these big rocks down. The only way to save it really was to do this. We had the Navy engineers come and look at it and everybody agreed that the only way to save it was to build a tremendous stone bulkhead for about an eighth of a mile, the whole length of the property, from the lighthouse at the point all the way down, to stop this erosion.

These were rocks that you could move only on flat cars

and heavy-lift cranes, and it was going to be an expensive deal, so we were negotiating. In the meantime, friction between the War Shipping Administration - really between Macauley and Waesche - had come to a head. This is hearsay, but apparently Macauley had a back door to the White House through Mrs. Roosevelt and having known the President himself. I think his wife and Mrs. Roosevelt knew each other. Anyway, in August of that year, the whole training thing was turned over to War Shipping and we were told to make plans to transfer over. At the same time another thing was developing.

The Navy needed a place for training their Seabees, and about that same time I was visited by a captain who wanted to know what I thought about the place for Seabee training. I pointed out the defects and all, but I'll have to admit I also encouraged him because I wasn't too happy about turning the training over to the War Shipping Administration.

Q: And they were not about to take over that base?

Adm. R.: Who? War Shipping?

Q: Yes.

Adm. R.: Oh, yes, War Shipping would have, but the Navy was looking for a place for their Seabees. What I'm saying is that I probably encouraged the Navy, although I think it was a good choice, as it turned out. I wasn't selling them a bill of goods. It met their immediate needs and they later developed it into quite a plant. I have never been back since they developed it, but they dredged out the harbor, it's a lot larger. That became and still is a big Navy set-up.

I turned the base over and turned the ship over to Dobson and then I was transferred to Alaska.

Q: The ship itself was turned over to War Shipping?

Adm. R.: Yes. I don't know whether it was still in dry dock or whether it was just refitting, after having the guns mounted, when I turned it over. I know we were still down at Long Beach.

Q: So, with this transfer of authority, you lost your job, really?

Adm. R.: Yes, I was completely out.

Returning to Hueneme for a minute. Shortly after War Shipping took over, the Navy moved in and ousted them from there. My recollection is that at the same time they had started a place I believe at San Mateo or some place in the bay for officer training. I may be wrong about this.

Q: "They" being War Shipping?

Adm. R.: Yes. I think they moved the activities that they had had at the base at Hueneme up there and I believe not too long after that they closed that part of it out because we were more deeply in the war and I guess there was a more suitable place. So that completed my time there.

My family was in Santa Paula, which is about twenty miles back in the delta from Hueneme.

In September of 1942 I was transferred to Alaska and left my family there in Santa Paula. I took command of the <u>Haida</u>, the ship that I had previously served on in Seattle and had taken to Cordova.

Q: She was now stationed at Juneau?

Adm. R.: Yes.

Q: And the picture in Alaska was quite different at this point from what it had been before?

Adm. R.: Oh, yes, entirely different. The Navy had established a base at Kodiak, which by now was a reasonably booming town for Alaska. Earlier in the war, the Japs had moved in to Adak and Attu, and, of course, we were busily trying - well, we had thrown them out, I guess, by that time. By the time I got up there they had been ejected. They were definitely out of Adak.

Q: The Battle of Midway had been fought and won.

Adm. R.: Yes, at that time. It's a little hazy to me now, but the Alaska proposition had been pretty well liquidated, except that, of course, there was still the fear of a recurrence. Although I agree that there is some question of what value it would have been, but the Japs really come into Alaska in the early stages of the war like they went south into Singapore and places like that, they could have swept across Alaska without any real opposition.

Q: Tell me, Sir, you were engaged in convoy duty?

Adm. R.: Yes. Actually, the ship was out when I arrived, so I had about ten days in Juneau, waiting around until she came back. The home station was Juneau and theoretically they were not supposed to come back to Juneau except to refuel. They came in about midnight one night and I took over command at two o'clock in the morning and at three o'clock we were on our way out to Pleasant Bay to take out the next convoy. Her principal job, and that's really all I did while I was there except for one incident - the ships came up through the inside passage and collected in Pleasant Bay, we'd have a convoy conference, and then steam out and take them to Kodiak.

Q: How big a convoy would this be?

Adm. R.: We could have as few as three or four ships and as many as ten to fifteen.

Q: With one escort?

Adm. R.: With one escort, and that was a snare and a delusion, strictly speaking, because the Haida was an old ship. In those days, I used to divide our ships into two kinds, the fast sinkers and the slow sinkers. We were one of the fast sinkers. We had a 5-inch gun, it's true, providing the submarine, if he appeared, would stick his neck up so we could shoot at him. If he didn't, we had no depth charges. We had no sound equipment.

Q: No detection equipment?

Adm. R.: No dectection equipment at all. But these merchant ships would sail merrily along, bravely protected by the Haida, and, hopefully, nobody would show up. Really, because the Japs were interested in other places, our greatest danger was the convoy routes that we were supposed to follow. I suspect they'd been drawn up by some helpful naval reserve officer who had probably been an engineer or something of that sort before he got into the Navy, because if you looked at them on the chart they were perfect. You'd come out through Icy Strait, head up to Yakutat, west to Cape St. Elias, and then down to Kodiak. The westbound was the inner one, you were roughly ten miles off any point of land, farther in some places, and then five miles outside of that was the westbound route, so the hazard was not the Japs but the opposite-bound convoy because up in that area, particularly off Lituya Bay, it's not uncommon to be set thirty or forty miles in a night. So, usually, when you picked up the opposing convoy it would be on the wrong side of you, if you weren't in the midst of it. That was really the trick. It would have been much more sensible, in other words, to steam straight across to Kodiak - of course, you were farther from land - across from Icy Strait. It would have been quicker - or at least have one of the convoys coming that way.

But we made the trips without incident. We had some scarey times occasionally, when convoys, east and west bound, got mixed up.

We'd go to Kodiak and lay over for two or three days, until they made up a convoy of ships that had unloaded at Kodiak, and then we would head back, get them in Icy Strait, and turn them loose. We were supposed to have a layover of twenty-four or thirty-six hours at the eastern end. Of course, it didn't make much difference to me because my family was down in California. This ship had been stationed at Juneau, so the crew all had their families there. There wasn't anything against it, except it seemed hardly worthwhile in many ways. It was roughly eight or nine hours' steaming from Icy Strait to Juneau, and we'd steam in and let the boys have a little liberty.

Q: They actually could have their families there? It was in the war zone, was it not?

Adm. R.: No, it wasn't called that. They'd had their families there since before the war so they just stayed on. I think by that time they had forbidden bringing families up there, if you got any replacements. I never questioned it because I didn't try to take my family up there.

One time, we did get chased out to the westward, but the convoy moved faster than we could move in rough weather, so after we were about halfway out to Cold Bay we were released and turned back. That was the only time I went to the westward of Kodiak.

The other interesting thing that happened up there was - this was after the first Battle of Savo Island, where the Navy ships had not only been gunned down but the paint had burned. So then the Navy came out with an order that every ship should be stripped of paint and they were going to apply non-fire paint. I remember particularly the distress with which several young naval officers came down - we were in Kodiak - to inspect our ship and tell us what we should do on the *Haida*, because the *Haida* had been built back in the early twenties and had partial wood bulkheads between all the staterooms and the wardroom. I was quite interested as to how these boys were going to solve this problem because if, for example, we had taken out the bulkheads, which was the only logical way to do it if you were going to do anything, it meant that in the wardroom we'd be just floating around in open space, as such. They had their orders but they didn't know how to carry them out so, in distress, they finally gave us up, particularly since I reminded them that amongst the Coast Guard ships we were a fast sinker. We really had no watertight bulkheads, except way below decks on the ship.

Actually, I think in Alaska this idea of stripping ships of paint was a terrible mistake, as the Navy found out. There was a cruiser in there and they stripped her of paint and about a week or so after they had stripped all the paint off the interior bulkheads, better than half the crew were down with colds or pneumonia, because what had happened was the minute that interior insulating paint had come off the bulkheads, with the cold outside and the heat inside, the bulkheads were running with moisture, condensation, and the decks were full of water. The boys were just wading around. They were wet all the time, and you just can't take that in Alaska. Later, of course, when they got their fireproof paint, things were better.

Q: Which says something about these across-the-board orders in the service.

Adm. R.: Yes. Probably in the tropics it was wonderful, but up in Alaska it was impossible.

Q: Is that something you were concerned about when you were head of the Coast Guard, across-the-board orders that pertained to your ships in so many different climes?

Adm. R.: Yes. You always have to keep that in mind. I find that is the big difficulty so often. You put out an order and it's a perfectly good order, it's logical, but there are conditions that it doesn't meet. It would be impossible to meet every condition in every order, but I think that when you do get a protest from somebody saying, "Well, now, look, this is impractical" and he has logical reasons why it's impractical, and I will tell a story of just why this might be. It happened later, after I became assistant commandant and was making trips to the Loran stations. You've got to be more open to objections, you might say.

Q: To be reasonable?

Adm. R.: Reasonable, and not say that's our order and we're going to stick to it. I've already mentioned the case where

I was first transferred to Alaska, years before, and because we weren't allowed to sell from the general mess we had to carry food up to sell. It was really ridiculous. There was no reason why the boys could not have bought from general mess and ships' supplies, except that up to that time it hadn't been done.

I was there then till just about Christmas, I think, and then the Haida was ordered to Seattle for overhaul. I don't remember who relieved us on patrol, but we were already down.

We were to have radar put aboard, so we went down to Seattle, to the Todd Shipyards. I wasn't there very long.

At that time we were building the Wind ships, the icebreakers, the first icebreakers.

Q: The Northwind and so forth?

Adm. R.: Yes, and I had been, when I was sent to the Haida, promised, or it was indicated - I had applied for - that I would have command of one of the Wind ships, so I was looking forward to being in command of an icebreaker.

We hadn't any more than got our lines on the dock in Seattle when the shipyard workers and Navy advisers all came down to tell us what they were going to do to the ship. We all gathered in the wardroom, the ship's plans were laid out, and that was when I learned that you've got to be very careful of acronyms and so forth because they were tossing these various letters around and I, being from the far north and not having been in on all this stuff, was completely mystified.

Q: Jargon!

Adm. R.: Yes, it's jargon, TBS and so forth.

Just out of curiosity, I finally spoke up and I said, "What does TBS (or whatever it was) stand for?" There were about fourteen of them and they looked at each other and there wasn't one who could tell me what it stood for. They knew what they were talking about, I don't mean that, but nobody had ever stopped to think what it stood for. But you know, they were placing these things, saying "This will go there" and "this will go here."

The other thing I learned there, nonessential information that you stack up as you go through life, there was a Russian icebreaker being overhauled, so in the light of my wanting to go to an icebreaker, I thought it would be a nice idea if I went and called on her. The foreman in the shipyard arranged that I could go over and talk to the skipper. I did, and he talked about icebreaking and I was gathering general information. He was very friendly and decided that we ought to have some refreshment, so he served beer, which was all right, but with the beer I found out that the Russians eat chocolates, which is an abominable habit, as far as I'm concerned.

Q: Sweet chocolate?

Adm. R.: Sweet chocolates, the kind that are wrapped in silver paper. At least, that's what he did, so that was my one and only call on the Russian icebreaker.

About that time the Coast Guard had changed as far as the Coast Guard was concerned. The preceding fall, we had taken over the full-time administration of the Bureau of Marine Inspection and Navigation which, as you know, regulates and controls the licences, certificates of merchant seamen and officers - licences of the officers and certificates of the men, and also is responsible for regulation of the merchant marine and the safety of the ships and that sort of thing.

You will also recall that at or about that time there was a big fiasco down at Guadalcanal where a number of merchant seamen refused to unload a cargo ship. This was treason and that sort of thing.

Q: This happened not only in one place but in many places.

Adm. R.: I remember the papers were full of it at the time, these terrible merchant seamen, getting five times as much as the men who were fighting ashore. The Navy, was properly, very much exercised about that, so they asked the Coast Guard, in essence, what are you going to do about it.

The procedure in the Bureau of Inspection and Navigation had been, at that time and they turned it over to the Coast Guard as such, that when an offense was committed by a man or an officer, whether it was disobeying orders or anything, an accident to be investigated or anything like that - let's say it happened in a foreign port or like at Guadalcanal, it would be logged and when the ship came back the shipping commissioner reviewed the log and this would be noted, then a hearing would be held. The only thing about this was - and this had been the procedure for years - that these were quasi-legal proceedings and by the time you got around to proceeding against the alleged culprit, any witnesses would have been dispersed on other ships all over the world so the chance of a conviction or proving a case was ultimately nil. In other words, maybe a year would elapse between an offense even being brought to a hearing and then, as I say, there'd be no one around or if they were around they probably didn't remember what happened, anyway.

So it was decided in the Coast Guard that something would have to be done to expedite this procedure, and this led to the setting-up of the Coast Guard hearing units. The first one was to be tried out in New York. The principle on which this was to work was that it would be staffed by officers and a yeoman who could act as court stenographer practically, who was able to take testimony, and each officer in there would be both a hearing officer and an examining officer.

Rather than wait for anything to be reported, the minute the ship came into port - this was done experimentally in New York - the examining officer would go aboard and examine the log for offenses, interrogate the crew, the officers, talk to - the unions had delegates, each ship had a delegate - the delegates. He'd talk to anybody who had complaint - the master has done this or the officers have done this or the food's bad. Assuming that he found someone reporting an offense, it would be minor, anything that was appreciable and merited consideration, he would call up the office and a hearing officer would go right down with a yeoman. Even before the shipping commissioner had paid the crew off and they were all dispersed, they'd call the people in and the hearing officer could decide on the spot what was to be done. These were what we call "in rem" proceedings, that is, they were proceedings against the men's certificates or licences, depending upon the situation. Assuming it was a minor case, you could give the man a reprimand, you could even go so far as to revoke the man's papers and take his papers right away from him.

It is true the fellow had an appeal. This was not final in the sense that he couldn't get his papers back. Or he could revoke papers for a limited period, anything at all.

Q: It was a positive step?

Adm. R.: It was a positive step, it was done right there. In other words, if his papers were taken away or revoked, say, for three months, he was going to be beached for three months because he had to have his papers to be signed on on another ship. Of course, with the pay that they were drawing at that time, the merchant seamen or the officers, that could be a sizeable penalty. In other words, he'd lose three months' pay. I think seamen at that time were drawing pretty close to $1,000 a month, so he'd lost $3,000 if it stood up. So it really was quite effective.

Anyway, I was ordered back to New York to head this up. It had already gotten started before I got there. Maybe it had been running two weeks. We had a fairly sizeable office there, I think we had about ten officers.

Q: And you were under the Third Naval District?

Adm. R.: Yes. Well, actually we were in the District Office building, but I never saw the Third Naval District, as I recall it. Yes, I do, too, I was in there once or twice. I had nothing to do with the naval district as such. We did come in contact with them through their intelligence on the merchant seamen, because that was another thing we had to watch out for along with this, so I was in the Naval District to that extent.

Yes, this was part of the Third Naval District because

the Third Coast Guard District was part of the Third Naval District because we were under the Navy.

That occupied me, then, until some time about April, I think. I was there about two months.

Q: Did that work out effectively?

Adm. R.: Oh, it was very effective.

Q: It really expedited things?

Adm. R.: It really expedited things. As I say, the ship would come back and the master would claim that he had something logged against a man and you settled the case right there. He could say "I didn't do it" or "I did do it," you know, plead guilty.

The advantage of it was, too, that even though you might put the man on probation, it was a mark against his record. Sooner or later, if this kept on long enough, if he was a proverbial malcontent, he would have built up a record of trouble aboard ship.

New York was the only place where this then existed. Of course, that was the principal convoy port on the east coast and it was a good place to try it out. We really put in quite a few hours there. During that period I never acted as an examining officer. I was always a hearing officer, if

I went out at all. Most of my time really was spent in the office, reviewing. Most of these cases were reviewed in the office as soon as they were typed up and brought in and they had to be approved, to see whether the administration was going properly and that sort of thing. But it was very successful because, as I say both - each officer was a hearing and examining officer - getting ahead of my story a little bit now. Following the war, this was ruled as being, strictly speaking, an administrative procedure that wasn't permissible. You can't be an examining officer one day and a hearing officer the next day. You've got to be a hearing officer all the time. I suppose it's the same idea as that you shouldn't be a judge one day and a lawyer the next.

But at that time the war was on and it was effective.

Q: Did you open other offices?

Adm. R.: Yes. Now we get into the next area of my story here.

Q: Oh, I see. The one in London was the same office.

Adm. R.: I think it was in early April that it was thought there were a number of problems developing in the British Isles that ought to be investigated, not only merchant seamen. So Admiral Chalker, who was assistant commandant, Captain

Shepherd, who had been the assistant chief of the Bureau of Marine Inspection and Navigation and had been brought over and made Coast Guard when they took over, Captain Norman B. Hall, who had been - or was - an explosives expert on ammunition, he had become the man in charge of ammunition-loading in the United States and we were getting reports that ammunition was arriving overseas in battered condition and that sort of thing, and I believe Commodore Dillon, but I'm not sure, and I, because I now presumably am experienced with this hearing procedure, were sent to England to find out whether it would be desirable - well, to correct procedures over there for ourselves in these various problems and to generally find out the problems and look around and see what was necessary.

We went to England for three or four weeks, studying the problem and talking to the British, talking to the Americans over there, as to whether there were problems. My job was to find out whether the British were having - and the Americans also - any problems with merchant seamen over there that could be handled locally rather than wait till they got back to New York. We went round to different ports and came to certain conclusions about all of these fields that we were interested in, one of which was, yes, as long as this was working in New York - I'm speaking now about control of the merchant seamen - there was no reason why it wouldn't be equally effective in England, if we wanted to send the details. This was going to be part of our over-all recommendation.

We even went so far as to make recommendations as to what officer should head the detail in the British Isles. Then, having gotten that far along, Admiral Chalker - I guess we all felt - by that time, you see, we were moving in to North Africa ready for the underbelly attack - we felt, well, if they were having problems in England would they not eventually be having similar problems in North Africa. So the first decision was that maybe we ought to ask for authority to go over to North Africa and study this, make a round trip.

Then, this board having gotten a little tired of British food and so forth made a decision which - I was the junior member and, after all, I had been in on all the conferences on the various things - so instead of five of us treking through North Africa why wouldn't it be a sterling idea for me to represent the whole board and go to North Africa and see what the situation was.

Q: What was your rank at that time?

Adm. R.: I was a captain. I'd finally made captain, but I was a relatively junior captain.

So they headed home and I headed for North Africa. I visited Oran, all through Tunis, and down to Rabat and Casablanca and talked to people. The same kind of approach was made.

Then I headed back, expecting to pick up my duties in

New York when I got back. I got off the plane at Floyd Bennett, I think it was then, and was met by one of my assistants in the New York office and I asked if the officer we had designated to go to London had left with his team yet, thinking while I was playing games in North Africa this had all gotten under way. He looked at me kind of sad and said:

"No. Haven't you heard?"

I said, "No, I haven't heard. What?"

He said, "You're taking the team back."

Apparently, my compatriots had sold me out when they got back to Washington! Not that I objected to it, in fact it turned out very well. So for the next two or three weeks I was busy putting together a team to take back to London with me. They did give me I believe a week's leave and I dashed out to the west coast to see my family, then back to head for England.

Q: Let me ask one question. While you were making this survey of the British situation and then in North Africa, did you not also consider the Murmansk run and the convoys?

Adm. R.: Yes, but we never considered sending anybody up to Murmansk because, you see, those convoys were being made up - most of them - either from Iceland or the British Isles and a lot of them were being made up up in Loch Ewe, which is on the west coast of Scotland. I later went up there, after

I was stationed in England. I went up there occasionally to talk to the boys when they came in from the convoys or before they went to find out how things were.

Q: You went to London in July of 1943?

Adm. R.: That's right. I took several officers with me.

Q: Did you select your staff?

Adm. R.: Within limits. I drew some from New York and I asked for one or two other officers that I knew. As a matter of fact, one of them was Commander Quentin Walsh, who had been with me at the whaling conference. Some of the officers were assigned to me. They didn't all go with me at the time. I think only four or five of us went over to set up the London detail and we set up a detail in Liverpool, one in Bristol, and one in Edinburgh. Excuse me, it was not Edinburgh, it was Glasgow. We did not have anybody in Edinburgh because there was no shipping coming in to Edinburgh. The ones up in Glasgow - since you asked early about Murmansk - were covering the convoys that were leaving England for Murmansk, also the ones that were coming in from Iceland direct to the northern ports.

There would be usually three officers to a port, so we had all together, not counting London, nine, and there were four in London, where at one time we had as many as five, but generally there were three or four.

Q: How did you go over, what transportation did you have?

Adm. R.: We flew over. My recollection is that we flew American Export. I think they were flying boats at the time. We may have gone by the Azores, I don't recall for sure. I do remember this. I was quite thrilled at flying across the ocean and I sat down next to a young man who was a State Department courier. If you recall, in those days, the State Department sent their dispatches by courier. They had a dispatch bag chained to their wrist. I asked him how many trips he'd made and he said, "I think this is my thirtieth trip." Of course, I was quite excited at flying, and I said, "Gee, you must find it enjoyable." He looked at me kind of sorrowfully and said:

"I'll tell you. I wouldn't take $2,500 for my first trip and I wouldn't give you a nickel for any one since."

As I flew more during the war, I began to appreciate his sentiments.

Q: There were certain hardships involved!

Adm. R.: As I say, I don't recall how I got back to England with my group. It could be that we went via Iceland in a Navy transport plane. I know on one of my trips I went through Iceland and had to put up there. Later, I'll recount another trip I had when I came back.

Q: The next question is did you have any difficulty in getting space in these various towns where you were setting up your offices?

Adm. R.: No. In all of these places there were naval liaison officers and in most cases they were linked in with the British Navy, so they'd have a room or so and that was all we needed to operate out of. Quarters for the people were a little more difficult. I know up in Glasgow the Navy liaison team had hired or rented a rather nice home. If they'd had coal to heat it, it would have been much better. The naval reserve officer in charge of the liaison group had a flagpole put in the front yard and had the ensign hoisted and insisted that the front yard was the quarterdeck and everybody should salute the flag on going through the gate, which disgusted my representative who lived with the group very much. He thought this was a lot of foolishness and I was inclined to agree with him.

I do remember one thing on my first trip. We landed in Ireland and had to fly from Ireland to Blackpool, I think it was, in a British plane. We landed at Shannon Airport and stayed in Limerick overnight, then flew the next day. I said to Blackpool but it was one of those ports. You couldn't see anything. The British had blocked out all the windows, so we just sat there like sheep in this flying boat. I think it was a big Sunderland that we flew over in, commercial.

We got our offices set up. We were in Grosvenor Square with the Navy. They provided us with space and we started operating. The additional personnel for the outer ports came over by ship. I distinctly remember that because they brought a lot of supplies, frankly, toilet paper and things like that. Anybody who was in England during the war knows the hardships of British toilet paper, even in peacetime, much less in wartime. It was really rugged. They brought several steamer trunks that we had ordered and had sent over.

Gradually we got our organization set up through the British Isles. It was very effective. We worked with the British. I had been appointed senior Coast Guard officer in theEuropean Theater. Let's see, that would have been in July, and the following fall - before that I might mention that we had a number of interesting cases, some of them funny and some of them not so funny.

One of the big problems that we ran into very quickly wherever we went - I had learned this on my inspection trip - was that when you asked questions "Have you any trouble with the merchant marine?" the one thing that particularly the Navy liaison, our own U. S. Navy liaison team, resented most was the fact that there is very little distinctive about the Navy uniform. They had learned this the hard way. And the merchant marine officers, in some instances, were almost identical - they wore almost identical uniforms. I don't know whether you know it or not, but the only distinctive portions of a Navy uniform at that time were the buttons and the hat device. Obviously to an uninitiated person, it's very difficult to distinguish a button device because it's so small and not many people know the difference in the hat device. So the great trouble was that merchant officers ashore in uniform might be conducting themselves - getting into trouble, and reports would come back that they were naval officers. I ran into that almost every place I went. That was one thing that I'd be asked to do, straighten out the uniform situation.

I also found out that the so-called misconduct ashore of merchant seamen was greatly overrated. Almost every place you'd go almost everybody would have a complaint about the merchant seamen and their conduct, in some cases merchant officers. I finally got to the point where I'd ask:

"That case you're telling me about, was that Two-Gun Heller?" He was a merchant marine captain who apparently thought he was from the Wild West or something and would go around around with two guns strapped on his hips and so forth and got to be known as - I mean he spread his notoriety pretty well through the British Isles.

There were cases like that, but generally speaking, although we had some very serious cases - I remember one occasion where we had a case of a man who had stabbed a crewman. We had hearings on him and the Army had him in a stockade somewhere in the middle of England. On a weekend I remember chasing all the way across to Liverpool and then driving about 75 miles to hold a hearing on this fellow and take his papers away before the Army lowered the boom on him, and things like that. Some of the things were funny and peculiar and led to many stories.

One of the most ridiculous ones that I ever had - you may recall the Army brought over a number of these big seagoing tugs, the old Army Transportation Corps. That was before MST was created. These fellows were under Army jurisdiction but they were civilians. They got over to Glasgow and they were in civilian clothes, but they decided they weren't making much headway with the local populace, particularly the girls in the bars, so the captains of these tugs - I suppose they had twenty or thirty men on them - decided they'd get themselves some blue coats and put four stripes on them and the engineers put on blue coats with three stripes.

I got a call to come up to Glasgow because what had happened was that the stewards and the cooks got to thinking this over and they saw that the captains and engineers were making more time than they were, so they decided that if four stripes and three stripes could do the job, they'd get blue coats and put five stripes on. I was asked to come up to Glasgow and settle this case of why the stewards couldn't wear five gold stripes on their sleeves. Obviously, I didn't go, but this was one of the more humorous incidents that came up while I was there. The captains and engineers were mad because the boys had put on five stripes and were doing better than they were with their four and three!

The following November it was decided that if this was good in England and New York - in the meantime, of course, the system had spread more or less in the main ports of the United States - possibly we ought to have a survey out to the eastward, so I was ordered to proceed out as far as India to make a survey of the requirements in that general area.

Q: Did this include the Mediterranean? Did you go through the Mediterranean?

Adm. R.: Well, you see, I had pretty well covered the Mediterranean on my first survey. At this time I think they were still fighting for Italy. Let me put it this way. We never did set up any units in North Africa itself. We did later set up a unit in Naples, but I don't think that by November we had cleared Naples. There was still fighting at Salerno. They may have gotten above Naples, but at least they hadn't cleared the port, so at that time there was nobody over there.

I had an interesting trip. Do you want the details?

Q: Well, if it has any bearing.

Adm. R.: It's kind of historical on the problems that we had.
In the first place, I had to get all my shots and yellow

fever was one of them. At that time, the British were giving their shots at a place called Welcome House and because presumably in their opinion, yellow-fever vaccine didn't keep, they'd open one bottle and you queued up for your shot, and if the bottle ran out they wouldn't open another bottle unless they could use up the whole bottle. I queued up one week and I didn't get my shot, so I decided I'd take a chance.

I headed out and got as far as Cairo and was put up in the old Shepheard's Hotel there. The Navy had their team at Shepheard's Hotel. The Navy had taken a large sort of dormitory room, so you'd go to sleep one night and you'd have somebody in the cot next to you and the next morning it would be somebody else. They were coming and going all the time. They indicated it would be some time before I could get out of Cairo to the south, to Khartoum, and on to the eastward, and while I was there this naval reserve commander came out. He'd been in the hemp business down in the West Indies and we got to be quite friendly, and he came in the hotel one day mad as hops. It seems that he had had his yellow fever shots approximately three years before and had come out with the assurance that this was all right, but the British had changed the ground rules. At that time, the U. S. said yellow fever was good for four years. The British had changed the ground rules and said it was only good for two years. He was on his way down to Mombasa or Madagascar, I suppose, to estimate the hemp crop or something like that. Anyway he would have to take his shots over and he'd have to wait two weeks for these to incubate. There's some rule that yellow fever shots take that long.

He said to me: "How are your yellow fever shots?" I didn't exactly lie but I said, "Oh, I think they're all right," not having had any I figured they were all right. So he said:

"Well, you'd better see for sure and have them renewed here." By that time I'd been there four or five days and I was pretty well fed up with Cairo anyway, so I said, "I think I'm all right. I'm not worried."

About three days later I was on the plane bound for Khartoum. I got in to Khartoum on a Sunday night. I recall it distinctly. It was about ten o'clock and I made my way into the operations office and said, "When can I get out to the eastward?" The fellow said, What's your priority?" Well, I was only on a Class 2. I'd learned a long time before not to throw your weight around with these Air Force sergeants. He said:

"Well, it's probably be three weeks before you can get out of here, at least."

So I said, "That's all right. If I have to stay here, I'll stay but I would like to get out sooner."

Then I got a bright idea. I said: "By the way, do you know anybody up in the dispensary. As long as I've got to be here three weeks I'd like to get the yellow fever shots." And he said:

"Sure, I've got a friend up there," so he called the friend and sent me up by car. This fellow was just dying for news from home. He wanted to know what the Dodgers were doing. So he goes into the icebox and gets the yellow fever shots and sticks them in my arm. Then he wanted to sit and talk and I said, "By the way, how good are those shots?" And he said, "I don't know what they do," so I said:

"Well, look, as long as you're making out the slip, how about predating it two weeks?"

"That's all right," so he predated it and we kept on talking about what the Dodgers were doing, what the news was from home, and all that sort of thing. Finally, about midnight, they took me up to the dormitory, put me under a mosquito net, and I went to bed. It seemed to me I had hardly gotten to sleep - I guess it was around 4:30 in the morning, and somebody was shaking me and saying, "Hey, do you want to get out of this place, really?" I said, sure. He said:

"Well, meet me down at the airfield at six o'clock and if you want to ride courier on some airplane parts that are bound over The Hump, I can get you on a DC-3 getting out of here."

So at six o'clock on Monday morning I was bound out of Khartoum in a DC-3, pilot and co-pilot up front, me sitting on about 500, - how I was supposed to destroy these parts I never quite figured out - sitting on a big packing case filled with about 500 pounds of airplane parts. We stopped one night at some God-forsaken island base down off of Aden, farther east than Aden, I forget the name of the island, and by Tuesday afternoon we were steaming in to Karachi. I turned over the parts to my relief, the relief courier. This little Pakistani doctor looks at my papers and I passed beautifully, my yellow fever shots and everything.

Now I come to the payoff on this story. It's rather a long story. The naval liaison officer picked me up and took me out to the home they had rented for their group and I got the same story about how they ought to have a Coast Guard officer there to straighten out these horrible merchant marine people and so forth and so on. I stayed with them and after dinner he said, "Do you want to take a ride?" I said yes, so we drove out into the desert. Karachi's pretty much in an arid area. About 15 miles out of town, we drove up in front of this big building that had a big stone wall. It was a nice building. It didn't look like a prison. The liaison officer gets out, goes in the back of his car, and brings out a case of beer and four or five packs of cigarettes and hands them over to the guard. I said:

"What's all this about?"

"Well," he said, "a couple of naval officers came out here about a week ago and they didn't have their yellow fever shots up to date so they're spending fourteen days in the pest house out here."

I just kept my mouth shut. I had had my shots two days

before.

From Karachi I went down to Bombay and Colombo, Ceylon, then came back to Madras and up to Calcutta and back to Delhi, then to Baghdad. At that time there was quite a lot of shipping. We were trying to support the Russians, so there was quite a lot of shipping coming in to Khorramshahr and quite a lot of tankers running out of there. I went down to Bahrein then came back to England and from England came back to the United States to make my report. I got a few days' leave on the west coast and then headed back to England.

Q: That was quite a tour, and what was the result of it?

Adm. R.: We established a unit at Colombo, Ceylon, and also one down at Bahrein or Khorramshahr, I don't know which. I know it was not as far up the river as Baghdad, at least I don't think it was. I never went out there again, so I'm not too sure. That was the result of the tour on that particular trip.

Q: Tell me something about your duty. You were on Admiral Stark's staff, were you not?

Adm. R.: We were simply a unit assigned to ComNavEu, Admiral Stark. I was part of the over-all staff which, as you can recognize, was at that time, a rather large grouping of officers. Basically, the Coast Guard unit was under a Marine division of the staff. When I first went over there was a Commander Jackson, a reserve officer from Philadelphia, a former Naval Academy graduate, who had gotten out and was in the shipping business, in charge. He was relieved by another commander.

I was there for the build-up of the invasion of Europe, went through all of that.

Q: What was your role in that? I mean, what was the role of the Coast Guard units?

Adm. R.: Basically, as senior Coast Guard officer in Europe, I was in charge of the hearing units and handling the merchant marine problems, as they arose. Admiral Shepherd came over and he was - then Captain Shepherd - assigned to the SHAEF staff and worked with a Britisher on merchant marine requirements. Knowing that the invasion was coming, my recollection is that President Roosevelt had indicated, or else they had requested, and there would probably be losses in the invasion possibly of the larger ships, if not a lot of the landing craft, they wanted patrol boats to save lives. Unfortunately, what they wanted was patrol boats that had diesel engines because of the possibility of explosions, whereas all of the Coast Guard boats, at that time - all the old 75-footers of the rum-running days had grown to 83-footers and they were all gasoline-powered. There were a lot of conferences as to how this could be met and in the end it was decided that there was no answer but to accept the 83-footers. I forget the exact number, but a number of 83-footers were shipped across and a base had to be established for them and that was done at Poole. Of course, there was a commanding officer and I assisted him, working on the staff in London to get this base set up and the boats operating.

The next thing that came up that required Coast Guard assistance was the Phoenix project. The idea was they were going to sink these barges to make harbors for the landing craft, and a number of our warrant officers were sent over to man the tugs and the craft that were going to be involved in the Phoenix operation.

Q: These were to be established after the invasion?

Adm. R.: Right after, but, remember, this was in late 1943 or early 1944 when we were preparing for D-day, which took place finally I think on June 5th.

We had brought up from the Mediterranean, because that operation was now over, a number of LCIs that were manned by the Coast Guard and they were to participate. As I recall it, there were three flotillas of LCIs. They were down at Portsmouth, and I had quite a little bit to do with them. I mean helping to get ready, trying to smooth out difficulties of supply and that sort of thing. They were going on maneuvers and so forth.

The thing I remember best about that is going down to their headquarters because while they were down there at Portsmouth they had Agatha Christie's home, which had been taken over by the government. One of the more enterprising artists of the group painted a postcard picture of the bar and I often wondered if Agatha Christie's home kept that mural that was painted over the bar, after she regained it, after the war.

Then we also had some LSTs, I believe one flotilla, that had been destined to move out through the Suez after the invasion and go on out towards the Far East. It had been turned around and brought back up. There were problems with them because they had not been winter-outfitted. When they arrived up there, of course, it was spring, but they still didn't have proper clothing for England, even in the spring, and there was a lot of backing and filling as we tried to outfit them.

The Coast Guard also was manning transports. The Wakefield, the old USS Manhattan, came in every three or four weeks and I had contacts with them.

Q: She was bringing over troops, was she?

Adm. R.: Bringing troops in. It was just a series of jobs.

It's hard to define, because one day it would be one thing, plus the fact that all this time we were working out problems with the merchant marine.

Q: And having hearings?

Adm. R.: Having hearings. At one time I had about seven in the office but sometimes we were down to two or three, and it was just a matter of handling day-to-day situations.

One of the things that happened, for example, was that we decided it would be good publicity to send Jack Dempsey over. You remember, Jack Dempsey was a commander in the Coast Guard. He came over for three or four weeks. I think he was taken in originally to help with athletics and so forth at Hoffman Island, which is not a Coast Guard training station - no, Manhattan Beach, I guess it was, that was our training station at that time. Manhattan Beach outside of New York.

I had quite an interesting time taking him around. It was surprising how popular he was - not surprising if you know Jack Dempsey. Remember, these were the days of Joe Louis. Jack was an excellent representative of the service and I thoroughly enjoyed the three or four weeks that I had with him over there. He was a prince of a fellow. Maybe not the best educated person in the world but a good diplomat and a very likeable person.

When the invasion came on, of course, our ships participated. We were manning at least one of the transports that took part. Four or five big ships went over. I don't remember the name of the transport that we commanded and that was Coast Guard manned and under our control. She was in the invasion. Then our public relations people insisted on sending over one or two photographers and I had problems in that area. We set up a dark room. Actually, some of the early pictures from D-day were taken by Coast Guard photographers. We had worked out systems to get the pictures back. Of course, they were cleared by the Navy, too. I don't mean that we went outside, although I did have one photographer - maybe all photographers are nuts, but this one was, and I spent some time keeping him out of trouble. For some reason or other he had gotten disassociated after we landed from our troops on Utah and Omaha beaches. He'd gotten up with the British on Juneau and gotten in to Caen before anybody else, and he came into my office after the expedition -

Q: Triumphant!

Adm. R.: Triumphant - in dungarees, looking like something. He meant well but apparently he hadn't been trained in military techniques.

Q: He was a lone wolf?

Adm. R.: Yes.

Q: Tell me the story of how Loran came to be used in connection with the invasion operation.

Adm. R.: I had never heard of Loran at that time. In fact, there was nothing out on it. It was just being developed by the Navy and the Coast Guard, I gather.

I was in town, wandering round Berkeley Square one day, and noticed this Coast Guard officer who had not reported to me. He was in, I regret to say, a kind of slovenly uniform - at least he wasn't wearing his uniform in a uniform manner. I haled him and asked him who he was and what he was doing in London. He told me and admitted - well, he said he had intended to report but hadn't, but he couldn't tell me. I asked him why not. Well, he said, he was there on top secret business. I said:

"I'm the senior Coast Guard officer and I'm entitled to know whatever goes on here in the Coast Guard, and I want to know."

He wanted to know if my office was bugged and said he'd tell me in the office. So I took him back to my office and, after showing him that the office was not bugged, he whispered to me that he was there on Loran, which meant nothing to me. Then he explained in general what it was. He was actually a very brilliant electronics man, as I later learned, a reserve officer who'd come into the service, and he'd been in on this Loran project. It was agreed that the three necessary stations would be set up on the northern island of the Hebrides and he was going up to the technical adviser. The British were to provide the labor for setting up the stations, and the equipment was to come from the United States.

Later I became quite friendly with him. In fact, a month later he was back in my office, crying because he felt that the security provisions at one island particularly were very lax. The manuals, instruction books, and so forth were lying around, and I think he was suspicious of the inhabitants, who, as you probably recognize, were mostly fishermen.

Q: Very simple people?

Adm. R.: Very simple people and he seemed to feel that maybe they wouldn't be above even encouraging the Germans - which I doubted - to come in and take the equipment and that sort of thing. I reassured him, told him that the British were just as much in the war as we were. I think he was still very unhappy about the laxness of the British in protecting the then-infant Loran system. That was about all there was to that.

There were continually people coming over, drifting through for one reason or another, on some special mission. Then, of course, after we got onto the continent and SHAEF moved on in to Paris, I had one reserve officer show up one day who had been a lawyer in the Treasury Department, particularly in the finance, and he was going over to be on General Eisenhower's staff, on the control of the finances of the occupied countries. He, I regret to say, was a sort of a brassy Jew. To a degree, a sort of a self-seeker, I think. Undoubtedly a very brilliant lawyer and very brilliant in his particular field. But I always remember that he came into my office in Paris and introduced himself, but the first thing I noticed was that he had on his shoulder the SHAEF shoulder patch. This was even before he'd gotten to Paris to join the SHAEF staff.

Q: And you didn't know the nature of his mission, either?

Adm. R.: He told me, but my first question was why the shoulder patch. He told me he was on SHAEF's staff and before I could get another in he began to give me an explanation of the SHAEF shoulder patch which, as you may remember, was a sword cutting the chains asunder and so forth and so forth. He was broken-hearted when I told him that, as far as I knew, in the Coast Guard there was no authorization for wearing any patches on the uniform, other than those designated, and to get the thing off in a hurry. And he did. Later we became good friends - well, I say "friends" -

QP You worked together?

Adm. R.: The interested side line on that was that he was a

lieutenant commander when I first met him and he expected to be promoted to commander. In fact, I guess he'd been recommended for it from SHAEF - this was later. He was in Paris and I was in London. I never met General Eisenhower, but the phone rang one Sunday morning early - I guess this was in the spring of 1945, before VE Day, it rang in my apartment early one Sunday morning and here's this fellow on the phone, wanting to know if I'd heard whether his promotion had come through. Remember, at that time, all the phones from France were scrambled and you always got this warning "Remember, the enemy is listening in." So I told him hell, no, I hadn't heard a thing, then after his last comments he said, "By the way, the General asked to be remembered to you." I said, "General who?"

"Why, General Eisenhower, of course."

I won't repeat on this tape what I told him over the phone, but, in effect, I told him to get the hell off the line because there was a war going on. Because, as I say, General Eisenhower didn't even know I was alive. This was typical of this guy's approach.

There were a lot of funny things that went on. The interesting part was that I was there through the V-1s and the V-2s.

Q: What was your reaction to them?

Adm. R.: I found the V-1s very interesting, if you can be objective when somebody else is being killed. The point being that if you were out and you saw one of these V-1s coming, it looked like a little Piper Cub, you'd stand there and watch it and you knew if the engines kept going till it more or less got over your head, you were all right because it never dived straight and when it hit you weren't near where it hit. At night, particularly, you'd see these little things coming along and the searchlights would pick them up and, of course, the ack-ack going, it was quite a thrill and interesting.

The V-2s were, in a way, less terrifying. On the other hand, if you happened to be close to them when they went off you really knew. You didn't hear the V-2 till it hit and if it was close enough to you to really do for you, well, you weren't going to worry about it one way or the other.

I don't know just how to give you an honest answer on it. My exec and I had an apartment together. My exec is now Judge Skelly Wright. He's a circuit court judge in Washington. On one occasion we had our windows blown in some, but they were quickly repaired.

A couple of the officers who were with me came in one morning. They lived right across from Hyde Park and one had hit in Hyde Park. I guess that was a V-1. It had blown in their apartment, or bedroom, and they came in covered with dust from the debris that had been thrown over them. They had to be moved out for a while.

The closest I came to any real problem was in Antwerp,

where a V-2 came down half a block or a block away. Of course, the great danger was not the direct hit. The great danger in all of those things was glass, because it either sucked the glass out of blew it in, depending on how the air was compressed and unless the windows were well taped or something or unless you had your black-out up you could get cut to pieces by broken glass. That was the real danger. I was only about half a block away when this one hit in Antwerp, in a store, as a matter of fact, fortunately, in the back of the store and, although the windows were blown in I wasn't hurt. They could be a bit terrifying.

I made trips to Paris. We had been in on the landing at Cherbourg and once they got the port cleared ships were going in. We had an officer there and later we had an officer at Le Havre. Of course, Le Havre was in terrible condition because the British had bombed it so terrifically. There were Navy units over there and Coast Guard units.

Later, we moved farther north and Antwerp was a part of call.

From D-day or from the time we established ourselves over there, that is, the Allies had established themselves, through the spring of 1945 I made the rounds of our units probably once a month.

Q: Did the Coast Guard suffer any losses in the landings?

Adm. R.: No. I don't think we suffered any in the landings

but we had no combatant troops there. Our boats picked up survivors. As a matter of fact, my recollection is that all together these 83-footers were operating out of Poole picked up over 1,000 people, some live from the water and some dead. There was a story of one boat that picked up a couple - I'm not sure whether they picked them up or whether they were asked by one of the larger transports to bring back two bodies, and they stuck these bodies down in the lazaret aft. When they got back to Poole, they took the cover off the lazaret and they practically fainted because one of them had not been dead. He'd come to in the lazaret.

Q: He was in the proper place, wasn't he? It was named properly.

Adm. R.: Yes. I could go on and tell you all kinds of stories about it and about the different things that happened.

Q: Did the Coast Guard help with the clearing of the harbor at Cherbourg, for instance?

Adm. R.: I don't recall that we did, no. I'm quite sure Commodore Sullivan was there, I remember talking to him, but I don't think we had anything to do with the clearing. In fact, we didn't have any equipment for that.

I know that we had something to do with the clearing of

Naples Harbor because, as I mentioned to you the other day in passing, a former bo's'un, by that time I guess a lieutenant commander DelPra, later Commander DelPra, had been active in that.

Just as kind of an aside, one of the funniest sights I've ever seen I saw when I was down at Poole, visiting one day in the spring of 1945. We were driving along a street in Poole and there were houses between us and the harbor. Many of the ships that the British had at that time and that were plying round there carried barrage ballons, and we saw this barrage balloon coming up the harbor, it would come down just about to the housetops and then it would rise maybe 30 or 40 feet, sort of progressing along. We couldn't figure out what was happening, with this thing that would come down and go up, come down and go up. So we raced down to the harbor and here comes one of our 83-footers. This was a balloon that had gotten loose and they were on their way back and had decided that this would be a nice prize to take home, so they tied it on the stern, lashed it to the stern. Well, of course, the balloon had just enough buoyancy that every so often the buoyancy would take over and lift the 83-footer out of the water. Then it would settle again, as the weight of the boat would take over. It was one of the funniest sights I've ever seen, an 83-footer struggling to bring this barrage balloon in as a prize.

Q: It was almost too big for her?

Adm. R.: Yes, it was.

For that whole period, after the rescue operation was over, they used the 83-footers as dispatch boats to carry mail and passengers back and forth across the Channel. Our boats were running almost a day-to-day cross-Channel service.

Q: That in itself was a fairly dangerous operation, wasn't it?

Adm. R.: Only supposing the E-boats could escape from the north and come down. By that time they'd been pretty well contained. They were fighting for their life, you see, after D-day, and falling back.

In the early stages, yes, there were problems.

I learned another interesting thing, incidentally, that I had not realized. The 83-footers when they first came out, we had to take them and run them at different speeds through the water so they could take pictures of them. I asked why this was because it didn't occur to me. The answer was that from a plane or from the Spitfires that the British were using the way they identified their own, what they used to call their HSLs, high-speed launches, against the German E-boats was the fact that the wakes are different at different speeds. At the altitudes they were operating at you can't identify a a boat by its silhouette, that is, a small boat, or even from the side. Of course, they were attacking at high speed, and so the only hope of being sure you were hitting the enemy and not your friend was to recognize the wakes. So that was why we had to run these boats at different speeds so they could photograph the wakes to educate their pilots.

Q: Very interesting. What was the maximum speed of an 83?

Adm. R.: I would say 18 to 20 knots. They didn't compare with the E-boats or the HSLs.

Another thing that I was quite involved in at the time was working for the Coast Guard and for the Navy in interchange of information with the British on all kinds of, well, not only safety gear but anything having to do with more effective safety. At that time, there was no consenses as to what was the most effective color, for example, to paint life rafts. Originally, if you remember, in the old days, life rings, if they had any color on, had red on them. Later, it was international orange. Inventors were always coming up with some new type of inflatable life raft.

Probably one of the most important duties I had, to me at least, and I should have mentioned this earlier, was a committee I served on.

Shortly after I arrived - the Navy had been doing this but they dropped off and I got on. You asked what I did on Admiral

Stark's staff. The British had set up a committee. The chairman was Admiral Leggett, who had been the navigator in World War I of the fleet at the Battle of Jutland. Commodore McKay, who had been a merchant skipper in the Pacific Far East, as I recall, Captain Beswick, an old Englishman who'd been a skipper for the Blue Funnel Line, and the American representative were the members of the committee.

I think in some things the English were ahead of us, in investigations, or had better thoughts. Our concept in this country has always been, generally speaking, investigate to try to fix blame, if there is any. Generally, that's all right, but sometimes you miss the real thing of what really caused the accident. In other words, you go on the concept that it's always due to misfeasance. Sometimes it's not.

What this group of ours was supposed to do was investigate accidents in convoy. We met once a week, and if there'd been any collisions in convoy or so forth, as soon as possible we got the participants in before us. They were assured and, as far as I know, this was never breached, they could say anything they wanted, they could blame it on their company, or anything it would go no further than our board, as far as anything they said was concerned. The purpose being to find out why the accident took place, not to fix blame, but to find out if convoy procedure could be improved. Once we assured them that what they said in this committee was in confidence, then we could get them to talk freely and then we really found out many things that were wrong with the convoy procedure - signals had gone wrong or they weren't clearly understood and that sort of thing.

It was a very interesting experience, working with these two Britishers and one Scotsman. Of course, they're all Britishers. Commodore McKay, actually, was an Elder Brother of Trinity House.

Q: I was going to ask if they were under the aegis of Trinity?

Adm. R.: No, this was under the aegis of, I guess, the Admiralty.

I might mention another practice that the British had which I thought was far more sensible than ours, although I doubt I would sell it. The British did this. If they had a job, say, a commander of a base and a retired full admiral or vice admiral wanted to come back to serve during the war and be "active duty," he could wear his uniform but he served on that base - let's say it was a commander's billet - at a commander's pay. He didn't come back on active duty as an admiral. I met any number of senior officers who were serving in relatively - officers past retirement age who were serving in relatively small jobs compared with what they'd had on active duty, to relieve officers of that rank to go to sea to fight. It always seemed to me it was much more sensible than calling an officer back and saying, okay, you've got your same rank and emoluments and so forth as you had on active duty.

Q: It makes sense in terms of service, doesn't it?

Adm. R.: Yes.

Going back to these committees, I never met any of the members but I was told that they had a committee in the Admiralty - I don't think the U. S. served on it - whose job it was to interrogate survivors of ships sunk in convoy, like we mentioned the Murmansk run and so forth, who were brought in later to find out how they withstood the rigors of maybe being two weeks or something in a lifeboat. I was told this on good authority. I think it was Commodore McKay who told me that in one case they had a murder by one of the survivors of one of those who - in fairness, I think in this particular case the man who was murdered had gone crazy and the other one struck him over the head, possibly in self-defense.

But the difference is that, in this country, had that come out in a board of investigation, the man would have probably been given a trial, at least he'd have had to stand trial. But in this case, the board evaluated it and looked to how can we avoid this in the future rather than subjecting this man who confessed very frankly he had hit this guy over the head and thrown him overboard because that was the only thing to do under the circumstances. It may not be justice but, as I say, the records were all - anyway, in that respect I think the British were ahead of our approach to some of the problems.

Q: Perhaps you could account for that in terms of their longer experience at sea?

Adm. R.: Possibly.

I worked with practically every agency. I worked with Scotland Yard because, of course, sometimes some of the problems with the merchant seamen involved investigation and that sort of thing. It was a very catholic experience. I sort of covered the waterfront in every respect. One time, I even accompanied Admiral Stark to Omaha Beach through a mistake. He had a young aide who had the same name as mine, Richmond. We went over on a British destroyer which had arranged to take Admiral Stark and several officers with him. I think Admiral Stark called up the duty officer and said, "Tell Richmond I'll want him to go along," and they duty officer looked down the list and found my name and called me. It was a surprise to me. I got my clothes on and headed out. When I got aboard Admiral Stark said, "What are you doing here?" I explained that the duty officer had called, and then it came out. He told me I could serve just as well as the other one and it was a very enjoyable opportunity to visit the beaches. We foured the beaches together, but it was purely accident.

Of course, I'd been to the beaches before with the Coast Guard, but that was my one moment, you might say, in high echelons.

I was returned to Washington, or I got orders, either five or eight days before VE-day. I've always regretted that I didn't have the opportunity to finish it out.

Q: Why didn't they let you stay there?

Adm. R.: I was ordered back to Washington, and, of course, everybody expected VE-day was coming but nobody knew when it was coming.

Q: You came back in May of 1945.

Adm. R.: Yes.

Q: Well, that was too bad, because you'd worked on preparations for it and you should have been there for the big event.

Richmond #3 - 257

Interview #3 with Admiral Alfred C. Richmond, U. S. Coast Guard
(Retired)

Place: His residence in Claremont, California

Date: Wednesday morning, 19 November 1975

Subject: Biography

By: John T. Mason, Jr.

Q: Well, Sir, at the outset this morning, you want to lap back for a moment and talk about an incident involving the Coast Guard Reserve?

Adm. R.: Yes. I recall one incident that I think is worth recounting, but aside from that, I think I'd better just review briefly the fact that the original act for the Coast Guard Reserve was created, as I indicated earlier, for two purposes. It was an attempt, I really believe, to block the Power Squadron getting quasi-governmental status like the Boy Scouts, and, secondly, to provide a medium by which the Coast Guard could acquire private vessels temporarily, largely for use on the inland waters where we did not have facilities for the patrolling of regattas and, to a degree, safely work. We were charged at that time with patrolling marine regattas and, with the growth of the number of small boats on inland waterways like the TVA lakes and other inland lakes that were being created by dams and so forth, it was necessary for us to be in charge and yet we did not have the facilities.

Now, the bill was hastily thrown together, as I recall it. It only had probably one hundred words in it and it simply indicated that we could acquire the facilities. As I indicated, the writing of the regulations for the reserve-to-be, which later became the auxiliary, was most complicated. There were problems such as if a man had a boat which was large enough to have him employ a full-time keeper or mechanic, engineer or something like that, what would be the status of this employee providing the Coast Guard took it over, hoisted a commission pennant on it for, say, three or four days of a regatta?

Q: It would be a yacht, then?

Adm. R.: It would be a yacht. I'm speaking of, say, a 60-foot cabin cruiser, where the owner had a caretaker or maintenance man on it. He wouldn't want to lay the man off, and as long as the Coast Guard was using his boat, he would not want to pay his salary. So, to overcome that, we wrote into the regulations a provision that this man could be taken in to the Coast Guard - maybe called a chief petty officer - which would allow us to pay his salary for three days. He was not enlisted or anything like that. It was just a provision. And out of that was created the term "temporary reserve." It was an innocent beginning, but in a sense we created a frankenstein that was to backfire on us to a degree after the war. I might mention just parenthetically that there were many problems in writing these regulations. None of the details had been incorporated in the act. It was just very general.

For example, in writing our regulations, we had such problems, as I indicated the other day as ownership, divided ownership, and that sort of thing. I mean, who would be in the reserve if you had four members. Would they all be in?

Another thing that troubled us - we never solved the problem and I don't suppose there is any answer - was that we invisioned that probably, as we set up these flotillas that joined, they would probably come from, say, a yacht club or a grouping of yachtsmen. But, just suppose, for example, that on the other side of the tracks was a fisherman who decided he'd like to become a member of the Coast Guard Reserve, as it was then called, it was pretty obvious that there were going to be some problems of caste, if nothing else. You couldn't set up flotillas of fishermen and flotillas of yachtsmen. To a degree, some of this did later haunt us but not to any great degree. Yet, on the other hand, we might in some instances want fishing boats. Those were problems.

However, now to get on to the one thing I remember that was a peculiar problem. We did turn out the regulations and they were reasonably successful, I think, but it wasn't long before, as we started to enlist boats and owners into the Coast Guard Auxiliary to accomplish our purpose, we ran into this difficulty. The insurance on any of these boats would be invalid under their then policy if the boat was put at the disposal of the Coast Guard. Remember now, when this boat was put at the disposal of the Coast Guard what we had to do was to hoist a commission pennant and, in effect, it became a government vessel and the insurance was invalid.

Q: To be resumed when they took the boat back?

Adm. R.: Presumably, but during that period it wasn't. Now we get into the question of what happens if the boat is wrecked, damaged, all of which were very real possibilities during the period that they were to all intents and purposes Coast Guard vessels. The only way you could give relief to an owner, because the Coast Guard had no funds - suppose a $100,000 yacht was sunk while in Coast Guard hands, the Coast Guard had no money to turn to the owner and say here's $100,000 for your yacht, go buy another one. Or, let's say it needed $50,000 repairs, as I also indicated yesterday, if we had the work done we would have to put it out to the lowest bidder who might not be the man that the yachtsman wanted his yacht repaired by, because, as you know, yachtsmen tend to patronize certain yards where they know the builders and that sort of thing. There were all kinds of complicating problems.

Admiral Waesche asked me to see what could be done about this and I traveled to New York, Boston and Connecticut visiting insurance companies. To make matters worse about trying to convince the insurance companies that their policies should be extended to cover the yachtsmen, this was right following Dunkerque. You recall all the publicity then current about how the British yachtsmen had rushed across the Channel and saved the retreating British army. Naturally, the minute you began to talk to an insurance man about the possibility, even though you minimized the possible losses that they might have, they were very chary and I couldn't blame them. Most of them said very truthfully that they could see no way out. I forget now all the companies I visited. I remember the Hartford Company and particularly Chubb and Sons, which was, I think, a sort of broad insurance brokerage company. I think they handled more than one company. There were several others.

Finally, somebody came up with an answer that seemed to solve the problem. The only way a yachtsman could eventually get relief for a loss, let's say, would be for the Coast Guard to introduce a bill in Congress. This might take two, three, four, five years to unwind.

Q: I would think, Sir, until that matter had been determined and settled that yachtsmen would have been very reluctant?

Adm. R.: This is what we were running into. The minute they found out that their insurance was invalid, the answer was no. In other words, for this reason, the Reserve was falling flat on its face, and that's why I was given the job of trying to see if it couldn't be worked out.

Somebody came up with an answer which, essentially, was this. The insurance companies - or some of them, I found the insurance companies very cooperative but, of course, they were faced with out-of-pocket costs. So somebody came up with the idea of possibly writing into the policy a provision whereby the insurance company would, in effect, pay off any claim resulting during this period, but would stand subrogated to subsequent relief by Congress. A number of the companies did circulate this information - if you want your boat to be a part of the Coast Guard, we are willing to put this proviso or addendum into your policy - and I believe some of the basic policies were written with it already in.

Q: It was mandatory then upon the Coast Guard, in case of damage, to have a bill introduced in the Congress?

Adm. R.: We would anyway, but, yes, I suppose it would be mandatory. After all, it was an obligation on the part of the government if, in the course of using a man's boat, to put it back whole. I mean it wasn't a question of the Coast Guard trying to evade responsibility because, obviously, if we'd caused the damage or the loss it was up to the government to replace the loss, but the only procedure would be to go to Congress and get the money. There was no fund that we could dip into and say, okay, here is compensation for your loss.

Let's say you had a boat out and you did $10,000 worth of damage to it, maybe somebody ran into you or you ran into somebody else, or you hit a dock, anything could happen, with this provision in his policy the private owner could have the repairs done and the insurance company would pay the damages, just the same as they would if he'd been operating the boat. Then they stood subrogated to any subsequent relief - and, incidentally, as I recall it, they even agreed that there would be no interest on this. In other words, in my fictitious case, they would be $10,000 out of pocket and maybe three years later, when Congress passed a bill that made the payment of this $10,000 from the government, presumably to the owner, they would collect the $10,000. As I say, I think when you consider the spirit of the time and all - you think of insurance companies sometimes as having no heart - but it really was a very cooperative effort on their part.

Q: One little detail. The congressional appropriation would be made to the individual, the owner of the boat rather than to the insurance company?

Adm. R.: Yes, not to the insurance company. It merely was an agreement in the charter. Frankly, to my knowledge, it was never exercised for two reasons. One, I know of no damage that arose to private vessels while we had them. It was simply just like you've got to take out insurance against fire burning your house down, but you hope the house never burns down. This is exactly what happened in our case.

Secondly, before this really got going to any great extent, we had a number of boats in by this time, we were in the war. During the war both the Coast Guard and the Navy took a number of boats, but we took the ownership of the boats, I mean completely.

Q: By condemnation?

Adm. R.: I don't remember just how they were taken. I suppose it was a form of condemnation. Well, as a matter of fact, as I recall it, the Navy had the _Corsair_.

Q: Yes, and she became the _Vixen_, I believe.

Adm. R.: I think so. All of those were taken over and the Coast Guard took a number of boats, but they, during that period, were owned by the government. Then, when they were returned to ownership after the war - some weren't returned, some remained and I suppose the owners were compensated - others were returned if the owners wanted them. I think there was a compromise adjustment, depending on how much the boat had to be restored, and if you could reach agreement it was restored and paid for, that sort of thing. I wasn't in on the details of the restoration of the boats, so I'm only guessing at that. But I know that both the Navy and the Coast Guard had boats and I think there were probably as happens on those occasions, one or two cases that satisfactory compromises or adjustments could not be made. But basically I think the whole thing worked pretty well.

That's what I wanted to revert to because I think it's quite an interesting aspect of the creation of the Reserve.

I might carry that a little further now, because then the war came on - this is going to lead into the postwar period - and it became obvious right at the outset that the Coast Guard would need to expand, and the medium by which it was to expand was a Coast Guard Reserve. They got authority to form a Coast Guard Reserve and the then Coast Guard Reserve became the Coast Guard Auxiliary. A lot of people don't know that today, but the Coast Guard Auxiliary for, I'd say, two years, was the Coast Guard Reserve.

Now we come to the Coast Guard Reserve. Really, the first officers who were taken into the Coast Guard Reserve under new regulations that had to be written for the Coast Guard Reserve - we'll call it the Coast Guard Reserve 2, to keep it clear here - I think I sat on the board selecting the first officers and many of the first officers that came into the Coast Guard Reserve were people who had been in the Coast Guard Auxiliary and wanted to get into the Coast Guard, so they came into the Coast Guard Reserve.

Then the Coast Guard Reserve 2, the real Reserve that we

have today, began to expand and began to enlist in the Coast Guard Reserve and take officers. Then the Spars were created, this was during the war, and they were obviously Coast Guard Reserve officers. And somewhere in that period - this was while I was in Europe - we finally stopped even making regular enlistments in the Coast Guard. Everything was done into the Coast Guard Reserve. I mention this now because it had a big impact in 1946 and 1947, at the end of the war, because all our enlistments from about I think 1943 were Coast Guard reservists. I think at the outset of the war we had about 900 officers - that was the number we were authorized but I think we were about 100 short - so about 800 officers and roughly 3,000 men. In the period of the war we went, as I recall, to between 10,000 and 11,000 officers and in the neighborhood of 100,000 men. Those figures are approximations only.

Some of the people who had been auxiliaries were then too old, had regular professions, and did not want to become regular reservists, in other words, fulltime, active duty reservists, and they are now auxiliaries. Some of them still owned their boats, some of the boats were taken over by the Coast Guard so what happened was many of them were made temporary officers in the Coast Guard, warrant officers, officers, and so forth. They used to give so many hours a week, patrolling the harbors and things like that, to relieve active duty personnel, whether regular or reservists, to go overseas or to do other wartime services. They might do two nights a week patrolling a harbor or something like that, and they had this temporary reserve status.

I can't now recall all of the various categories, but before the war was over this temporary reserve provision - they were allowed to wear uniform and some of them were actually paid for their services, but it became a very convenient way to meet certain problems of personnel. In fact, the most ridiculous one, as it later turned out, and the one that probably caused us as much trouble - the Navy was having a lot of trouble with - or industry was - with plant guards at various manufacturing plants and industrial plants around the country. Again, I'm only telling hearsay on this. I was in on the aftermath but not the beginning. Somewhere along the line the Navy convinced the Coast Guard - they wanted to bring these plant guards under military control and, mind you, these temporary reservists were only quasi military, so they convinced the Coast Guard that the way to do this was to take all these civilian plant guards, put them in uniform and make them temporary reservists of the Coast Guard. That was how far down the line we used this temporary reserve thing that had been started innocently, and that's why I say it became a frankenstein to really haunt us. I might as well finish this up now.

After the war was over, these people were not obligated - some of the temporary reserve officers even got overseas during the war, usually on inspection trips or maybe a junket or two to see what was going on - maybe I'm supercritical in that. After the war, as you recall, the two things that were most treasured, or that everybody wanted, particularly the enlisted personnel - you see, we use this temporary reserve now for men, officers, and everything, had been using them. As I recall, there were seven categories of temporary reserve from these people who actually worked with the Coast Guard, operating small boats on a temporary basis, all the way down to the plant guards. I can't tell you offhand what those categories were now. There's probably a record of them.

Anyway, the one thing you got when you got an honorable discharge was the so-called ruptured duck and that was, hopefully, a sort of open sesame to the returning serviceman for a job. If you had an honorable discharge and a ruptured duck, you got a little preference. So quite an agitation built up among many of these temporary reserves because they wanted honorable discharges from the Coast Guard, but they hadn't been in the Coast Guard. We did give them a release or something like that, but that wasn't enough because, after all, an honorable discharge is a nice paper and they wanted the ruptured duck. My recollection is that even as late as 1948 they were still agitating. I think they even tried to get a bill in Congress that we would have to give them an honorable discharge. I think a couple of them even entered a court suit to try to force this giving them an honorable discharge and a ruptured duck, which we opposed bitterly.

That was one of the early problems of the postwar period and that's why I wanted to revert because I think, without knowing the background of how this built up, all the turmoil doesn't make much sense.

Furthermore, in the closing days of the war there was one other complication that entered the picture. Admiral Waesche thought it would be desirable to form a Coast Guard League modeled after the Navy League. In retrospect, and this is not to downgrade the Coast Guard League because the people who've stayed with it have been very loyal and very helpful, but basically I think it was fundamentally an unsound idea. I think the comparison between the Navy League and what later became the Coast Guard League - if you really analyze it is an error. I may be wrong but I think the Navy League was basically founded on the support of people who service the Navy. I mean the monetary support behind it came from them. It is true that the rank and file, the chapters, and so forth are usually people who served in the Navy or who are interested in the Navy for one reason or another, had children in the Navy, and that sort of thing. To support it, financially, however, whether you call them ship chandlers and ship yard people, these are the people.

The Coast Guard did not have fundamentally that kind of backing. We weren't big enough. When I was commandant, there was an effort to try to get the shipping companies to do for the Coast Guard League - and we were moderately successful -

what I've just indicated industry and others were doing for the Navy League. But it was never very successful and, by that time, the League was going downhill. Now, I believe the remnants of the Coast Guard League have joined in with the Navy League. I think it's all sort of amalgamated.

Many of the people who were the founders of the Coast Guard League were these yachtsmen who were temporary members of the Reserve and people who had a general interest in the Coast Guard plus ex-Coast Guardsmen, but they were also infiltrated by a lot of nonyachtsmen temporary reservists who tried to use the Navy League - I mean the Coast Guard League - as a medium to espouse their demand for honorable discharges and the ruptured duck and that sort of thing. It was a very confused picture following the war.

Q: Let me ask this question. Would it not have been much more sensible to have put these temporary types into the regular Reserve, when it came into being, rather than insist on maintaining a temporary reserve status alongside the regular reserve status?

Adm. R.: I suppose it would have been.

Q: What were the objections at that time to that step?

Adm. R.: I can't answer because I only came in on trying to

clean the mess up. But, take the plant guards, for example.

Q: Well, they just came in later, to complicate things, because the Navy wanted them under control.

Adm. R.: That was during the war, and we're talking now about from 1942, 1943, and 1944. As I say, this was a progressive thing. As I recall it, I think one of the categories, although they never made many demands, was all of the Pilots' Association members, the port pilots. They didn't want to come into the regular Reserve, because if they came into the regular Reserve they'd be on government pay, and they were making more money as pilots. They weren't going to give up their jobs as port pilots. It was quasi-military authority.

There were a lot of complications in this that I don't think were realized at the time. I often wondered with some of these temporary reserves wandering around, had they been captured, what their status would have been. Strictly speaking, I think they'd probably have been shot as spies. Fortunately, most of them were in the United States and we were never faced with that situation, because they were not military, strictly speaking - that was the whole thing - they were civilians. I go back to the plant guards. They were employees of the companies for which they worked.

So there were a number of these categories like that and what you asked would not have been practical. I think this was simply a handy, temporary expedient which they grabbed onto to meet an immediate problem without ever thinking of the potential consequences. That's the best answer I can give you.

Q: I think, maybe, for the sake of continuity here, you might go on and talk about the Reserve, any aspect of it that developed during your period in command, to make it a complete unit.

Adm. R.: I think probably I can do that best really by picking up at the close of the war, when I came back, because it's all part of this mixed problem. I'll have to jump a little bit back and forth on it.

I came back and, for roughly ten days, I was finance officer. Why, I don't know. They called it finance and supply in those days. Then we reorganized and I don't remember now whether we set a new division up as the Planning Division - it later became Planning and Control, so for the purpose of continuity I'll call it Planning and Control.

Frank Gorman was in charge of it - Captain Frank Gorman, and I was one of his assistants. There were four or five of us in the office and I was his principal assistant. This is now the summer of 1945.

We were faced with the necessity of getting down our strength and we came back to the Treasury Department. You've

Richmond #3 - 273

got to understand the implications of this. We're in the Navy, having been there since just before the war broke out, the November before Pearl Harbor. Then we're back in the Treasury Department and in the nine months between then and July 1st, 1946, we had to come down in strength from about, as I recall and as I said before, 110,000 men and 10,500 officers, down to a strength of about 17,000 men and 1,500 officers. We had ships overseas. We had people overseas. And, remember, since we had been enlisting reservists from as early as, I think, 1943, the great proportion of these enlisted men were reservists and any regular personnel that we had were probably by then chief petty or warrant officers. In other words, we didn't have any regular ordinary seamen, basically. Furthermore, we were hit with the then demand of anybody who had left a business to go into the war or left a profession, to get out. There was this pressure.

This was probably one of the most hectic periods that the Coast Guard ever went through. Bringing ships back, decommissioning them, trying to commission our remaining cutters, trying to run our remaining cutters, largely with regular officers and warrant and petty officers. It was a hectic time, but we did manage I'd say by July 1st of 1946 - we weren't down to the objective strength by that time, but we definitely made it in, I would say, a year to eighteen months after that time.

We had been manning the transports, LSTs - of course, those

ships were easy. All we had to do was turn them back to the Navy and walk away from them. We had been manning the Loran stations and we still had to keep those operating. Of course, we didn't have as many. Most of them were pretty well battered and run down. It was really a very, very hectic period.

You wanted me to continue with the Reserve and I might as well while I'm about it.

It really developed into this. As I recall the picture now, by 1948, 1949, and 1950 we had no enlisted Reserve personnel. I think we may have had 300 or 400 men who had kept their Reserve affiliations. We had a list of about 5,000 officers, many of whom had no interest in the Coast Guard and never cared whether they heard from us or not, but some who wanted an active Reserve, who liked their affiliation with the Coast Guard and wanted to push it.

We knew we needed a Reserve. The question was which way to go on this thing. As I say, we had a paper list of roughly 5,000 officers and maybe a few hundred men, not more than that, if we had any, but nobody that you could call up, really, if you needed them.

To show you this need, I have to revert to another thing that came up.

I've indicated that I was now in Planning and Control. Frank Gorman was in charge. Another complication arose that fall, and that was Admiral Waesche was sick and really Admiral Chalker was running things as Assistant Commandant. I can't remember whether Admiral Waesche had retired at that time or was simply home sick. I guess he had passed on by that. Anyway, we were to get a new commandant in January and there was a degree of political in-fighting. As I indicated earlier, Frank Gorman should have been the man and would have been the man to be commandant on the basis of intellectual capacity, had he been able to handle liquor.

I won't go into the details of the political in-fighting that went on and the different names that came up. But Admiral Joe Farley emerged as the commandant and became commandant, as I recall it, on January 1st, 1946.

In January or February we presented the Coast Guard budget for the first time since the war - that was to be the budget for the ensuing fiscal year, obviously - before the Treasury Post Office Appropriations Committee, understanding that the preceding year we'd been before the Naval Affairs Committee, as part of the Navy budget.

The chairman of this committee was John Tabor of New York, who was known in Congress as a hard-boiled economist. He was fair but a really tough individual to face. I forget who else was on the committee at that time.

Q: Tabor was the over-all chairman of appropriations.

Adm. R.: He was but he also headed up the subcommittee on Treasury. Dirksen was there then and, although I respected him a great deal, he could be pretty hard-boiled.

I don't remember what we were asking for but my recollection is that it was somewhere in the neighborhood of $80,000,000 or $90,000,000. Remember that some of these people had been on the same committee and heard the Coast Guard when it was a small outfit, so they were attuned to lifeboat stations and revenue cutters and a budget probably in the neighborhood of $30,000,000 or something. Now here comes this overblown, although still cut down from wartime strength, budget.

Frank Gorman had for years been the spokesman before the committee and so Farley gave him the job of speaking.

Admiral Farley was, I think, a greater commandant than probably many people at the time thought he was. I grew to respect Admiral Farley very much. He was a very sound thinker, a bit slow at times to come to a decision, but I don't know that that's always bad. His one weakness, if he had a weakness, was that he hated to talk to Congress, or maybe he hated to talk generally in public. In a private conference he was fine, but he did not like to present either legislation or any presentation before a committee, any committee, legislative or appropriations.

So, we went up the first day and Frank - Admiral Farley read his opening statement, as was customary, and then Frank Gorman took over and went through the day. We were to report the next morning so we went up there and we sat down, I regret to say, Frank Gorman was not there. For the record, I think he was disgusted. He had hoped to become commandant and had not been selected. Anyway, I guess the night before he decided to drown his sorrows and he drowned them to the extent that he didn't show up. Then the roof fell in, because Admiral Farley, instead of picking up the ball, turned to me and said, "Okay, Richmond, you have it."

That was the beginning of my presenting budgets before Congress. I was scared to death, I have to confess, but there was nothing to do but carry on, so I did, and for the next almost sixteen years I presented the Coast Guard budget. That was my indoctrination under fire, and I had had really no experience before congressional committees.

I will say that I suspect that even John Tabor realized that they were faced with a novice and was relatively lenient. They didn't lower the jib boom too much on me. We lucked through, I'll put it that way. They could not, of course, understand why we needed all these various things. It just wasn't in the realm of the old Coast Guard. But we got through with a reasonable budget, enough to run for the next year. I think that was the budget that established -

Q: The postwar status in terms of personnel?

Adm. R.: Yes, and even though we told them we were still in the process, they couldn't understand why we couldn't get these ships back and the men off of them and all that. And, at the same time, and part of it probably was brought about by the fact that they were being importuned by anxious parents who wanted their sons back in the family fold - they were getting messages "why does the Coast Guard hang on to my son, why is he still over in the Pacific," and that sort of thing.

About a week or so after that Frank - I don't know, but he didn't come back to duty, he retired shortly thereafter, and I ended up as head of the Planning and Control section with all the problems of bringing the Coast Guard back to postwar status, and there were lots of them.

Getting back again to why we needed a Reserve. At about that time the Navy had set up a board of about 100 captains who were supposed to evaluate the needs for a future war, should we have one and, in the process meeting the various problems that obviously came up in a thing like that. They came to the question of port security.

Now, as you know, the Coast Guard is charged with port security and, of course, had conducted port security during World War II in all the ports of the United States. My recollection is that in New York alone we had 4,000 men just on port security, guarding and attending the different ports of New York. So this board, in making its study of war responsibilities, came to the question of port security and they took an easy answer. It was one sentence, "Port security is the responsibility of the Coast Guard," which is basically correct.

Remember, too, everybody was still a little uncertain as to the future. They were basically correct but there was nothing said as to how the Coast Guard was going to discharge this duty in the event of a war.

You will also remember that in that time we were never quite sure which way the Russians were going to jump. We'd been allies but not friends at that time. I remember Admiral Farley being awfully patient because here we were faced with the problem of having a responsibility which we truthfully were not then prepared - after we'd gotten down to size - to discharge. He was awfully patient because every time he and I had a conference on future plans for the Coast Guard, I'd usually start out with "What would we do if Joe struck tonight," not meaning Joe Farley but Joe Stalin. I pointed out that, to take New York alone, if we took the yeomen off the desks, stripped the ships that we had in New York of men, we could probably muster about 125 to 250 men to guard the docks of New York. And if you took the yeomen off the desks, then you wouldn't have anybody - or some of the yeomen - then you wouldn't have anybody to mobilize to add up, so you're in a vicious circle. In the same way, the ships wouldn't be able to operate because you'd probably be taking half of their crews. So what are you going to do.

Q: But, of course, in that set of circumstances, you'd almost automatically become a part of the Navy again?

Adm. R.: That's true but the Navy wasn't going to give us men to do it. Of course, I was building up the other because the question was to be prepared.

It became obvious that we ought to have some sort of a Reserve and at this point - and I'm talking probably about 1948 or 1949 - it became apparent to us that probably what we ought to have was some sort of Reserve, if nothing else, particularly geared to port security. Several plans evolved, but nothing specific. One plan was to maybe take in 1,000 men and train them but it wasn't very practical, but we had the basis for a Reserve and, as I said, a paper list of 5,000 officers, of whom probably as few as 1,000 were actively interested in the Coast Guard. Some of them were actually agitating for duty of some sort.

Q: But, as time went on, that list diminished.

Adm. R.: We were being pushed, in a way, by a few loyal Reserve officers who wanted to continue their affiliation with the Coast Guard. We had no enlisted force, which we really needed, particularly if we were to go into a port-security proposition. I think it was in 1950 that this really started to jell as to ideas of what kind of reserve we would try to develop.

In the meantime, some of these reservists, not being on active duty and we were not able to give them any active duty and not being directly under our control, began to agitate in

Congress at the same time they were pushing us towards it. But I think it was in 1950 that we finally went to Congress with a request for money. I was Assistant Commandant at the time we made our first request. We did get a moderate sum to start enlisting men, training men, to amplify the reserve.

Part of our problem was that we were being met with the argument that, after all, the Coast Guard is a reserve of the Navy. We never considered ourselves as such. We felt we augmented the Navy but were not necessarily a reserve. Therefore, why have a reserve on top of a reserve. We ran into arguments like that. We pointed out that during the war it had been necessary to augment our fleet and our ships to battle conditions, which required a lot of men, and we finally evolved a system that later became known as port-security units, ORTUPS, as we called them, and ORTAUGS. ORTUPS was Organized Training Units Port Security and ORTAUGS were for augmentation of the ships.

A lot of funny things happened. As I said, some of the reserves were agitating. Really, one of the men who did the most and with whom I later became very friendly was Walter Handy, who worked in the Treasury Department. Walter later became a vice president of ROA, Reserve Officers Association. Some of them had joined, I guess, the ROA naval units. I remember a bunch of them descending on me in the office one day. They came in and said, "It's all made. We're going to be taken care of," and I said, "That's fine, but how do you know?"

They said, "Well, we've been up to see Senator Saltonstall and Senator Saltonstall is with us."

I said that was fine. Communication is a wonderful thing if you understand what you're getting into, so I said, "What happened? Did you see Senator Saltonstall?"

"No, we didn't. We saw his administrative assistant and explained the situation and he went in and saw the senator, then he came back."

I said, "All right, and what did the senator say?"

"The senator said 'You can depend on me.'"

I started to laugh and they got mad. I said:

"Okay, that's the answer, but what are you going to depend on the senator for?"

For the first time it dawned on them that politicians can give cryptic answers. This is like the oracle of Delphi. You have to be able to interpret these answers.

That's just a humorous aside. But, anyway, we got the reserves started and set up training units and enlisted men in the Reserve. Some former enlisted reserves came back in. We set up training units both for port security and for vessel augmentation. It had gradually evolved over the years. One of the congressmen on the appropriations committee became greatly interested in the Reserve. In fact, I guess he was finally given a plaque as the father of the Reserve. That was Gordon Canfield, of New Jersey.

From the time I was Assistant Commandant through Commandant, almost the whole time, either Gordon Canfield was chairman of our subcommittee or Vaughn Geary, of Richmond, Virginia. Both of them became very close to the Coast Guard. I considered them both very good friends. They worked for the Coast Guard. I don't think they gave us anything that we didn't deserve, but they knew the Coast Guard. In many ways, Vaughn Geary was just as much a friend of the Reserve as Gordon, except Gordon had been chairman the year the Coast Guard Reserve got its kick-off and was always interested. He was probably a little closer to the Reserve than Vaughn, but basically they were both great supporters of the Reserve.

Of course, the Reserve built up. We finally established port-security units around. It was a fight throughout the whole time and I guess still is. In fact, I think even a couple of years ago there was some talk of an economy drive, just before the Coast Guard went to the Department of Transportation, and of doing away with the Reserve, but a fight was made and it's still in there. And I think it's a necessary adjunct to the Coast Guard. At first, I'll have to confess, the training was pretty fragementary and sometimes I think we did wrong things. Later, we took in the crews and trained them aboard ship for the ORTAUGS units. During my regime as commandant when we decided to build up the forces for port security, it was used as what it was meant for, to augment the Coast Guard when we needed men. We had that six-months program, if you recall - the Navy had it, too, we'd train officers for six months and then we'd have them on standby. For the enlisted people in the Reserve, it was a convenient way of enlisting for two years, then we'd have them in ready reserve. I don't know whether this has been dropped since I left, but then the regular enlistment was four years and a lot of people didn't want to enlist for four years.

During the Korean conflict, when we had to develop port security, the Reserve was very valuable to us in augmenting the services when we could not necessarily get people to enlist for four years or did not want to make a career of it.

As you know, what you hope to get always is a career man, even a four-year man - you're losing money if you lose a man at the end of four years, I mean really to capitalize on the training that you have to give your technical men now. You want men for your petty officers and so forth who are going to re-enlist and, hopefully, make a career of the service. On the other hand, there come times when you have to expand and then these expedients of two-year enlistments or use of reserves are valuable. I don't recall that we ever called the reserves to active duty, as such.

Q: That's the question I was going to ask you. When the reserves were called up for the Navy and so forth, on that one occasion, I think it was in connection with the Berlin crisis, did the reserves in the Coast Guard get called also?

Adm. R.: I wasn't in Washington at the time, but I don't think so because that was a different proposition. I don't think the Coast Guard's services were needed. But when we went into that port security program during the Korean situation, we did need to expand the service. There's always this problem of fluctuating size. Reasonable fluctuations in size don't hurt a large service, but when you're dealing in terms of 20,000 men and you have to fluctuate by 4,000 or 5,000 men, you're talking about 25 percent of your personnel and you have problems.

As I say, the Reserve system was an excellent medium of adjusting on that because they were short-term people. Most of them were definitely not making a career of it. They could, though, and we did induct some of them. As you recall, when the first draft law was passed every young man had eight years' obligated service. That didn't mean he had to serve eight years, but even the boys who enlisted in the regular service for four years were subject for four more years. My recollection is that what we did if they decided to take their discharge was put them in the ready reserve for the fifth year and then they went to the standby reserve. But it did give us a potential there and if we had a real emergency, a war or something like that, they could be called up and called up fast.

Q: You mentioned several times the reservists and their organization attempting to enlist the support of Congress for this or that. Did theCoast Guard authorities welcome this kind of political intervention, or did they resent it?

Adm. R.: No. We did not resent it, providing it was properly handled. I don't think, in fairness, that the Coast Guard Reserve ever really forced our hand after the Reserve was started. There may have been one occasion that backfired but, generally speaking, it was not widespread through the Congress. It was usually confined to people we could talk to like Gordon Canfield or Geary or other members of the committee. They did not bombard the whole committee with petitions. I suppose at times letters came in, but they were usually limited. I can't say there was any criticism of the Reserve in that respect.

Of course, at the time I mentioned we needed and wanted support, good support, for what we were trying to sell to Congress.

I don't remember the exact year, but it was before I became Assistant Commandant, I think it might have been 1948, another development came along which also probably helped us a little bit with the Reserve. As I mentioned before, it was very hard for the subcommittee, having known the Coast Guard - what the Navy used to refer to and I guess others as "the hooligan navy" - the prewar Coast Guard, to adjust to the postwar Coast Guard because we were way down from our wartime strength but we were still twice as big as we had been. We were now in loran and we were now in ocean weather stations, which, incidentally, was a fight all of its own, whether we should have weather stations or whether we shouldn't, and we had more ships, we had more men. The only thing we were really beginning to cut down on was the lifeboat stations. What we were doing was substituting for the old so-called beach patrol station - as you probably know, at one time, there were so many stations along the east coast and I guess they did it to a degree up on the lakes. In the early days of the life-saving service, even when I joined the Coast Guard, they had stations every five miles on the Jersey coast, along the Carolina coast, probably as far down as Georgia. Farther down they had stations but they were farther apart and intermediately they had what they called houses of refuge, where you could take refuge if you were wrecked on the shore.

But, getting back to the five-mile stations, they used to patrol the beach. You may have seen pictures of the boys patrolling the beach. They had a time clock or a checking clock halfway between the stations and the man would walk two and a half miles up the beach and meet the guy coming down. In other words, there was continuous patrol. As the sailing ships disappeared and shipping became more mechanized, that need disappeared. Furthermore, the problem now was not the big ships as much as yachts and so forth. Then better propulsion came into being in yachts and things like that and also for our boats. So there was a gradual transition from the old lifeboat stations, of which at one time there were over 250, as I recall, to the inlet stations where you used larger and faster boats, probably our 75s, 83s, and, later, the 95-footer boats.

We entered the war with the old Coast Guard, a lot larger than when I came in, but still pretty much a lifesaving, revenue cutter, rum-war Coast Guard. Now we've come out and we're into new things - weather ships in both the Atlantic and the Pacific, the Loran system to be maintained, which they didn't understand too well, a whole new story, in fact.

Finally, I think it was in 1948, Congress decided, in essence, that a study should be made of the Coast Guard. Another thing I might mention that had come in, of course, Loran was part of it, but the aids-to-navigation system. They were not familiar with the lighthouse service. The lighthouse system had come into the Coast Guard in 1939. They might have gone through one appropriation with us with the lighthouse service before we got into the war, but not more, and that wasn't enough really to familiarize them with it. The peculiarity of the lighthouse service had been that there were very few officers in it. I think they ran the whole thing with about 80 superintendents - they weren't officer, they were commissioned when they came in. Their tenders were run mainly by warrant officers and civilian employees. It was pretty much of an autocracy with a few haves and a great many have-nots. We had larger tenders and we had chief warrant officers on them and larger complements. There was more work. We had these buoy depots where we put officers.

It was easy to understand why Congress just didn't recognize all these changes. So they put in our appropriation bill, as I recall it, an order which said that a management company should be brought in to study the Coast Guard. The company would be chosen by the Secretary of the Treasury, the chairman of the appropriations committee of the House, and the chairman of the Senate appropriations committee. Everybody was asking what's the Coast Guard doing this for, and so forth. I talked to some of the committee clerks and they told me that they were going to smoke us out. In fact, one of the committee members told me they'd see what we were into now.

I said, "Okay, I think it's a wonderful idea because it will be one of two things. You're going to find out that what we're telling you is right and we need what we need, or else you'll find we've been kidding you, in which case you can kick us out and get somebody else. And that's basically the way the thing ought to be run."

He said, "I guess you've got something there."

Anyway, the Coast Guard was given the job of finding a management company. We studied the field and really made a sincere search, and we listed forty companies. We thought we had every company in the United States. We listed, as I recall it, the Heller Company as the first choice.

Q: Walter Heller?

Adm. R.: Walter Heller, yes. Walter Heller later made a study of Congress, I think, and I think he became quite an adviser up there. We thought they probably had the best reputation of anybody. We put the companies in order of priority, as we saw them, and that was number one. We sent the list up to Congress and to the Secretary - Snyder was the Secretary at the time, and he and Tabor and the man from New Mexico, Senator Hayden, I think, who were the chairmen of the committees, got together and, lo and behold, we got word that the Ebasco Management Company would make the study. They weren't even listed. I never knew how they got chosen. They were a New York concern.

The story on Ebasco was that there was the Electric Bond and Share Company and they had been doing their own management studies and there was something about anti-trust or something. Anyway, they had to squeeze out and had split off their management group and it became the Ebasco Management Company.

That was all right. We didn't care who it was. They made the decision. Probably it was as well they didn't take anybody from the Coast Guard list, as a matter of fact, because of the way it turned out.

Ebasco came down with a group of men and we worked with them. We assigned I. J. Stephens and he was right with them the whole time. He traveled over the country. They turned out a volume that was about two inches thick. I wish I'd kept one of those things. As a matter of fact, as we went through, they pointed out a lot of things, some of which we knew were wrong, and almost all the internal things that they pointed out that would improve efficiency, if they were good we didn't wait for them to come out in a report, we just went ahead and implemented them. If somebody comes along and gives you a good suggestion, why wait for somebody to pass on it.

They turned out a 35-page summary of this volume that was two inches thick, and there were a number of recommendations. As I say, by the time the report came out, about a third of them had already been implemented. A lot of them were trivial, some of them good. Summing the whole thing up in words on one syllable, the whole two inches, it came down to the fact that they found that the functions of the Coast Guard were manifold and that it required so much personnel and services to do them all, and Congress ought to specify, come out and say what they wanted the Coast Guard to do and then give them the money and personnel to do it. In other words, they didn't say you're wasting money or anything like that.

For example, they mentioned Loran and said that if Congress didn't want Loran to be continued they ought to say so. In other words, they indicated that the Coast Guard was operating in a lot of dubious areas that weren't spelled out, and then they made an estimate of what this was going to cost, which was roughly twice or three-quarters more than was in our current appropriation. We never did get this definition of our duties. Some of them we did. I mean we didn't get a comprehensive definition of the duties, but we did get some legislation we needed and we did get a more sympathetic ear from the appropriations committees from then on.

We were given the task of trying to implement those things that we could. As I said, probably a third of them had already been implemented by the time the report came out.

One of the things that they did recommend and later turned out was that we should change our auditing, in effect get a CPA in to reorganize our whole finance system and also get a supply man. We undertook to get that and we got an outstanding man for the CPA. He had worked with the General Accounting Office.

One other thing I might mention that was in this, too. The first budget that I defended and the second budget contained I forget how many appropriations, and it was sort of ludicrous because you had to tell, for example, even like in your offices how many CAFs you had. You had to tell how many you were going to have, a guy in charge and so many assistants. These were civilian employees and this gets pretty ridiculous. So one of the things that they recommended, maybe we'd already started this ourselves, we did get permission to change our budget presentation so that we had only four appropriations. Operating expenses had personnel money and operating costs in it. Before that we had personnel, operating, you had to tie the two together. This way, we had operating expenses that covered the board. We got it down to four appropriations, which made it much simpler to present and much easier to understand. We had Operations-Acquisition, Construction and Improvement, Retired Pay, which should be properly taken away from the operating expenses, and finally the Reserve appropriation.

I guess we were down to three and the first year the Reserve appropriation was in operating expenses, but I think the following year we had it split out so that it could be viewed separately from strict operating expenses.

That was a big break for us, really, because it put us on the way up. As I said, at this time I was in planning control. I'm trying to think of other problems that were taking place at that time.

One kind of an interesting aspect, slightly humorous in a way, although it could be considered serious. Sometime during the war we had set up to go into the South Pacific, dog teams. By that I mean sentry dogs. They were still in existence after the war, but we finally disbanded them. Also during the war, out on the West Coast we had a horse patrol for a short time, patrolling those beaches that could be patrolled. So we had these boys with German shepherds with police dog training.

Q: What would they do in the South Pacific?

Adm. R.: The same as they did in Vietnam, sentry work. You can train them for sentry work and that sort of thing.

I guess at the first Truman inauguration, I have some movies of about 150 of these boys with their dogs moving down Pennsylvania Avenue in the inaugural parade.

Anyway, this had to be disbanded. There was no more need for them. These dogs had been given by private owners as a war effort, with the condition that at the end of the war, the dogs would be returned to the owners. That caused a problem for two reasons. One, some of these boys, and I never knew why, ended up in China. I suppose it was about the time we were trying to salvage Chiang Kai-chek. Anyway, some of these boys with the dogs ended up in China and either they lost the dogs - I suspect what happened was that, food being short, the dogs got eaten by the Chinese, not by our boys. They were stolen, probably, and eaten by the Chinese. Anyway, some of the dogs didn't come back. Well, you know, it's pretty tough to try to explain to an indignant owner why his dog wasn't returned. At least, you can't tell them they were eaten by the Chinese or anything like that. It doesn't help.

Really, the most trouble we had was that these dogs all had to be de-trained, and they were, or so we thought. This is something I learned after the fact. When you de-train a dog that's been trained to be a killer or an attacker, you're never quite sure just how good the de-training is. If, inadvertently, somebody happens around and maybe gives a signal that the dog has been taught to obey, you're apt to have some of your friends attacked. And we had one or cases of that, where the people wrote in. In fact, I think there was one case where the dog did so much damage he had to be put away, and the owners felt that they were entitled to reimbursement from the government because we hadn't done an adequate job of de-training. That was just one of the sidelights of some of the problems that arose during this period.

In the meantime, as I say, we were trying to reorganize. We were fighting the battle of Loran. The U. S. was committed to Loran, but if Loran was to continue, and we personally thought it was a necessary military thing if we had another war, or in any case, for our planes that were flying - when I say "we" I'm using an editorial "we," meaning the United States. Ships had Loran and we wanted to keep the Loran system going, but it was also recognized that this was an expensive system and probably we would not be able to continue it simply as a military adjunct, and, after all, it did have value for use as a commercial system.

Q: What were or are its particular values in the commercial sense?

Adm. R.: Several. In the first place, of course, it's a reasonably instant navigation system and much more accurate than star sights and so forth. On two stations, if you can establish a line of position, for example - well, if you were a fisherman off the coast and had a Loran set and established yourself on a line of position - say, you're off San Diego and you want to hit San Diego - you're not going to flub around, you just stay on that line. It's just like going down the street, you run on that line, and maybe you save a day's steaming time with a load of fish over your competitor, who may be zigzagging all around on his sights and so forth. That's a very crude and simple example.

Of course, we were thinking of it more in terms of large ships, at that time. Although I gave the crude example of the fisherman, it got to the point where fishermen were putting Loran sets on their boats when the price of the receivers got down to where it was a reasonable investment.

At the same time, the British had a competitive system, Decca, and in many ways, particularly in close-in work, I have to admit that I think now - well, I thought then, too, in many ways - Decca was preferable. I've seen Decca work in the Thames River. It was quite a problem because Decca was trying to sell equipment over here, or to sell the system, and there were innumerable conferences. The State Department was involved in it, the Navy was involved in it, and obviously we were involved in it. Also, at that time it was further complicated by the fact that there was another system whose name I can't remember that some of our people were trying to promote. In theory, it would have been wonderful. The basis of it was that you could plant a transmitting station, probably one or two, in the middle of the country and it would go all over the world. They claimed great things for it and they wanted money to start it, but it never got beyond first base. Of course, the airlines wanted it because it would work over land.

You see, Loran A is no good over land, basically. The Air Force at that time had been working around in the closing days of the war with something known as Loran C. There was a Loran B, which was considered for a short time - there was quite a little study on it - because it would handle the harbor problem. Loran A can be botched up by land masses. It's a line-of-sight deal and therefore you get - well, it isn't line of sight, I'll take that back - but land masses will throw it out, so it wasn't really good for harbors. But Loran B could be. As I say, Loran C had proved ineffective. It had two advantages. The stations didn't have to be as close together but it required more equipment. It hadn't been effective. Later, it was developed and now I don't know whether there are any Loran A stations even left. Loran C was just coming in when I retired. We had put in three or four stations or more likely twelve Loran C stations by the time I retired. But back in the days I'm now talking about, it had not been successful. Later it was made successful. What it did during my regime was confuse this whole problem of Loran A.

In the interest of navigation generally across the ocean, we were fighting for expansion of Loran A to service the trans-pacific and trans-atlantic flights.

IATA, the international aviation group that meets up in Montreal, were in this fight. It was just a confused picture. I really can't give you a detailed description of it.

Also, there was a great deal of activity in what you might call search and rescue. Everybody was experimenting with new devices. We had a search and rescue agency right there in Washington and they were pushing, properly so - the search and rescue agency was being operated by the Coast Guard, and we were still working on improved flares, improved lifeboats, improved exposure suits, improved signaling devices, kites, Mae Wests, improved radios for cranking out an SOS, and particularly involved in the establishment of the weather stations over the Atlantic and into the Pacific. Then, of course, the big question was, well, how many ships do you need to man a weather station. Theoretically, you needed three ships per station, although we never attained that. The ideal of three ships was to have one ship out, one ship going and coming, and one ship having its relief in port. They stayed out for twenty days. It's not the nicest duty in the world, slugging around in one position out there.

Then there came the question of the division of the spoils. Beyond the chop line in the Atlantic other European countries contributed ships. In the Pacific we did the whole thing. I guess the Japanese did have one or two stations later, after MacArthur took over, up near Japan. But in the mid-Pacific, the Coast Guard did it all. In the Atlantic, we had stations west of the chop line. I believe the British and the French had some to the east but they had to work out their own schedule.

Q: Was this the chop line that existed for convoys in World War II?

Adm. R.: I don't know. It was an arbitrary line.

Civilian transatlantic aviation was just getting going and, as I say, the airlines and the passengers wanted the idea that down there would be a ship if they were forced down. About that time, a plane up off Newfoundland came down and we managed to get them all out and bring them in. Then I think there was one plane lost. But, with one thing and another, all these were debates.

Another thing that was going on at this time that we were engaged in - MacArthur was the supreme commander in Japan and he had a Coast Guard officer on his staff and, as you know, they were trying to set up the government. They weren't allowed to have a navy, but they set up a defense command. Essentially, the regulations for that were the Coast Guard regulations written in Japanese. They did the same, they brought the lighthouse into the thing. I don't know how it is now, but up to the time I retired, they were still working with the Coast Guard, using our types of ships, generally speaking, because Captain Frank Meals was on MacArthur's staff and was told to draw plans for this agency, the seagoing part of it. I don't think he had anything to do with their shore business. So it was modeled right after the Coast Guard. If you got their brochures, flyers, and so forth, you'd have thought they were put out by Coast Guard Headquarters, except for the Japanese language on them. I mean the pictures of their ships and their procedures and all.

As assistant commandant and commandant whenever I went to Japan, I always conferred with their director and superintendent of engineering and that sort of thing. I think now they have some sort of a navy, but they didn't have any navy then and this was their defense command set-up.

Q: Now do you want to deal with the Coast Guard Academy?

Adm. R.: Yes. As I told you, the Coast Guard Academy when I was there had been at old Fort Trumbull. Then, in the early thirties, they acquired land up near Connecticut College, up the river, practically across from the submarine base at Groton, and they built the Academy for 100 cadets. The Academy was built actually to house 200 cadets because, thinking in terms of the 1930s, long before the war, nobody visualized the Coast Guard would ever need more than 200 cadets. That probably would be the maximum growth.

When the war came along, it was obviously inadequate. The Academy continued to function. They crowded the best they could but they also started using it as a reserve officers training place. The 200-man facility was obviously inadequate for cadets and reserve officer trainees, so they put up a lot of temporary buildings. At that time the area was very limited. It's built on a hill leading down to the Thames River. These buildings were squeezed together and, very frankly, were a terrific fire hazard. If a fire had ever started in there we'd have burned up any number of people. They had four dormitories, for example, that were right together - two-story wooden barracks - separated by maybe 20 or 30 feet, and in that New London weather and the heating you have, it really was quite dangerous. Nevertheless, we lucked through.

Shortly after the war was over, to meet our officer requirements, we had gradually expanded the Academy to 400 and, at the time I was commandant, it was up to 600. For a while these barracks buildings stood idle. They were not removed, but eventually we had to house cadets in these wooden barracks and to use the wooden auditorium, because the original auditorium in Hamilton Hall probably only housed 200 or 300 people. This other, I guess, housed about 1,000.

This whole time we had this expansion of the Academy. We wanted to expand it but there was no way we could do it at the time. It finally hit me during the time I was commandant, during the Eisenhower administration, actually. I realize all this is not in sequence, but it's probably best to keep the stories together.

A classmate of mine was superintendent. We all had deplored this situation, it was dangerous, we wanted to expand the Academy, but we couldn't get the money. The Academy had been growing steadily, we were up now to about 600 cadets. They had a parents day and the parents were up there and this classmate of mine made a speech to the parents in which he said, "I can't tell you to write to your congressmen, but I can't tell you not to," which was a negative way of saying please do. He called attention to the situation, and I think he knew that we had put in that year for a new barracks building to replace some of the old ones in that year. But one morning the roof fell in on us as all these congressmen began to call up and say "What's this about the Coast Guard Academy?" That was the day that we'd gotten word from the White House through the Treasury Department that we had to cut back 10 or 15 percent in current appropriations and cut back our acquisitions appropriation for the next year.

Q: Was this in the late fifties?

Adm. R.: It must have been around 1955.

To make a long story short, we had to answer the congressmen with our tongues in our cheeks, and I had to talk to the superintendent of the Academy.

What made me think about this was your question whether the Reserves ever gave us trouble in Congress. They never gave us half the trouble that I went through on that particular occasion. Eventually it worked out. We finally did get a new barracks.

Then we had a study made by an educational group and they made a good many recommendations. We'd asked Congress for money to have this study made. A great many improvements were made at the Academy and now, of course, it has expanded greatly over what it was when I left the service. I think they now have about 900 cadets there.

The group that made that study was specially adapted to study universities and things like that and they made certain recommendations about changing our arrangements and buildings. That led to our being able to acquire more land and build more buildings. By that time we'd already gotten a new dormitory. The boys were all out of the temporary buildings. The temporary buildings had been removed. As a result of that study the Academy was able to expand to more ample space. We had to condemn land to do it. We usually went on the basis of not strict condemnation. I can't think of the term now but I will fill it in at a later date. It's a Declaration of

Taking. Anyway, that was the way that we took most of the land at that time, through this quick procedure. I gather that's the way we've gotten most of the additional land there since I left the service. There was one last piece that we took down in the park before I left, where the gymnasium went in, was seized that way. So much for the Academy.

Returning for a moment to the problems of Loran through 1947, 1948, 1949. Most of the buildings, particularly in the South Pacific, had been simply quonset huts and the chains that had been put in had been put in, in many instances, on a temporary basis to spearhead the invasion forces and that sort of thing. Furthermore, we had, as I recall it, no Loran systems in the Caribbean at that time because there was no need for them. We did have some, as I recall it, in Alaska, but they had been quonset huts. Deterioration had set in in most of these, particularly the ones in the tropics.

In many instances we relocated the Loran stations more in line with the needs of particularly transpacific aviation and also of the movements of our troops back and forth in the postwar days, because we were still out there in Japan and Okinawa. We're still in Okinawa. Transpacific aviation and military aviation. So that meant doing away with some of the stations. Among those we kept, I remember particularly those in the Philippines. At that time we had three stations to the south and three stations to the north. Most of those had to be rebuilt, so we were in the battle for funds.

Q: This was a reassessment of the whole picture of Loran?

Adm. R.: Of the whole picture, and we were adding stations, too.

Q: How did you do this? I mean did you do this in consultation with the Civil Aeronautics people?

Adm. R.: Yes.

Q: And the Navy and Army, or what?

Adm. R.: The Navy and Civil Aeronautics primarily, and our own evaluation of the traffic and the traffic pattern. We had stations along the west coast that had to be rebuilt. The idea really was to cover any potential transpacific aviation lane, with one exception which we did have plans to do, but I don't think ever got implemented, and that was the one down to Australia.

Q: Some of these air routes were not exclusively ours but involved other nations. How, then, was this handled?

Adm. R.: Let me back off just a minute. Primarily our consideration was not commercial aviation. That was secondary. Certainly, we hoped that they would use it and they did use it. What we were primarily considering was protecting our own military aircraft flying these routes, because they were the ones basically that had to land to start with. The commercial people came along and, as new planes came out, they put Loran on because it was there and it was instantaneous navigation. When I say "instantaneous," that's relative, but Loran was a new concept. Of course, during the war it had been a secret deal, nobody understood it.

Again, getting into this subject of language, I remember on one occasion I was before the Senate Appropriations Committee - subcommittee - and I'd been a little bit exasperated because old Senator Green, of Rhode Island -

Q: Theodore Green!

Adm. R.: Theodore Green, a very fine gentleman, but I'd been expounding on the need for money for ocean stations. We figured at that time an ocean station was costing approximately two million dollars a year to operate, personnel, ships and all. For a Loran A station in those days with an officer and fourteen men, we had a round figure of about $125,000, which we'd throw out to explain how we got to the grand total and so forth. Remember now, I said a Loran station and an ocean weather station.

After I thought I'd made a very, to me, excellent presentation, I had a wonderful lesson in the fact that words seem something to one person and may mean something different to somebody else, because after I got all through, I remember old Senator Green looking down at me and saying:

"You know, I just can't understand why one station can cost $2,000,000 and another station only $125,000."

Well, it was obvious that he had no concept of what I was talking about as far as stations were concerned. Another thing they simply did not understand was what Loran was. On one occasion, again before the Senate committee, I thought I'd be real smart. It worked, so I guess it was smart enough. I took a chart with Loran lines on it - my children were small then and had some little boats, so I took one of their toy boats, laid the chart out on the desk in front of the Congressmen - before the senators, I should say, and put the boat on the chart, on one of the lines. Then I said this was the situation. It would be all right to take sun sights or star sights if the sun was out, but I said, if it was in a fog - and with that I dropped my handkerchief over the boat - I said he's going to be in trouble.

It helped. For the first time, I think they got the idea that this little electronic device, Loran, was valuable. And, I said, it was equally applicable to a plane. Not only that but with the Loran system, in about a minute a man can establish his position, assuming he's within the limits of these stations, whereas even with star sights he's got a good ten to fifteen minutes which, on a plane - well, with planes it could be quicker because they deal with a different system of navigation, but basically, I said, it's a question of knowing your position better. It really helped.

About this time, I adopted or recommended a practice which I think helped us more than anything else. Some questions arose, I believe it was around 1948 or 1949, when I was presenting the budget, about certain things. It occurred to me that this language difficulty, which I just mentioned, was really hurting us largely because the congressmen just didn't know, had no concept of, some of the duties of the Coast Guard. So in a kind of expansive moment, I said, wouldn't you like to, in effect, go and see for yourself some of these units. At that time Congressman Geary was the chairman and it later turned out that he loved to travel and see. A lot of people accused me later of having junkets, but if these were junkets they were well worth it. I know that some congressmen are known to have taken junkets.

Right at the outset, Congressman Geary and I sat down and I said:

"Now, look, if we made these trips, I mean these trips are going to separate the mice from the men."

"That's the way we want it," he said.

So I traveled to Europe with the congressmen and I traveled to the Pacific with them. I had an unwritten rule. I never went any place and said now we need so much money for this or anything. I never tried to sell them on the trip. My own object was to take them there and let them see.

Q: Educational!

Adm. R.: Educational. I think they appreciated it. In other words, there was no soft sell or that kind of thing. But it did have this advantage that later, if you were posing an appropriation for a particular thing, and if you had had the congressmen there and if they started to question it or if some question arose about it, you could always say to the congressmen, in effect, "Now, you remember Mr. So and So, you were there last year. You saw the place." In the first place, they probably didn't remember, I'm not saying they did, but no congressman's ever going to admit publicly that he doesn't remember, so it's "Oh, yes, yes." I don't mean that you necessarily got what you were asking for.

But another thing that comes up in appropriations was very difficult. You see, you only have probably at the maximum to present - when I left the Coast Guard I think our appropriation was around $300 million - here you are presenting an appropriation bill in terms of a few hundred million, we'll say, and you'll probably have at the most two and a half days of hearings before one committee, before the House subcommittee, and probably maybe not even a day before the Senate committee. Our committee worked hard, but remember that you knock off for lunch. In the first place, you use up probably an hour for your opening statement, which has been prepared and in which you outline the various appropriations and what you intend to do with them, and then you get into the questions. From then, your day is broken up by quorum calls, some of the congressmen will leave, they're not all there all the time. Sometimes you may be down to just one committee member, and sometimes they'll rush out, so that you may sit for a half-hour while they go and answer a call. So it probably works down to the fact that you have, at the most, ten hours of actual testimony and you're lucky if you have that much. I'd put it closer to six or seven hours, in which you've got to present a pretty full picture which they've got to evaluate.

Remember that they are asking you questions, not all of them relevant because particularly if you've got a new member or a member who's a bit flighty, as I had once. For example, right in the midst of it, he wanted to know - a plane had been forced down - and he wanted a learned dissertation on why it wouldn't be a good idea to stuff the wings of the plane with ping-pong balls to keep it afloat. This was serious. But this is what we were confronted with. A lot of your time is wasted by irrevelant questions. I remember in the early days before we streamlined our budget presentation and we had all these different appropriations, we had in this appropriation bill $25,000 to buy new matresses for bunks and that sort of thing, and it seemed that one congressman - I don't remember his name now, I think that was the only year he was on the committee - had been at an Army base and he had seen some rebuilt matresses. We had them priced, so many mattresses so much and so forth, and he had seen them at probably half the price.

Q: Reconditioned?

Adm. R.: Reconditioned mattresses, and he couldn't see why we shouldn't get reconditioned mattresses and save, say, $10,000. Well, this was all right. The question was definitely relevant, but then he wanted to carry on. This went on for a half-hour, I know, during this hearing, arguing with us about being inefficient, to the point where I almost yelled at him. Cut the $25,000 out entirely and let's get on, because, after all, we were talking at that time in terms of $80,000,000 or $90,000,000, and it would have been better to simply scratch the item right then and there and said, okay, we don't want them. But, no, he wanted to make a talk for the record, and so a half-hour of valuable time, as far as I was concerned, was wasted. This is part of the difficulty that you run into in presenting a budget, and this was part of the thing where I was lucky, in that most of the committee that I worked with - of course, new members would come and they wouldn't have the background of the others - but I was very fortunate throughout my whole tenure practically to have as my chairman either Mr. Geary or Mr. Canfield. They had traveled, not necessarily always together, but on different trips and had a knowledge of the Coast Guard. And even if we got new members who hadn't always traveled with us, they would defer to the chairman in practically every instance.

Q: But they were the continuity?

Adm. R.: They were the continuity that carried us on, so, as I say, I was very lucky in that respect. But I really think we owed it to these trips which a lot of people say were a waste of money and junkets and so forth. I will say for our committee that they went. I'll grant you that we had a good time on our trips when we weren't working, but they worked. I'll give you an example.

I know of one case where we took them up to Scotch Cap, which is at Unimak Pass, where you go round the tip of Alaska, up into Bristol Bay. The Aleutian Islands start there. We had a Loran station at Sarachef, which is on the north side, and we had a landing field where we landed our amphibians - we had to fly out there in an amphibian, and the landing field was one that the contractor and ourselves had made. It was simply loose rock. You had to land in daylight because the only guides you had were oil drums filled with rocks that marked the runway. In other words, it was sort of primitive, primitive in the last degree. Then you had to drive twenty miles north to Sarachef or twenty miles south to Scotch

Cap. Scotch Cap was a light on the south corner there of the coast, and that's the one that the tidal wave in 1948 that hit Hawaii - the light, I think, was 118 feet above sea level, and when the tidal wave hit there - I think the light might have been higher and the basement was 118 feet, but it could have been the other way. Anyhow, the keeper made a mistake - in thinking that the safest place would be in the basement of the light. He took his four men and went down in the basement of the light. The tidal wave rolled across and ground the whole light into dust and the men were crushed in the basement of the light. So we had to rebuild Scotch Cap light, and when we did we built it farther back up on the hill. But that's how high that tidal wave rolled across there. It was over 100 feet when it hit on that bluff.

Getting back to my story. I wasn't on this particular trip. I was in the hospital at the time. This was the trip that my friend Frankie Kenner took, but he told me about it. They landed and they had to go from the landing strip to Scotch Cap in a weasel - that's the amphibious jeep type of thing. They had two weasels. Part of the time you have to run the beach, cross creeks, and go out into the surf. That's why they had to use a weasel, and they had to cross these streams that run down off the tundra, but they didn't have enough room for the congressmen to sit. You always think of congressmen riding round in limousines and so forth. Gordon Canfield told me himself that he rode out in the back seat of the weasel lying across the knees of Congressman Geary and, I think it was Hernandez, of New Mexico, twenty miles, lying across the knees of his compatriots.

I tell this story only to show that these trips were not always pleasure trips, even though we had a lot of fun on them when the work was done. Gordon Canfield used to tell the story about how, on this particular trip, he got out there and he was talking to one of the boys on this light and he was very much enthused. He asked the fellow what he read. The fellow was honest and said, "Well, I enjoy reading the Congressional Record."

Gordon said, "How do you get the Congressional Record?"

"Well," he said, "I subscribe to it."

He must have been the only person in the United States who subscribed to the Congressional Record, and Gordon was so impressed that he said:

"Cancel your subscription."

And Gordon used to tell this story about how he came back and ordered the Congressional Record sent to this boy at Scotch Cap.

We went practically every place with the congressmen. I took them to Europe. I also found out another thing. If you're going to make a trip with congressmen, never take senators along. We think of rank in the military service but, if you haven't worked on the Hill, you probably don't realize that there is a degree of jealousy -

Q: Rank and condescension!

Adm. R.: - and on this particular trip - this was about the first trip we took - we went to Europe. We had the House Appropriations Committee and Senator Kilgore, of West Virginia, and he decided to take his wife along.

We flew over, we had a DC-4 at that time, with one congressman and we met the rest of them who came over on, I believe, the old Mauretania, and then from there we flew them all over Europe and then flew them back. Senator Kilgore decided to take Mrs. Kilgore, which didn't help matters, any. Every time we arrived at a place, we were met by our own representative, if we had one there, and if we didn't have one we were met by the consular representative. Well, obviously, the senator was senior and I was head of the party and so the consular agent or the ambassador's representative would want to put the Senator and Mrs. Kilgore in the first car. The others would be portioned out among the remaining cars that you might have.

Admiral, then Captain, Kenner came to me and said:

"Look, this thing is going to backfire. These congressmen are getting madder and madder."

The first thing we learned was about Senator Kilgore and Mrs. Kilgore always riding in the first car. We couldn't do anything about that because we didn't control the scene from the State Department, and I could understand why they would naturally give preference to the senator. But I did learn that the thing to do was for me to bow out gracefully from the front car and start jumping into different cars behind.

The biggest crisis we had on that trip, and I tell it as a humorous story, was that we had one congressman who was a bit of a hell-raiser. He'd been a superintendent of schools out in Indiana. The first thing he told me when I met him was that he wasn't going to be horsed around by any guy in uniform and I said:

"That's perfectly all right, Sir. If you want to miss the plane, I'll just leave some transportation requests and you can catch up with us."

Well, we always gave them the time to check out and told them we expected them to have their baggage down by a certain time to check out at a certain time. The first time he came down after that, he arrived on time. We hadn't gone very far, several stops, when he came to me and said:

"This is the first so and so trip that I've ever been on where when they say they're going to leave at a certain time, they mean it."

He finally got to the point where he'd sit in the plane and we were fifteen seconds later getting out wheels up he'd complain.

We went to Greece on that trip and the King was still there, and the congressmen had an opportunity to meet him.

Q: King Paul, wasn't it?

Adm. R.: Yes, King Paul. And the minister of interior had given a lunch at the Yacht Club and the boys had had a little too much retsina, all the congressmen and so forth. Some of them were Democrats, some Republicans, and they were getting kind of argumentative on home politics, but they were also eyeing Senator Kilgore. He was sitting a little bit apart because he wasn't in on the House arguments, anyway. The minister of the interior got up and made the usual flowery speech about how he was so happy to have this congressional delegation present and so forth and so on, the typical type of thing that you give. This was all being interpreted out of Greek into English, and I could see the congressmen getting more restive all the time, and I was getting more restive because I knew that if Senator Kilgore responded, then, every one of them would want to respond, and I was afraid before they were through something would be said that would forever rupture Greek-American relations, and if it didn't it would certainly rupture the trip.

So that poor minister had hardly got down before I was on my feet, and I started in to thank him on behalf of the congressional delegation. I was sure all wanted to extend their own personal thanks, but it was late and we couldn't all have this wonderful opportunity, they had enjoyed his hospitality. I poured it on with everything I could, but all the words were

to all of them - "You're not going to have a chance to talk."!
And with that, we broke it up.

The funny part was that this congressman from Indiana came to me afterwards and said:

"Richmond, that was the smartest damned thing you ever did, because if that so and so Kilgore had gotten up, I was going to get on my feet and I was going to tear him apart." And he would have, too.

This was some of the fun of traveling, but I learned my lesson then. If there was a senate trip coming up - of course, we had with us, too, the clerks of the committee, that was another thing. We always tried to take the clerk of the committee with us because they really are the people who mark up the bills. I don't say that they know the answers any more than the congressmen tell them, but they do the work. You, having been there, know the story.

We had Harold Merrick on that trip. Maybe you know him?

Q: No.

Adm. R.: Well, he was from the Senate, and the House guy was Rusty Orisan.

It was a lot of fun traveling with them. We didn't make all the trips we hoped to. Mr. Geary and Mr. Canfield and I got around quite a lot.

Q: Well, now, on March 9, 1950, you became assistant commandant of the Coast Guard, assistant to Admiral Merlin O'Neill, who was the commandant. Do you want to take up the story at that point?

Adm. R.: Yes. That preceding two or three months there'd been kind of backing and filling as to who would be assistant commandant. We couldn't get a decision from the Secretary of the Treasury. I knew that Merlin O'Neill had put forward my name, but I was still functioning as the head of the planning division, and, when I was appointed to the assistant's job, it was agreed because of my having handled the budget and reorganized it to an extent that I be given the additional title of Chief of Staff, although it was more adding the duties to the assistant commandant.

Q: You might tell me now, what are the duties of the assistant commandant, in contrast to those of the commandant?

Adm. R.: In a sense, you might say it was almost the same as the vice president to the president. Strictly speaking, to help implement the policies, primarily, however, to function as the commandant in the absence of the commandant on official business or otherwise. To head the administration of headquarters, if the commandant is out of town or sick or in any way incapacitated.

The assistant commandant's job by becoming chief of staff at that time - I think after my time it was divorced again from the assistant commandant, and we actually set up what had been the planning and control office as the chief of staff's office, and officers were assigned separate from the assistant commandant as chief of staff. But, at that time, as I say, I wore both hats.

I don't remember too much detail of this period, other than the same battles that we had been fighting through the 1946 to 1950 period. They were continued in many ways, with one additional problem that began to come up. That, of course, was the Korean conflict, which was getting hot just about that time.

We were involved primarily with the question of port security and, at the same time, we were still having our problems with the expansion of Loran and weather stations. In trying to improve our Loran stations, improve our service, trying to improve our personnel on the Loran stations, I think I ought to explain that the policy was to put men out on these Loran stations for one year. Most, if not all, of the Loran stations were in relatively isolated localities. In many cases, they were on islands where there were not even natives and, although we tried to supply them every two weeks or so, it wasn't always possible. There were a great many personnel problems, with the transfer of personnel.

During that period as assistant commandant, I made a

number of trips, particularly to the Pacific, but also to the Atlantic stations, or the east coast stations and the Pacific coast stations. But out in the far Pacific, primarily. They were arduous trips and yet very interesting. We found out a great many things. Many of the stations had been ill supplied when originally put in commission, in the sense of furniture and things like that, and we found a great many morale problems with the boys out there. Although they could usually be brought down not so much to isolation, to the isolation of the station, but to the question of the boys' future, particularly in respect to relief.

I found that if a man was supposed to go out, say, on a certain date and he was delayed as much as a week or two weeks or even three weeks in getting relieved, not only was he disappointed at not being relieved on time, but it had a bad effect on the whole crew, even boys who maybe had eleven months to do, because from then on for the next eleven months they'd be worried about whether they were going to get out on time.

Q: I suppose they felt, as a group, that they were really off on the sidelines somewhere and not that important?

Adm. R.: They did, and they felt that nobody was interested in them. I think these trips, which started the first year I was assistant commandant, did a great deal to build up morale because, for the first time, I think they felt that headquarters was interested, that somebody back in Washington knew their problems. I usually took with me about five officers, invariably specialists, like an electronics man, an engineer. People often asked me what can you learn from visiting a station for just a few hours or staying overnight - in many cases, we had to stay overnight - and the answer to that is that, in a way, you can learn quite a lot if you know what you're looking for, and in a general inspection of a station, plus if you've got experts, you can look for the critical points that you want. And it's really better than if you went and stayed a long time because, on these trips we might inspect as many as twenty-seven or thirty loran stations. Well, if you stayed, say, a week at each one, you'd be gone too long and, by the time you got to the last one, you'd have forgotten what you had learned on the first station, even with notes. So it was much better to make quick visits and get a bird's eye view. Then, with a little experience, you can pretty well spot trouble spots and spot them very quickly, especially if you have a competent staff with you.

Q: You can see through the spit and polish, which is prepared for your arrival?

Adm. R.: That's right. Just as an interesting sidelight on that, Admiral Kenner - I guess he was a captain at that time -

and I always did the operational inspection.

In the late fifties, before I became commandant, I was still assistant commandant, I had quite a hassle with several assistants of Senator McCarthy over the judgment of the people, but not the Coast Guard, in putting a certain type of evaporating equipment aboard the Courier, which we were going to man. They were convinced - they were trying to make us say that as a result of this mistake, because that's what it was, it was not the most efficient - for some reason we didn't like it. Anyway, they were trying to indicate that this was a Communist plot and, of course, my own opinion at the time was that you make plenty of dumb mistakes without having them inspired from Moscow. But this all fitted in with the general pattern of the times.

By the same token, we were having, as were all government agencies, some problems with personnel whose records might be slightly questionable, not necessarily Communist-affiliated but you had to clear all your records and that sort of thing. It was a rather difficult time from that standpoint, but I don't remember any specific cases, except one where we had one hearing examiner who, incidentally, had been overseas with me during the war and I knew was absolutely non-Communist. But he unfortunately had a rather bad reputation for drinking quite a little bit. Those things were gradually cleared out.

In the meantime, we were trying to evolve a policy of how to deal with this port security. This evolved while I was assistant commandant and into the time when I became commandant, but it started at that time obviously because there was a suspicion that the Soviets might attempt to blow up one of our ports with an atomic bomb. The first approach to it was that, maybe, the thing to do was to restrict the major ports but leave some of the minor ports open. I think they were going to leave one minor port - this policy was not being evolved necessarily by the Coast Guard, this was in contact with the State Department and Treasury and everybody else - to leave one minor port.

Q: To leave one minor port what?

Adm. R.: Available for Soviet vessels. Of course, no Soviet vessels were arriving. This was a potential. But the idea was that if, say, a Soviet vessel was coming and you thought there might be danger, you diverted it to this minor port. The only catch on this was - and this was the Coast Guard position somewhat enunciated by me, I guess - that this was kind of a stupid policy because how do you explain to the port that you choose - I believe it was some small port up in New England, Portsmouth or something like that - that you'll send a Soviet ship in up there when you won't let it go into New York because you suspect it's got dangerous material aboard. Of course, their answer was, well, it's a smaller port and therefore presumably it wouldn't get blown up, anyway.

Q: There wouldn't be so many people blown up!

Adm. R.: There wouldn't be so many people blown up. And that was my whole argument. After all, it's kind of hard to explain to the mayor of a small town that he and his townspeople are expendable. So that policy sort of died aborning. And about the time I became commandant we evolved the 24-hour system, but, of course, it was never publicly put out.

Q: And the 24-hour system was what?

Adm. R.: The 24-hour system was simply this. Keep in mind that no Soviet vessels were coming and nevertheless the Soviets were still a friendly nation, even though you were suspicious of them. Therefore, you could not do to them what you weren't doing to somebody else. So the principle of this thing was that every ship entering a port of the United States - I think even our own - had to give 24 hours' notice. Now, as you know, with the shipping information that is available, it's possible that they were coming in at such and such a time. Most companies have agents and the agents know when the ships are coming, so we didn't feel that this was any great threat. The theory of this thing was that if any ship suddenly appeared off your port unannounced you could deny it entrance. It didn't make any difference what nationality it was. But to do this, you had to have vessels on patrol all the time, otherwise how would you know when somebody slipped in.

So for the ten major ports we evolved this theory and

adopted it. Of course, the 24-hour business was put out but nobody really knew the reason other than that we were trying to control shipping and that sort of thing, and it gave us a leverage on any unannounced visitors getting in to port, on the assumption that an announced visitor would be all right. Now what would have happened, and it really did happen in the end but by that time things had calmed down, but what would have happened had a Soviet ship come - I don't think we ever finally had come over and announced it was coming - I don't think we ever quite came to grips with. I think that was a question that would have been decided at the time. As a matter of fact, later, Soviet ships did start coming in, and on the west coast we had a few problems with Communist ships. I don't believe they were Soviet, I believe they were Chinese Communists, and we had to take some drastic actions to divert them in some way on some excuse or another.

Q: I take it that that was a time when we didn't have investigative reporters who wanted to look behind your 24-hour rule to discover the reason why?

Adm. R.: Apparently not, and, as I say, there was really nothing radically wrong with what we were doing. It applied universally to every ship. As I recall it, I believe even our own ships had to report. All it meant was just setting up a reporting center to take this information and assimilate it.

Later, we also kept a record or ships on the high seas out to a certain distance. So we had a pretty good line-up on anything that was off our coasts, and I think it was in the interest of the then-suspicion. I think it was a sound system and well justified, and I think it was effective.

As I say, had we had any trade with the Soviets at that time and ships coming and going, it could have gotten embarassing. I forget which was the first ship that came in. Wasn't there a ship that brought Khrushchev to the United Nations for a visit?

Q: The Gdynia?

Adm. R.: Yes, I believe it was the Gdynia. She finally came in and, of course, it was announced and there were no problems. Obviously the ship wasn't going to blow up with Khrushchev aboard.

I suspect that even at that time had a reputable Soviet commercial - well, of course, no line is strictly commercial under the Soviets, but I mean a regular trade ship wanting to bring passengers or things to the United States, a Polish or any other Communist country, and it had been in legitimate trade, I don't think there would have been any great problem in accepting it. It was to catch the ship that might try to sneak in with a bomb in its hold. You'd know it was there but nobody would pay much attention. It was more to put us on the alert than it really was against a surprise attack.

About the time I became commandant we needed more vessels for our port-security fleet and we needed to maintain them. The Secretary of the Treasury at that time was George Humphrey, who was a difficult man to deal with unless you understood his psychology. On one particular occasion I was called over to meet with the Secretary to plead the case of the vessels for port security, he feeling that it was absolutely unnecessary.

Q: This was a proposed program for - ?

Adm. R.: This was at the time we were amplifying and building up this fleet.

I went over to the Assistant Secretary's office and the two of us went to the Secretary's office. The Secretary's custom was when you had a proposal or project he immediately started in on the Assistant Secretary and myself - the Assitant Secretary had asked me to do the talking on the project - telling me that it was unnecessary, this was utterly ridiculous that any enemy would try to sneak a bomb in by ship, and, if they did anything, they'd fly it in by modern bomber. Secretary Humphrey was quite outspoken as to why he thought this was a stupid idea. Finally, after quite a tirade, I asked the Secretary, as a businessman, if I could show him how I could blow up ten ports simultaneously in the United States at about one-third or maybe less than the cost of his bomber fleet, admitting that it could be successful, would he be interested, as a former businessman. He said yes, go ahead and talk.

So I explained to him that very frankly if I were sitting on the other side and wanted to bomb ports in the United States as cheaply as possible, it would be perfectly possible to pick out ten old broken-down merchant vessels, hide a bomb in the hold of the ship, cover it with fake cargo, put aboard a crew who, as a whole, would not have to know the destination or the contents of the ship, send them out under sealed orders to get them in position off the various ports at a given time, and order them in to the various ports to arrive at a specific time, even with time enough to give the crew a chance to get ashore, if necessary, and with one or two trusted agents to set the bomb on a time device. Also, if you wanted to save your personnel or save some of them at least, there would be very little chance of detection of the ship on the high seas because, as you know, it's very difficult to determine either from the air or the surface, except by close visual contact, what a ship is, and even then it almost requires boarding to know on the high seas what ship you're passing. There's always a possibility of false flags and changed names.

We had the experience of the German ships during the war that did just that - in both wars, as a matter of fact.

Q: You mean the raiders?

Adm. R.: Yes. He grasped the thing right off and rang the bell for his secretary. When she came in he dictated a favorable memorandum to Bobby Cutler, who was then head of the National Security Agency, advocating the adoption of this program and coined something that I hadn't thought of, what he called the Trojan horse theory, which it became known as colloquially amongst us.

And so we did get this port-security program set up. We had some problems with it in the later years as trade began to broaden, but at the same time pressures were going down and some of the minor ports that were exercising this were trying to get ships to come in and trying to encourage trade with Communist-related countries. They couldn't understand why there was some reluctance to let these ships come in, but it was gradually worked out and nothing ever really developed that backfired on the thing.

Now it may seem to have been an unnecessary precaution and maybe money unnecessarily spent, but I think you have to put yourself in the times and in the spirit when everybody was suspicious of the fact that the Russians might, or the Soviets might, deal us a blow behind our back, as it were. When you come right down to it, the thinking behind the DEW line and the various strategic defenses that have been set up airwise were originally based on the same concept.

Q: Of a sudden and overwhelming attack.

Adm. R.: Yes, and plans were laid to scramble if a fleet of Russian planes crossed a certain line. There was a line drawn down through the Atlantic, very close to the chop line. There were extensive plans for countering even a sortie, if any large number of planes was seen coming our way.

Q: Part of the DEW line extended was the Atlantic patrol, the air patrol.

Adm. R.: This wasn't as unreasonable at that time as it now appears in retrospect.

Another problem that plagued us a great deal during this time was explosive loading, the carrying of ammunition. We had controlled this during the war. You may recall, I don't know what year it was, the Perth Amboy explosion?

That explosion caused us quite a little bit of trouble because this was another case where the Coast Guard's authority was limited, and yet, when it took place, why hadn't the Coast Guard taken certain actions. Some of the facts are vague in my mind now but, essentially, in the Perth Amboy explosion what blew up were land mines and various things that had been shipped from a factory in Ohio, and they were on barges to be taken out and loaded aboard ship. I guess they caught fire and these land mines and things, which apparently were poorly packed, let go and considerable damage was done.

Well, the limit on the Coast Guard's authority was basically that we controlled the loading on the ship and we could control where the ship was loaded. Although we had extended ourselves to trying to watch as it was loaded on the barges and things like that, there was some question, in my mind at least, whether we really even had that authority, although I suppose, once it was on the barges, it really did become basically our authority.

I don't think it's been corrected to this day, unless a lot's been done since I left, but the fault lies in laxness in federal control of explosives right from the point of manufacture until they are moved to their point of destination, whatever it is, out of the country. True, ICC requires that explosives be marked properly and that sort of thing, but there was not at that time and I doubt if there is now any federal inspection like there is in a meat factory or something like that, at the manufacturing plant to see that explosives are properly packed and properly shipped. True, once they're packed they have to be marked and the company can be caught for not marking them properly.

But, again, once they're put on the road or the railroad there's no control over those explosives, so they can be put on a siding or left dangerously. Then, when they get to the point of destination, before shipping out, suppose the Coast Guard finds something wrong with them, what do you do? You turn them around and send them back inland where they can do more damage. How do you handle this? There was nothing clear on this, and it was a horribly mixed-up mess.

We had set up explosive-loading areas where the ships that were going to take it out of the country had to be, and those were always set out reasonably safe from populated areas, so that if a ship blew up you'd lose only the ship. We had tight control on the ships because we could tell them how to stow it and that sort of thing.

We tried to get legislation. We were bucked a great deal by the explosives industry, DuPont, for example. I went round and round with their representative. They were particularly interested in the shipping of dynamite. Let me back up a moment.

It is true that many cities had ordinances against loading in other than limited areas.

It comes back to me now. Another confusing element in this thing was that the only guideline we had for what were safe distances and quantities of material was, as I recall it, "American Explosive Distances," or something, which is an arbitrary formula that had been worked out a number of years before by the Army Ordnance Department and established distances between bunkers. In other words, you could have so much explosive power but it had to be separated by so much distance. We had used this as a guideline - it was the only thing available, really - for most of our control of explosive-loading areas.

But, as I started to say, New York City, I know, had

ordinances that only so much explosive could be taken through the city or across the docks.

Q: Certain bridges restrict it.

Adm. R.: Many of them did, yes. We were successful in tightening up, we were never completely successful. Most of the legislation we were trying to get was blocked or was slowed down, at least, by the explosives industry, particularly in the shipment of dynamite. They said that dynamite was safe.

Just about that time, I remember, down in Venezuela a large truck train of dynamite had blown up and killed a number of people. They laughed that off. Later, there was a big explosion up in Oregon, where a truck of dynamite had been left and caught fire or something.

Dynamite, I agree, is generally stable but it can also be unstable, and that is the great trouble with all explosives.

We were successful in prevailing on some areas down in Florida, or some of the companies, to establish a special loading place down in an isolated area of Florida, south of Pensacola. I believe it was somewhere near Panama City. But we never were able to lick completely or solve this question of shipping explosives. We had quite a hassle, for example in Pensacola. Pensacola had an ordinance. It was being shipped out in barges from Pensacola and the ordinance amounted essentially to the fact that explosives had to be brought into town between, we'll say, four and six in the morning, each truck had to be ten minutes apart coming through town, if it was a train, which was fine. There was nothing wrong with the ordinance, except that it overlooked one thing and I had quite a fight over this. It goes down to the loading area where the trucks now park, which is, we'll say, a city block, right in the center of the city, and here it sits, and they're all gathered together, until such time as it can be loaded on the barges and moved out. In other words, if this thing had been devised so that each truck came in, it went onto the barge, and out to the ship, that would have been one thing. Yet, people couldn't see why this was dangerous.

It was a very complex thing and I have to admit that, although we worked hard on it, I never successfully licked the problem.

Q: Let me ask, and this of course is, I believe, since you retired, has the Coast Guard been involved in these efforts of the Army to dispose of its poison gas?

Adm. R.: I can't answer you because I don't know. I wouldn't be surprised. Let me put it this way. It would be definitely involved if it was shipped by water any place, because even while I was commandant we were having a lot - you see, while

I've been talking about explosives, I've been talking in terms of dynamite and TNT and things like that, but there are other dangerous elements shipped such as chlorine gas and, of course, they're shipped under regulations. But we did have some cases while I was commandant of escaping chlorine gas and having to evacuate certain places. I think there were some tanks lost in the Mississippi River at one time and there was quite a problem with those.

Any time that any shipment involves either the oceans or the navigable waters, yes, the Coast Guard, unless it's been relieved of the reponsibility, would be involved.

Q: It wouldn't be involved in, say, air shipments across the nation, would it?

Adm. R.: No, as far as I know we were never involved in anything like that because, of course, it was out of our province. I don't know, really, if there's any satisfactory answer to it. Then, it was highlighted when the ammonium nitrate being shipped out for fertilizer blew up at Galveston. This was reclaimed ammonium nitrate, we later learned, from Army ammunition. It was being shipped out, and fire broke out, as I recall it, on a ship next to this ship and spread. I forget how many lives were lost. Then, of course, everybody wanted to know how this could happen. Mind you, this was fertilizer that was being shipped. Nobody had thought that ammonium nitrate, as such, was explosive. All kinds of pressures grew up as to whose fault it was, which was never settled. Then experts began to appear and discuss whether ammonium nitrate is dangerous or not dangerous. My recollection is that we were authorized about $100,000 to have tests run and one thing and another.

We immediately prohibited all shipments of ammonium nitrate which, since some places along the coast - I think Charleston, South Carolina, was one place that was shipping it or else getting it in - anyway, this caused all sorts of problems because they were being deprived of business. It was really a mess. The records showed there had been one other known explosion of ammonium nitrate at a plant in Germany, but the process was different and this wasn't a plant, anyway. Then, of course, there were implications that in reclaiming this ammonium nitrate the Army hadn't done a good job, which, of course, wasn't our responsibility. But it led to a big hassle with members of Congress. Some of them wanted one thing and some wanted another.

It was finally resolved with the belief, that, if properly handled - oh, I think there was some talk that maybe the bags it was shipped in were conducive to making ammonium nitrate explode. All kinds of tests were run, but I don't think any basically conclusive answer was ever worked out, other than that under most conditions ammonium nitrate is inherently stable. As I say, it's used as a fertilizer.

That was one of the problems that came up. Another one that caused a great deal of grief, though of a slightly different nature, while I was commandant. This fellow had bought an old schooner - a Chesapeake Bay bugeye. He was out of Baltimore and he was running weekly vacation cruises. In most cases, this is a reasonably safe thing, but out in Chesapeake Bay they got in a storm and they fetched up in about seven feet of water off Fairhaven, which is close to Chesapeake Beach, as I recall. She went to pieces and six or seven people were drowned. It was quite a fiasco, and, as usual, it became a question of why had the Coast Guard let this fellow go out.

The answer was that as long as the fellow was a sailing vessel, he was not subject to inspection even though he was carrying passengers. He did have a motor dinghy which he used to take passengers out fishing from the boat, and also, if the wind died, he'd sometimes push the schooner around with this motor dinghy. We had warned him that if he used that for navigation he would be subject to our inspection. His ship was old and we felt it was probably not in too good condition, anyway. He'd been warned.

But there's a basic defect - or was, and I suppose it's still there - in the navigation laws. You can't stop somebody from violating the law. You can pick them up and bring them in and they pay the prescribed penalty for their violation, but if they've got money enough, they can turn around and go out and do it again the next day. They don't have to comply with the law if they want to break it. We tried to point this defect out, but I don't think they ever got very far in convincing Congress that something better ought to be adopted.

Another case we had caused a great many headaches. These things don't start big but they take up an awful lot of time and really divert from a lot of the business of the service. You probably remember the Yankee, which used to sail out of New England and take people around the world. She belonged to a man called Johnson and was a good, safe ship. As a matter of fact, I heard that a lot of the pictures that his paying guests had photographed on these cruises before the war were invaluable to the Navy at the outset of the war because he had taken the Yankee in to South Pacific islands that our people knew nothing about. I gather he turned over a whole album of pictures for navigational purposes. It became almost a guide book.

But, with the laws, we finally found out that, strictly speaking, with the tonnage of the vessel, he was in violation of the law, carrying passengers and that sort of thing. Again, here I'm hazy on all the details. He sold the Yankee and went across and built another boat that I think he operated out of Europe. He sold her to a man in Chicago who had made a trip with him and who I think probably was competent to handle her. He was going to do the same as Johnson, maybe not as elaborate. I think his idea was to make short cruises during the summer along the coast.

Q: On the Great Lakes?

Adm. R.: No, still on the coast. After he got it, we called attention to the fact that he couldn't operate this way. He had his money sunk in the vessel and he took it to his congressman and we fought it back and forth, but there was no way out. I think he did operate it, anyway, and we had to cite him. It was a mixed-up mess. There was some question about the tonnage which revolved around whether it was under 100 or over 100 tons. I think it had been built one way and then they'd made alternations which changed its displacement.

Another fiasco we had was with the Boy Scouts, which came about in an odd way. The Boy Scouts, as you know, have a group known as the Explorers, Sea Scouts. The Sea Scouts are Explorers. I think now they're divided into three groups, the Sea Scouts, the Explorers, and their aviation group.

There was a group down at Alexandria that had obtained an old 75-footer of ours for their Sea Scouts, and the fellow in charge naturally wanted to give these boys experience and have a lot of fun at the same time. He decided that maybe a trip to Florida through the inside passage would be very nice, and it probably would have been if this thing had held together. The idea was that each boy was to defray part of the expenses of this trip. So I suppose the boys went home and told their parents they were going on this trip. Pretty soon we began to be flooded with questions from parents, is it safe to let my son go on this 75-footer. So we sent an inspector to inspect her and he came back and said no, the vessel wasn't safe. It hadn't been kept up well. Those were gasoline motors and there was gas in the bilges. Of course, that could have been cleaned out. He said:

"I don't think it's in too good condition, but it could be fixed up."

Well, we passed this word, but, as we looked into it, we began to realize that by letting these boys pay, he was, in effect, charging - he was carrying passengers for hire, not as a passenger ship, but as a motor launch, which required him to have a motorboat licence - a motorboat operator's licence, I guess, is what we called it. So, we passed this word and the word about other requirements, too. As usual, things get twisted and the first thing the papers came out with was that the Coast Guard is going to require everybody who runs a motorboat for hire, like charter fishermen and so forth and so on, to have officers' papers. There's a lot of difference between taking a licence for a third mate and taking a motorboat operator's licence, as you can readily understand. Then the roof fell in on us.

That was one of the problems and that led us to begin to look around at this whole Sea Scout thing. I had a very good friend who was head of the district area and I called him in one day and we got to talking. I said:

"How well do you really control these Explorer-Sea Scout groups of yours?"

He said: "We don't have any control. We get an old Navy liberty boat or a Coast Guard lifeboat or something."

And I said, "Yes, that's what we've just found out," because, looking around, here's what was happening. We'll say they get one of those old 50-foot running boats of the Navy and, you know, it's open. The boys don't like that so they decide to deck it over. Then, having decked it over, they put a house on top, and pretty soon the center of gravity has gone from down on the keel up to the masthead. I'm exaggerating, obviously, as I always do, but these things were definitely unsafe. I talked to this fellow and I said:

"Frankly, I think you boys are out on a limb on this thing because sooner or later - hopefully this won't happen, but sooner or later one of these is going to go out, capsize, and a lot of boys are going to be drowned, or some boys will be drowned, and then you've got a suit on your hands."

He saw the logic, so then we entered in and helped them draft some regulations so that any time any boat taken over was altered in any way, they'd come to the Coast Guard and ask us to inspect it and give it a test of seaworthiness. I can't say it did, but I hope that move did end up in saving some lives.

Q: A very constructive step.

Adm. R.: I'm convinced that sooner or later some of those boats would have been in trouble. We found some that looked like cartoons of Dr. Suess' houseboat or something.

Q: Also with a nonprofessional as a leader of the scout troop.

Adm. R.: People just don't realize that you get in a little rough water and all the kids run to one side and over they go.

So that was another hassle we had.

Probably one of the biggest problems we had was in the boating field.

Q: You mean private boating?

Adm. R.: Private boating, and it came about largely because of a wartime development. I have already mentioned that, even before the war, yachting, or rather boating, had become much more common than -

Q: Much more available to the ordinary man.

Adm. R.: Yes, and at that time, before the war, if you had an outboard motor you spent 90 percent of your time pulling the starting rope for every 10 percent that you were able to cruise, if you ever got started at all. If World War II didn't do anything else, it made the outboard motor grow up. In other words, as you recall, the Navy came out with those barges that were really pontoons and then they developed these big outboard motors.

So we came out of the war with three things against us in this boating problem - or for us, perhaps: (a) an improved outboard motor that was reasonably reliable - it's come a long way even since then but even then it was reasonably reliable - and not too expensive; (b) boats that were not too expensive. I mean we were down now to where the working man could afford - $2,000 for an outboard and boat; and (c) we had opened up in the interior large bodies of water - for example, down in Texas the Snake River, Red River to the north, and others, TVA. You can go all over the country. These bodies of water were opened to people who basically were not familiar with water. If you grow up, we'll say, along the coast, you grow up with an appreciation of what can happen when that water gets mad or you've really got a rough storm. You learn to keep a weather eye out. But now we've got reasonably big bodies of water out in the middle of Kansas or Texas, any place in the midwest, and here's a farm boy who now has at his disposal a 20-foot boat, a 10 or 25 horsepower motor, 90 percent of the time perfectly smooth water, but no great knowledge, maybe not even a knowledge of how to swim. You've got problems.

There's one other thing, too, that entered into it, and that was that along with the outboard motor and these runabouts came the trailer. Remember, before the war, if you owned a boat in Baltimore, you were pretty well restricted to the upper regions of the Chesapeake Bay or along the coast, you might go down the coast ten miles or fifteen miles. That was the limit of your cruising, except that you might go down the inland canal to Florida, if you wanted to take a month. But basically your cruising was your home port.

Now you've got a little cabin cruiser or a boat and you can load it on your trailer and if you want to go out to Tennessee, or if you're in Tennessee and you want to go to the ocean, you can. So you have a mobile boat fleet, if you want to call it that, and problems were multiplying fast. It really wasn't until I would say four years before I retired that we finally got the motorboat numbering acts through and safety requirements, because people were being killed off right, left, and center. And there were many other problems. Water-skiing had come in and people were having their legs cut off - not everybody, obviously. There were cases arising of improper operation, both at the coast and inland, more inland.

I know of one very tragic case, a Sunday school picnic on a river, a fairly large river, and this minister arranged for the kids to get on a raft or something. Sure, they got off the beach a little bit, they all run to one side, the raft tilts, and you've got them all in the water. Two or three of them drowned. Poor judgment, but certainly nothing malicious. Just stupidity, I guess. It wasn't really stupidity even, it was a lack of knowledge of how dangerous water can be.

Q: You were dealing with land-oriented people.

Adm. R.: And, as I say, we hadn't become educated. Furthermore, we had problems with the sale of life preservers. First, the lack of knowledge of the requirements as to what you had to have in the different sized boats, and second, dealers selling more surplus materials. It was a glorious mess. You could talk almost for hours on the problems that were in it.

Then we got into the question of registration of drivers and operators of boats. That was a tough one because - I'm talking about small boats now, I'm not talking about boats carrying passengers for hire, which were covered, I'm talking about you own a boat, should you have to get an operator's permit. The analogy was that, after all, you have to have an operator's permit to drive a car. In other words, we got into the question, you might say, we had fifty or sixty years ago with cars. If you recall, in the early days of automobiles, some states did not require an operator's permit. The registration carried with it the authority to operate the car. Now, of course, every state, I'm sure, requires you to show your proficiency.

So we got into this hazy line. When we got into the numbering acts, should the boats be require to be numbered, registered and numbered, and should we have operators' permits. Operators' permits are still not required, as such, and although I think I did argue for them at the time, I'm not convinced that they are entirely essential. No, I think I always did oppose more or less operators' permits because I don't know of any common denominator that you could use to really evaluate operation. For example, if you can drive a Volkswagen you can drive a Cadillac, to all intents and purposes. Furthermore, if you know to stay on the righthand side of the road and stop at a stop sign, you're reasonably proficient. But being able to operate a 15-foot runabout doesn't necessarily qualify you to operate a 45-foot cabin cruiser. So, giving operators permits, what standards could you really use?

All these things were complicating factors in the development. Different congressmen had different ideas. It depended on who was singing in whose ears at the time. But we finally did get the Motorboat Act, we got the states to move in on it, and, as you know, now if you own a boat you have to have it numbered by the state. We tried to leave it as much as we could to the states, but with Coast Guard over-all control. I think it's been reasonably successful.

Q: It's quite interesting, the complexity of your problems

as the complexity of ordinary life grew in the post World War II era. Your problems grew apace. There is one other that comes to mind and I wonder if this is under the cognizance of the Coast Guard. That is the passenger airplanes when they're flying over the water. Of course, one is always shown how to operate or how to put on a life vest and that sort of thing, in case there's an emergency landing on water. Does this come under the aegis of the Coast Guard?

Adm. R.: No. But I will move into that field now, which is also parallel. It started while I was commandant.

In the first place, remember now, we're going back twenty years and, of course, planes weren't then what they are today, and there was always a chance of a potential ditching at sea and that was why we were operating the weather stations, not only to give them a fix in their navigation as well as with Loran, but also to be there, hopefully, if there's a ditching. And, of course, most of the planes in those days were carrying these inflatable life rafts and that sort of thing, in case they were forced to come down and abandon.

We found that most of the training being given to their pilots and stewardesses at that time was being given - well, I know of one case in San Francisco where they'd take them out and inflate a life raft in a swimming pool. Then they'd get in them and look at the equipment. This ties in with what I said earlier about our search and rescue outfit. Earlier, we had been trying to develop various forms of safe rescue if a plane was down and it was possible to get the passengers out, because, generally speaking, if a plane has to land in water, if the pilot is able, he had a pretty good chance of bringing the plane down and the passengers getting out. It isn't like flying into a mountain where you've got trees and rocks. If you can land it flat, the plane will probably stay afloat, unless it's just broached open because of a hard landing or something like that. It will probably stay afloat for a half-hour, an hour, or even longer in some cases, depending on the damage. So, there's a good chance of the passengers getting out without too much damage.

We started setting up and trying out - we ran a few off the east coast, but basically we'd go out to Honolulu - search and rescue exercises. We ran two or three a year and we invited the various airlines, officers, pilots, stewardesses, to send representatives out, and they did. We'd give them a day of lectures on the various procedures, techniques, and what they were going to do. Then we would put them on one of our major cutters, take them off Honolulu, and we'd put out four or five of these inflatable life rafts. In many cases, the companies would send their own equipment out. We'd divide them up into crews and put them over into these life rafts and let them rig the kites and try to go through all the rigmarole - put out the dye and the various things.

At the very first, we found out two things - they found out that going in a life raft, even in a mild slop is a lot different than going in a life raft in a swimming pool. In fact, you'd be surprised at the number that got seasick. Some of them enjoyed it, and all of them felt it was well worthwhile because it was a practical application of what they might have to face with their crews - or, rather, with their passengers. I might say parenthetically that one of the first groups was a stewardess who was on a plane that came down off the Oregon coast - later. And what we tried to do after the first one was to get a speaker from the airlines themselves who had gone through a ditching and could tell his experience. And I remember this girl saying - I believe one person, an elderly gentleman, died of a heart attack but he was the only casualty - that she credited the fact that having gone through this drill before was the one reason that she was able to get her passengers into the life rafts. She gave full credit for this. She said she would never have known what to do or how to do it otherwise.

We got them all back and then, that night, we'd have a plane simulate a ditching. We devised our own method of putting down a sea lane of lights. We also used helicopters, we showed how we would work with a helicopter. At night we would lay down these lights. At first, there was a lot of consternation about the fact that these lights might set off gasoline that was on the water, but we disputed that and proved that it was not a danger. Also, the lights we devised were far enough above the water, so that they wouldn't set off gasoline that was on the water, we showed that they wouldn't. Then we showed them what to expect if we had to help them at night, how to come in and make their approach and land on the water.

It was very effective, and I took congressmen out several times to those missions and they enjoyed it a great deal and thought it was a good thing. I think it was.

Q: This sort of indoctrination continues?

Adm. R.: I don't think so because, you see, the weather stations aren't there, there have been no ditchings, and I think they've given it up. I have not heard of any search and rescue exercises recently.

Q: But, of course, they still on the planes at the outset of a flight -

Adm. R.: That's different. That's a depressurization proposition. They don't tell you any more than that. You get that going across the country.

Q: But they also will tell you about the life preserver and how to put it on?

Adm. R.: I guess they do over water, too. I haven't made an

overwater flight for some time. Those are company instructions to the passengers, yes, but as far as actual ditching is concerned, I don't even know whether these big planes carry life rafts any more. I've just been out of it, but I don't think the Coast Guard is running search and rescue exercises any more. For one thing, of course, the time of flight is so much reduced now. It's only five hours to Honolulu, and in the days I'm talking about, you know, you were up eight or nine hours, probably. We were flying planes 200 or 300 miles an hour, as compared with 500 now, or something like that. If you have a tail wind, you can do better than that.

Q: You mentioned the use of helicopters in these demonstrations. I know the helicopter isn't an integral part of your story, but were you instrumental in seeing that the helicopter was used more frequently in your search and rescue operations?

Adm. R.: Do you mean me personally?

Q: Yes.

Adm. R.: No, not personally. A very good friend of mine was instrumental in first bringing the helicopter to use in the Coast Guard. Then I knew Erickson, who was the developer of many features that made the helicopter a very valuable tool for search and rescue.

Q: He worked closely with Sikorsky, of course?

Adm. R.: Yes, but if I am correct, I think Erickson was really one of the first people to develop a system for the capability of blind flying with the helicopter.

Q: My question pertained to your part in it?

Adm. R.: Except for supporting efforts to get the number of helicopters we needed to adequately service our stations -

Q: That's what I mean.

Adm. R.: As budget officer presenting the budget for so many years, the answer is yes. I actively supported the program, as I did our whole effort in aviation.

As long as you've raised this question, also on types of helicopters. In other words, we tried to keep abreast of the very best type for our use. At times, we had different ones in the service. At one time, we had the Piasacki's, the old Flying Bananas. We had Sikorskys. Practically every air station that we had was equipped with a number of helicopters. And we were active in trying to develop the use of helicopters from ships. Of course, the wartime cutters and the cutters we got before the war were not fitted out for that purpose, so we were limited there.

I had always wanted to fly a helicopter, but I was not in aviation, and by the time I got to the point where I could demand it I was past the age limit.

Q: Now, you're going to talk about some phase of the activity of the Bureau of Marine Inspection?

Adm. R.: Yes. As I mentioned earlier, the Bureau of Marine Inspection and Navigation had been transferred to the Coast Guard, as I recall, in 1942, during the war, under a temporary wartime act. At the close of the war, I think it was in 1946, the President was given authority to readjust departments and that sort of thing. Anyway, the Bureau of Marine Inspection and Navigation was put in the Coast Guard on a permanent basis. At this point there were brought together under one head four governmental related activities, all primarily interested in maritime matters, the regulation of safety and the saving of life on the waters. Namely, obviously the Revenue Cutter Service, which stemmed from the original Revenue Marine and its creation was, as you know, even before the Navy's - not the Continental Navy but the U. S. Navy. That is why the Coast Guard traces its history from 1790, the first Congress. The Lifesaving Service which, as I recall it, had its beginnings with volunteer lifesaving stations along the coast and dates from the early nineteenth century and had been put under government control probably in the early 1800s. The Lighthouse

Service, which had come into the Coast Guard. The Lifesaving Service and the Revenue Cutter Service had been joined in 1915 to make the Coast Guard. The Lighthouse Service, which started with volunteer lights in a rather local way, had been brought I think in 1819 under federal control and joined to the Coast Guard permanently in 1939. Now in 1946, the Bureau of Marine Inspection, which had been the old Steamboat Inspection Service, came in as a permanent part of the Coast Guard.

All of their personnel, mainly former merchant marine officers, were given commissions varying from lieutenant commander up to captain. Admiral Shepherd, who had been the second man in the old Bureau of Marine Inspection and Navigation, about that time made admiral. He was in charge of the office of marine inspection.

Frankly, there was friction, as there always is when two services are brought together. Some of the former bureau people were unhappy at being in the Coast Guard but, generally speaking, I think the transformation, although gradual, was made without any undue friction. Some of the diehards that might have dragged their feet gradually dropped out and, by the time I became assistant commandant, I think we had a pretty smooth-running organization. Everybody seemed to work in readily and easily. By the time I became commandant, there was no differentiation. Admiral Shepherd was a very efficient head of the Office of Marine Inspection. He was well known in shipping circles and he tied the Coast Guard in. We had been together in England during the war and he was a very close friend and we worked together very closely.

Throughout the whole thing we became more and more involved in international maritime affairs. I forget the year that the International Maritime Consultative Organization, which I'll refer to as IMCO, was set up, but there began to be conferences. At most of those conferences, both he and I and other officers of the service were present.

There were other facets that required our attention. All the conferences that I attended on IMCO were in London, and that led to a revision promoted by the Coast Guard in the United States of the Treaty on International Safety of Life at Sea which, I believe at that time dated back to about 1930. I think that was when the last meeting had been held. It was becoming more and more obvious, with the modernization of ships, that a complete revision of that would be necessary.

So a conference was scheduled and probably two years or a year and a half before, we began to organize teams of industry, labor, and specialists to try to establish prior to the conference a U. S. position to take to this conference.

Q: This conference was scheduled for what date?

Adm. R.: The spring of 1960 is my recollection.
IMCO was getting ready for the preliminary conferences on some of the problems having to do with shipping.

Q: It was kind of a parent organization under which - ?

Adm. R.: No, I wouldn't call it a parent. IMCO is really a function of the United Nations.

Q: I see, like the Commission on Human Rights?

Adm. R.: Sort of like that, yes. It's a throw-off from the United Nations, under their auspices.

Whereas this Safety of Life at Sea conference was for the purpose of revising the earlier regulations -

Q: The earlier one is the one you told me about as being at the outbreak of war?

Adm. R.: No, that was the whaling conference. Actually, I think the first Safety of Life at Sea conference was brought about largely by the sinking of the Titanic, so it must have been right after World War I. Then I think there was one either in 1928 or 1930, but I could be wrong. Not having been a part of it, it's hazy to me.

Anyway, knowing that this conference was coming up and knowing that we were going to attend -

Q: In 1960?

Adm. R.: In 1960. As I say, I had been going to these meetings with Shep and other officers on IMCO, and we began to develop our U. S. position, hopefully to put our ideas across.

The International Safety of Life at Sea protocol, or the treaty itself, is not just a simple treaty, because it goes into ship requirements, lifesaving equipment, engine room - actually, I think there are eight or nine chapters, and all of these are technical, specialist deals - and labor, to a degree, although labor is, of course, basically under ILO, the International Labor Organization, and that sort of thing. But labor had a part in this because living conditions aboard ship and all these things were involved.

All these things were part of this conference, so it was necessary to have some pretty firm ideas on what we were doing. For example, one of the things we had to thrash out was our position with respect to shipping lanes in the North Atlantic. As you know, there are specified shipping lanes because of the ice conditions that ships going east and west follow. There were questions as to whether we needed lanes any more and various problems involved with that. The engineering requirements and that sort of thing were probably the most technical. I think our full U. S. delegation, although not everybody stayed the whole time, was about 60 people. England probably had more people, and some had less, so it was a large conference. It was broken into separate panels meeting at different places and then there'd be the general conference.

Q: Plenary sessions?

Adm. R.: Plenary sessions.

That occupied quite a little bit of our time in 1959 and 1960. In fact, I would say the last three or four years that I was in the Coast Guard, I was probably out of the country with my various trips, both to conferences in Europe and my trips to the Pacific, on an average of three or four months a year. I'll now say parenthetically that you can see why an assistant commandant is -

Q: A fully operating billet.

Adm. R.: Yes, he can be because he has to carry on. Even though you may be in touch with him, he's still the boss as far as running the shop is concerned.

Probably that year preceding I was almost weekly spending a day or two just sitting in with these various committees. Lots of them met in Washington, some didn't, on construction and various problems that might come up at the conference, and trying to evolve a consistent U. S. position.

We had made a complete study of the previous convention or treaty and earmarked the items - and the British had made a study and sent us the various things that they wanted changed and told us what probably would be their position. We were doing the same to them, so as to minimize the time that would be needed for discussion.

At the conference, of course, we did not attain all the U. S. positions. It's obvious you don't. I think this can be made as a general statement. I think the U. S. standards - well, even before we went to the conference - of construction basically and safety features were much higher than probably those of any other country. Therefore, we went with the avowed objective of trying to make the treaty mandatory, that the over-all required standards would come up to our ideas of safety. Obviously, with all the countries there, we were not going to win because economic factors are going to force other countries to say we just can't afford certain things. So you have to be in a position where you can compromise.

Q: Did you and your delegation have the authority to compromise on the spot and not refer back to Washington?

Adm. R.: The answer to that is when I say "compromise," maybe I use the wrong word. You are working to develop a document that will spell out certain standards for maritime shipping. Now, what is desirable in that? This will eventually be accepted as a treaty and it has to be approved by the Senate. Therefore, we could compromise as we wanted to, but the Senate might turn it down. The whole time I was there, however - do you know Cox of Gibbs and Cox? He's the one that designed the United States. He's passed on now, but he was quite an autocrat and once or twice a week he'd call me from New York and give me a lecture on not giving an inch to any of them on our construction standards.

Well, this was very nice but you can do only one of two things. You can either say, "Boys, do it as we do, or we'll walk out," or you've got to compromise. And who knows whether we're entirely right.

I don't know whether it's fully understood that any ship coming in to the United States could be subject to inspection, a foreign ship - our own are inspected before they go out. But a passenger ship from France comes in is subject to inspection unless France, or whatever country the ship comes from, is a signatory to the Convention on the Safety of Life at Sea. If they are and they've been inspected at home and they've got posted a safety certificate by their inspectors, the same as our ships have here, they're not inspected. That's accepted. Do I make my point?

Q: Yes, I understand.

Adm. R.: That is really the purpose. That is what you're striving for, but we can't say, "Okay, boys, unless your ships meet our standards, you can't come in to our ports." We could, but it wouldn't be practical.

We were over there, I guess, three months working on this. I was the first vice chairman of it. The Russian was the second. Of course, being in England, an Englishman was the chairman. I attended some of the sessions, some of the technical sessions, but generally only the plenary meetings, which were held maybe two or three times a week. I was in conference practically every day with the chairman on the problems that were coming up, where we had to give and could take.

After the conference, I came back to the States, and there were certain other conferences for IMCO.

Q: Before you talk about that, what about the convention? Was it adopted by our Senate?

Adm. R.: It was, yes.

Q: How long did it take?

Adm. R.: It seems to me it was the following year. We had to go before I think it was Foreign Relations, but I'm not sure.

Q: Our delegation or you as head of the delegation?

Adm. R.: As head of the delegation, I did the talking. There was a State Department representative present. All I remember about that is that the only quarrel we had was with my old law professor, who is now Senator Fulbright, who thought it was horrible that we wasted the time of sixty people over there to get this done. According to him, we ought to have been able to do it in a couple of days. I wonder if he ever had looked at the convention, because when the document was printed up it was about 200 pages of mostly technical data. I'm sure he never read it. I question whether he looked at it or any of the complexity of it. Also, he was sort of echoing this idea why do we have to give anything to these people.

Q: That was probably reflecting his personality more than anything else!

Adm. R.: Yes, plus the fact that this was a chance to make a little speech for the record.

Q: Tell me something more about the IMCO meetings that you attended. There were at least four of them, were there not?

Adm. R.: My recollection is that IMCO met at least twice a year, which started about two years before the convention. I went to every meeting and I retired in 1962, so there were three or four after the convention.

Generally, after the convention, they were to see what progress was being made, although sometimes other matters would be discussed. I recall that at one IMCO meeting we had quite a hassle over safety provisions of the ships that were operating in the Red Sea and around there. We had some tankers coming through there and we were interested.

I can't remember any specific problems other than that at one time there was some question about who was to be the new secretary general of IMCO and, looking forward to retirement, I had some aspirations but it was pretty apparent that there would be some objections from several of the European countries - not to me, personally, but to an American. Oddly enough, though, I think the Russians would have supported us. However, with that there was a sort of implied idea that if they supported the United States for the next secretary-generalship, when the place became vacant the United States would support them. As it turned out, I think it finally went to the French representative, who was a very fine gentleman whom I knew in IMCO.

One other organization that we eventually got into has an interesting history. It had been established in Europe and is an organization known as the International Association of Lighthouse Authorities. To fully comprehend this, you've got to recognize that in many countries the lighthouses are not subjects of the government. For example, in England, as you know, Trinity House is not a governmental organization. It's a private organization with government sponsorship. I believe the Duke of Gloucester is the master, but that's an honorary title. They own property. They get revenues from the property they own in different places and they charge light money. In fact, that was one of the big problems during the war that we had to work out. They had some rule that ships carrying mail have to pay more light money than other ships. Of course, every merchant ship coming over had bags of mail on it, and Trinity House was charging American ships light money for two or three bags of mail and there were screams and howls. It was finally resolved, but it was just one of the little things that come up.

Of course, I'd been very close to Trinity House. They were members of IALA.

And other countries. In France, for example, the lighthouses are supported by the Bureau des Phares.

Anyway, they wanted the United States to become members of IALA, and there was every reason that we should, except that we were a governmental agency. And here we get back again into this Communist scare. When IALA was created, they wrote to every country that had lighthouses and invited them to join IALA. That meant that they had written to the Communist Chinese. They'd also written to the Nationalist Chinese on Taiwan, which, I believe, had joined, though I'm not sure about that. When the facts came out - remember, that the Secretary of State at that time was Dulles, who believed that anything that had any relationship with Communist China and, I guess, to a degree, with Russia, was tainted - we got a flat, specific negative that the United States could join.

Yet, nevertheless, we were invited to attend their meetings.

It wasn't that the Communist Chinese had joined. It was the fact that they'd been invited to join and might join. They'd never even gotten an answer back from the Communist Chinese. As far as I know, they never have. In any case, we were what I suppose you'd call ex officio members. We sat in on their meetings - some of their meetings. And, as I say, as a result of my wartime experiences in London and in my business over there, I always had very close contact with Trinity House and they tried to prevail on us. Every two or three years, they would have a meeting. This would be about a three-day meeting at which papers would be given on lights, various improvements in navigation, and so forth and so on. There'd be quite a lot of entertainment and one thing and another.

Although we were not members, that led to the United States inviting IALA to hold a meeting in the United States, which they wanted to do. I was asked if we could invite them, even though we were not members, mainly because they wanted to come to the United States. They had been to several places in Europe. So we did, and we put on quite a show in Washington.

Q: Who financed it?

Adm. R.: The delegates financed themselves. The Coast Guard

financed part of it out of trust funds, the money that we had for special events. We transported them around and we took them out on tenders. We took them over to Atlantic City. The American Pilots' Association put on quite a party for them. I even took a few of them up to the Coast Guard Academy, but that had nothing to do with the delegation.

Q: How big a conference is it?

Adm. R.: I would say we had about 150 to 200 people all together. We had representatives from India, Korea -

Q: Taiwan?

Adm. R.: I don't remember that there was anyone from Taiwan, when I come to think about it. Of course, France and England, Holland, Germany, Denmark, Italy. I can't remember whether there was a Spanish delegate there or not.

By this time, I might say, Secretary Dulles had gone. Fred Scribner was Under Secretary of the Treasury and I had talked to him. In fact, he came to some of the meetings. We finally wore down the opposition and it was agreed - we had the last plenary session, as I recall it, over in the auditorium at the State Department, and in the final moments of the meeting we got word that authority had come through for us to become official members of IALA.

Q: Chris Herter had a different idea?

Adm. R.: Oh, yes. It was really ridiculous, you know. After all, we weren't fighting these people, and lighthouses are for the protection of life. It's one thing to shoot a guy, but why wreck yourself on his coast.

IALA had a rule that its president for the succeeding term - it seems to me that the other conference had been five years before because the term is five years - the country that hosted the conference their representative would be the president of the conference for the ensuing period. So, in the last few minutes, I was suddenly elevated to the chair of the conference. They had decided that the next conference was to be in Italy. That was the next big conference.

They had what I guess you'd call a board of directors consisting of France, England, Germany, and I believe, Holland, and the United States, even before we were official members. It met annually in Paris. So every time I went to IMCO I would go over to Paris and we'd have a day or two of meetings to discuss matters of concern to IALA. Until I retired, then, I was president of IALA. I mention this not because of that but because of the curiosity of trying to fit the Coast Guard, a governmental organization, into this organization that, strictly speaking, is non-governmental in any place that I know. It might have been governmental in India. I'm not sure how India handled it.

Another problem that plagued us for years was oil pollution.

Q: That gets to be a larger problem as the years go on!

Adm. R.: Well, even going back to long before the war, we were patrolling Los Angeles Harbor, Wilmington, San Pedro, and Long Beach, both for refuse, garbage, and that sort of thing, and for oil. The laws vary. The law that applies to the Great Lakes is different - or was, at that time - from the one that applies to the coastline.

I went down to Florida, for example, because we got screams from down there because oil was coming in on the beaches and wealthy New Yorkers were going down there, going out for a morning swim, and coming back with their feet soaked in sludge. Some of the hotels even had a morning rake-up and, in case they missed any, would have a barrel of kerosene that you could dunk your foot in to wash the sludge off. They were actually employing rakers to rake the beaches. And everybody said why can't the Coast Guard do anything.

Obviously, there are a number of problems with that, one being that because you find a bunch of sludge on the beach and because a ship that you might or might not be able to identify has been seen off the shore, off the Florida coast, or any place, doesn't prove that that oil that has come in has necessarily been dumped by that particular ship. It's the old story that you've got to catch the man with his hand in the till sort of thing. Furthermore, even if you gathered evidence or could get the evidence, you still had to turn it over to the engineers for prosecution and, in turn, to the U. S. attorney. So, by the time you went through this laborious procedure your chance of conviction was about one in a thousand. It wasn't a happy situation. We were getting the brunt of it, but more and more other countries were becoming involved because there had been some very bad spills. There was the Torrey Pines off the British coast. This, I think, was when you first began to hear of ecology because people had pictures of these poor seagulls, and it was pitiful. They couldn't fly because their wings were smudged with oil and they'd lost whatever it is that keeps them afloat.

We were being pressed, so in the spring before I retired I was at this big oil-pollution conference and, again, was the chairman of the U. S. delegation.

Q: Was this under the aegis of the United Nations?

Adm. R.: No, I don't think that was because it was not under IMCO. It was another conference like the International Conference at Sea. There had been conferences before but this was the first full-scale one.

It was a conflicting problem, too. You know, there's never anything easy. I'll put it this way, it's seldom that anything is black and white, there are always gray areas. For example, the American Petroleum Institute was able to bring figures to show that oil in salt water under certain conditions of temperature emulsifies and actually provides food for marine growth. The ecologists would come along and say it's terrible, the fish are dying. And I think probably the answer is that there was a little truth on both sides, depending upon the condition. But there had been tests run to show that oil will break down, but it's got to be pretty far offshore. As I recall, it probably would have to be in the Gulf Stream where the temperature is reasonably high, for it to do this deterioration, the breaking-up of this molecular structure.

It was an interesting conference. I don't know whether we accomplished much. One minute you'd be buttonholed by one group of people and the next by another. I guess I'd retired before whatever treaty we got out of it ever came to be considered.

The fall before that, I had a very interesting experience. The administration was changing at that time. I retired in 1962 and President Kennedy came in in January of that year. But in 1961 - No, Kennedy was already in.

Q: He came in in January of 1961.

Adm. R.: Yes, he was already in. I'm sorry. He had not

changed our Assistant Secretary, Flues, who had been the Republican administrator. Assistant Secretary Flues had been kept on and I guess Secretary Dillon had been kept on, too, because he was still Secretary.

Anyway, we acquired the C-130s so we made this trip around the world. It was the first time a Coast Guard plane ever went around the world.

Q: And you were a passenger?

Adm. R.: Yes. I took the Secretary and we visited the West Coast, some of the Loran stations, and Japan. We also took with us a Secret Service representative and a Bureau of Narcotics representative who had served in Lebanon. We did not take a customs officer, but in Japan we picked up a customs man. All of these agencies were under the Treasury Department, and as far as Hong Kong it was all Coast Guard and Customs.

Then we went down to Taiwan, where we were interested in the question of opium, which is a matter for Narcotics and Customs. I'm not sure that they call it Narcotics now. It's another division, but that's beside the point. The Secret Service was interested to a degree in narcotics but mainly in counterfeiting and that sort of thing.

So we flew to Taiwan, the Philippines, Bangkok, Rangoon, India and held conferences. In Rangoon, Burma, for example, I had conferences with the Burmese Navy. They had acquired some of our 83-footers and, like the Boy Scouts, were building houseboats on them and having certain problems. Then we stopped in Iran, Jerusalem, Cairo, then went up to Paris, where I renewed my acquaintance with the IALA people. I guess we came straight back from Paris, but we may have gone to London. I don't think so, though. It was a very interesting trip. Now that I've said that, I'd like to go back a little bit into aviation.

Two or three years before, we had been flying over the years originally PBYs and PBMs and the Grumman amphibian. You're probably familiar with all these?

Q: Yes.

Adm. R.: Obviously, practically all the PBMs had gone by 1950, when I became Assistant Commandant. I think we still had one or two until 1954 or 1955. The PBYs, I guess, had all gone by 1950 because we'd replaced them with the Grumman amphibian, the Albatross, as it was called. I guess some of them were still being flown in the service, but they were getting obsolete.

Q: In the Coast Guard?

Adm. R.: In the Coast Guard service, yes.

We had no real transport planes. Well, we'd come out of

the war - the first one was a B-17 that had been fitted out by somebody, and Secretary Snyder flew that. It was primarily the Secretary's plane. I suppose the commandant flew in it some but not much. Then, as our transport plane, we got a plane that had been General Eisenhower's, an Air Force transport. It was a DC-4 that had been fitted out for General Eisenhower when he was General over there. It had eight bunks in it, two staterooms with four bunks each, and quite good seating capacity. We flew that as a transport plane. Most of my early flights were in that.

Then, for local use, we got two Martin RMs. We used those back and forth across the country and for local flights. They were reasonably satisfactory, but it was obvious that we ought to have for search and rescue a larger plane. We had an aviation study board to study our requirements. There was quite a debatable question as to what did we require. In other words, what was our area of responsibility? It had never been defined. We knew that if you were in trouble five miles off the coast we'd go and get you, but 500 miles? 1,000 miles? What would be the limit of our responsibilities?

Well, those of us who felt that after all if you're in the search and rescue business, sea rescue, from the humanitarian standpoint there's no end to your responsibility. If you could get there, go, and you ought to strive that way. Other people said you ought to limit it to 1,000 miles. That gets to be a kind of hairy problem.

Q: It gets pretty arbitary!

Adm. R.: Yes, it's arbitrary, because if you say, gosh, that guy's 1,100 miles, let him drown, that, to me, is sort of a foolish thing. Or do you sit there and debate is it 990 miles or 1,010 miles? Of course, I don't think these people were serious about an arbitrary chop line, but when you do put lines down like that you do create arbitrary distinctions.

Anyway, we had a study made of our requirements and the general consensus was that we should go for broke and get the best we could. Then the question was what. I've always said that we finally got our program started thanks to a case of 'flu, because Humphrey was the Secretary at the time and he could be pretty hard-boiled, particularly on economy. He had the theory that there must be dozens and dozens of planes left over from the war, why don't you boys go and get some of them. There were dozens and dozens of planes, but some of them were older than the ones we were flying. Furthermore, it would have taken a mint of money. You see an airfield with 500 DC-4s sitting there and it makes you think, well, why can't some of these be used.

We finally decided on the C-130. I don't know whether you're familiar with it or not?

Q: Yes.

Adm. R.: It's a large Lockheed cargo plane that has the ramp in the back and can carry a tremendous load, relatively short landing space. They've since developed it beyond that, but it was a big plane.

We weren't getting any place in getting this through the Treasury Department. There were other planes besides these Lockheeds that we wanted. We finally decided if we had fourteen of these we would be able to do an admirable job. And we wanted so many helicopters - a complete revision of the Coast Guard aviation picture. But this aviation report wasn't getting to first base. It was lying there in the Treasury Department.

We were pressing the Secretary and one day the Secretary didn't come in. He was home sick with the 'flu, and I asked the Assistant Secretary if it couldn't be sent out to him - he'd sent for some papers, so I said, "How about including that with them?" So it was sent out to him and it came back approved. That's why I've always said that Coast Guard aviation was based on a case of 'flu. I don't know whether he was so weak he wasn't able to resist or what! Maybe he thought it was easier just to approve it, maybe he wasn't feeling like arguing in his usual manner. That was how we got started.

Of course, this didn't answer our question about transport planes, because we'd laid up the DC-4. Then we got a bright idea, which was later adopted by the Air Force, I believe, in a modified way. We said: "Well, look, we've got a big plane here, a turboprop capable of going" - there was some question whether we shouldn't convert one of them, and I said, "This I don't like because you're tying up a really expensive piece of equipment for a limited purpose. Furthermore, just about the time you want to use it for that limited purpose, you'll probably find you've got a sick engine or something."

So we put our heads together and decided that the thing to do, if it was practical, was to develop a pod to go inside. We gave some general specifications to some outfit down in Miami, Florida, and it came up with a pod -

Q: What was that? A capsule?

Adm. R.: A capsule that could be broken down like one of these houses that you throw up.

Q: Prefabricated?

Adm. R.: Prefabricated, yes. By slight modification of the planes for bolting-down, I think five men were supposed to be able to put it in in a day and take it out in about four hours. By putting similar bolts in each plane, we had the capability of putting this pod in any one of the planes and when it wasn't being used it could be taken out and stored

Richmond #3 - 378

at the air station, and you had your planes for regular Coast Guard use. That was what we flew around the world in, the C-130. It was a noisy plane and it wasn't the most comfortable. For example, all the C-130s had ports on the side, then, because of the curvature of the pod, you had to kind of funnel through the ports, so you really couldn't look out of the ports very well. You could look out, but it wasn't like sitting next to a window and looking down. We had capacity for fourteen people. As I recall it, we had two transoms which you could lie down on, and I guess there were three double seats. No, I guess we could carry probably up to twenty. It was quite nice. Then, the whole rear end of the C-130 was still available for carrying supplies or for storage or anything you wanted.

Q: This is out of sequence, but it's an interesting piece. You are going to tell me about the Coast Guard statue that's in the Battery.

Adm. R.: The Coast Guard Memorial Statue, yes. Ellis Read had been engineer-in-chief. I think he'd been one of the promoters. Sometime after the war, the idea was broached of having a Coast Guard memorial statue and they commissioned a fairly well-known sculptor to do this. I guess he submitted whatever sculptors do, a model or something, and it was accepted. I believe the money was raised by contributions, but

I'm not even sure of that. In any case, we ended up with a relatively large statue of what appears on the Coast Guard stamp, two seamen. So this statue was done and delivered.

Then came the question of where it should be placed. I think probably from the very first we'd hoped that it would be placed out on the Battery, but before we could get permission -

Q: Is the Battery federal ground?

Adm. R.: No, it belongs to New York City, but it was down near our old Battery barge office. We had to go to the City of New York and get permission, and it had to be approved by their Fine Arts Commission. So they took a look at the completed statue. Apparently the commission had one woman member and she took one look and, as I understand it, let out screams. She said "This is terrible, it's vulgar, or uncouth. The features of the wounded man aren't good," and one thing and another, I suppose as only artists can do.

To make a long story short, the commission couldn't agree on our putting it any place. It was stored in our supply depot up at Brooklyn, under canvas. Now the question is what do you do with - I don't know what we paid for it - a statue that's been bought, paid for by contributions. There was some talk of taking it up to New London and putting it at the Academy, but that's isn't exactly a public place where this should be commemorated. We debated it back and forth. This started back right after the war and I guess we had the statue before Admiral Farley retired. O'Neill was now commandant and I was assistant commandant. We facetiously considered putting it on a cutter and taking it out to sea and dropping it overboard, if it was as bad as this one member said it was, although, frankly, we didn't think so.

Then, I think we got word that the commission had changed and the woman was off of it. But before we would try this again, I think I was the one who suggested it, but whoever it was, we went down to the Mellon Art Gallery - a Coast Guard reserve officer was then administrating the Mellon - and I talked to him. I said, "Look, do you know somebody who is reputable to be judge." So we flew him up to New York, took him over to the statue, pulled back the canvas, to get, in effect, an expert opinion. If it's really bad, we don't want to put it up. He looked at it for a while and said it probably wasn't the last word in statues, but it wasn't all that bad. It wasn't uncouth and had strong, dynamic lines, these were the terms he used. In effect, he gave it the nod.

Now, we're in the position of approaching Mr. Moses who, I think, was the head of parks or something in New York, wasn't he?

Q: Yes, he was head of parks.

Adm. R.: We asked him to have the commission look again, which they did and, without the woman, they decided that it wouldn't ruin the Battery. And so, in due course, we got a place and got it mounted. Then it came to the unveiling.

This is a little aside from the story, but the day it was to be unveiled we were all on pins and needles for this reason. It seemed that the sculptor, at the same time he was doing this thing, had fallen out with his wife and he'd gone to Mexico. On the other hand, after all, the sculptor was proud of his work, so he was invited to come back. He came back and snuck into town, or so we heard. Anyway, he was present, but all of us who were present at the dedication sat there on pins and needles, expecting any minute to have - I don't know who serves warrants -

Q: A warrant was out for him?

Adm. R.: Yes. I don't know who serves back-alimony charges in New York, but fortunately the thing went off without a hitch. So now the Coast Guard statue stands in the Battery, and that's the story of it.

Q: Forever more!

Adm. R.: Yes, forever more.

Q: In connection with art, you also told me off-tape about

the survey you caused to have made of the wartime art.

Adm. R.: At one time we wanted to do some decorating at headquarters and I knew that there was a good deal of Coast Guard art, some of it free-lance and some of it asked for during the war. We had the whole lot in storage in the basement of the Coast Guard Library. I had wanted at one time to withdraw some of it to decorate some of the rooms at headquarters, some of the offices there, and I had run into opposition from the people who were then in charge of it, because, they said, it had to be kept intact. I had gone to the Academy and looked at this. Some of it was good and some of it was horrible, some of it was bloody war scenes that you wouldn't want, anyway, as decoration. In any case, it was almost impossible to find out what was good or bad because they were stacked side by side and after you look at a dozen pictures you get pretty well flaked out, anyhow.

So I conceived the idea that the only thing to do about it was to have a record of it and, at one time, and I don't remember exactly when, I directed that we go up there and make color slides of all these to keep as an index. My recollection is that this was done, although I never myself reviewed such an index. If so, it should be in the files at headquarters even yet, or maybe, at the Academy, but I think at headquarters because that was the purpose, to find out what we had.

Q: That certainly was a very constructive move on your part.

Adm. R.: Well, there were several hundred pictures, none of them framed - there might have been some of them framed.

Q: All right, Sir, we start with an account of legislation which you had always on tap in Congress.

Adm. R.: Throughout the roughly sixteen years that I was working in headquarters we were always involved with some degree or some problems of legislation. Of course, as you know, our legislative committee in the House was Merchant Marine and Fisheries. I guess in the Senate it was Commerce and Senator Magnuson was chairman of it most of the time. But by the time the legislation got over there, we didn't have as many dealings with the Senate side.

Q: It usually originated in the House?

Adm. R.: Yes. A number of important bills were put through in that time. Probably the most important, although it went through the Judiciary Committee, was the recodification of all the Coast Guard laws. Also, following up on Ebasco, we had certain remedial legislation to make definitive certain duties of the Coast Guard.

Another piece of legislation and we had two goes at this

was setting the size of the Coast Guard. I think in the first round we set it at about 3,000 and then we finally got it boosted to 4,000. Admiral Waesche, during the war, had four stripes and, as I recall it, Admiral Farley had four stripes and reverted to vice admiral. Anyway, Admiral O'Neill was a vice admiral as commandant. Of course, when I took over as commandant I was vice admiral, and we were successful in getting the legislation through that boosted the rank of the commandant to four stars.

Q: And the purpose of this was to put you on a par with the other services?

Adm. R.: No, not entirely. In a way it was, but we'd been that during the war and we felt that it was merited. Also, it made really for a better distribution or kind of a ladder - four stars for the commandant. We also made the assistant commandant, who had been a rear admiral a vice admiral. Now, the area commanders are vice admirals, so we now have three vice admirals. The whole problem of admirals in the Coast Guard was a very touchy one because shortly before the war we had only one admiral, who was a rear admiral, and that was Admiral Waesche, and the other commandants before. Then the engineer-in-chief was made a rear admiral. I believe at the outbreak of the war we had three. The assistant commandant was a rear admiral, the commandant was a rear admiral, and the engineer-in-chief.

Then, we had a fairly good number during the war plus even some commodores. As you remember, the commodore rank was brought back during the war.

When we came out of the war we got legislation which made the rank of admiral in the Coast Guard, but then we were into this question of the percentages. I believe at first we were only allowed about nine and gradually built up. I think at the time I retired fifteen years later we were up to twenty-two. That's the figure that sticks in my mind, but maybe we didn't have that many - one admiral, one vice admiral, and about twenty rear admirals. Of course, now they have more than that. Our objective was to have one rear admiral in every district, and at the time I retired I think we had one district yet that did not have a rear admiral in charge.

Q: And this act elevating the commandant to a full admiral became effective in 1960, did it not?

Adm. R.: Two years before I retired.

Q: Halfway through your second term?

Adm. R.: Yes.

Another important piece of legislation that we managed to get through was a selection out. I forget the year we got it through but '58 sticks in my mind and it might have been a year either way. Before that, a captain retired for age only. There was no limitation, and, of course, as far as admirals were concerned they were in and if they'd been chosen at an early age, why, promotion was blocked. There was stagnation and we needed to speed it up.

At that time I did not feel that we were prepared to go to what you might call the Navy system where, as you know, if you're a captain with thirty years' service and have been passed over twice, you're definitely out. I mean you're put on the retired list. I didn't think we were capable of having that. So we got a piece of legislation through - as I say, I can't remember exactly the year - which, in effect, had a retention provision in it to this effect. We selected for retention the captains, rather than selected them out. It was the same thing, but only a percentage could be selected for retention, so it was possible for a captain who was outstanding yet who had not been selected for flag to be kept on beyond thirty years. In fact, if he kept on in the percentage that was selected for retention, he could go on until he came to retirement age. But in the last year that I was commandant it was becoming apparent that we were running into stagnation all along the line in the Coast Guard.

You see, part of this had been because of the war and the bringing in of officers, and we had a big hump. It wasn't a case one class coming along after the other with natural attrition or anything like that. We had taken in a large number of temporary officers way back before the war when we first expanded during the rum war. They were pretty well assimilated. But then, following the war, when we were in terms of, say, 3,000 officers and this is now in the fifties, only ten or fifteen years after the war, we'd taken in some reserve officers and officers who transferred over to permanent status. And so we had a hump in the middle ranks. Therefore, junior officers now coming up were blocked by these officers who might be another ten, fifteen years in the service before they reached retirement age.

So we convened a board. Admiral Kerrins was the chairman of the board. This was known as the Kerrins Board. The bill to implement it was in the process of preparation to go to Congress at the time I retired. It actually was enacted and Admiral Roland will be able to tell you more about its effect when you talk to him. But it was enacted, as I recall it, after I left. There were provisions that I didn't like in the bill. I thought it was too drastic. I felt our problem was in the commander and captain grades and even lieutenant commander. I felt eventually we might come all the way down the line, but my own feeling at the time was that the problem was in the hump caused in the captain, commander, and lieutenant commander grades. Therefore, we need not go below those ranks to start eliminating to even out the line. Probably, some day they might have to, but that ought to be another step in this attempt to even out promotions. But the general consensus, I guess because more people thought they were more right than wrong - and we did go all the way down the line. It always seemed to me it was pretty drastic to take a lieutenant, say, a boy from the Academy, who has not a bad record - obviously if he has a bad record there's good reason to eliminate him, but you don't need an elimination system if his record is really bad - but basically it always seemed to me kind of hard to put a man on the beach after maybe eight years' service with a year's pay and a thank-you, after he's given that much time to the government. I never was convinced at that time that there was a pressing need for going down. But, as I say, they eventually did and apparently it's working out, so perhaps in afterthought I was wrong.

Q: I take it that you were the last of the commandants to serve for more than four years?

Adm. R.: Yes, to date, and I rather suspect that they will never again have more than a four-year term, and I think probably that's basically right. I was fortunate. I mean I'm glad that I had the opportunity, but it's the old story that too much tenure in office could be bad for the service. Maybe a new broom can always help. I don't think the service went back during my second term.

I was trying to think of other legislation, but it was

a continuing round of legislation on various things.

It was during that period that the question came up whether it would be desirable or necessary to get authorization for equipment before asking for an appropriation. I did not particularly like it, but I admitted there was some merit in it and in some ways it gave you a little leverage to go to the Bureau of the Budget with a request, say, for an icebreaker or a ship. I really think it came into focus at about the time that the problem over atomic-powered ships and that sort of thing came up, because it became a question of the desirability and the necessity of the Coast Guard building another icebreaker, an atomic-powered icebreaker.

Of course, the Coast Guard was always involved again with the Merchant Marine and Fisheries Committee on matters having to do with merchant vessels. Lots of times we came in with testimony of that nature. Probably one of the biggest problems we had was over pilotage on the Great Lakes.

The Great Lakes had a system whereby there were essentially first, second, and third mates, except that on the Great Lakes you had a master and pilot. You were a pilot on the Great Lakes. About that time, the St. Lawrence Seaway was opened and that raised a new problem because foreign ships were coming in and going as far as Chicago and the Canadians were piloting through the Welland Canal and other places, but the problem came up of how pilotage of these ships should be handled on the Great Lakes. Or whether these ships should be required to take pilots. In effect, you see, the ore carriers really didn't have pilots in the sense that we usually think of a pilot, being a man who comes aboard as you enter port and then leaves. I mean they were actually personnel of the ship.

We tried to get legislation through that would make it an effective system of pilotage. There were definite problems in this respect. Whereas you usually think of pilots, say, for New York Harbor where it's no problem. The man rides in on the ship, gets back to the pilot boat, or comes out on the next ship coming out. But here we're thinking in terms of taking ships from the entrance of the St. Lawrence Seaway through the lakes. The ship might be bound all the way to Detroit, to Chicago, and it was an entirely different proposition. They were small ships and the shipping companies claimed they didn't need pilots. We tried to evolve a system of pilotage that would be effective, and get legislation. We were fought sometimes by the lake carriers. Some of those lake carriers claimed they didn't need them and it was unnecessary.

I don't know what the final answer was. During my period we were not successful in getting mandatory pilotage, somebody extraneous to the ship. I think since then in certain portions they have provided required pilotage.

Q: I would imagine that the foreign skippers coming in would want pilots, would they not?

Adm. R.: There was divided opinion. We got testimony from both sides. Some had worked the lakes and the answer was no. Others, however, did want pilots. Of course, there was always the possibility of picking up somebody, if they felt they needed to be backed up on the run. But I think after they'd gotten through the seaway and through the Welland Canal most of them felt that they were capable of running the lakes without any help.

Another situation that arose was really a very touchy one. Sometime during the Eisenhower administration, the head of the Bureau of Immigration, who was a retired general but whose name escapes me now - in the Immigration Department they were at that time and I suppose still are to a degree having a great deal of trouble with the Wetbacks, the Mexicans, who came across the border. Their policy was when they picked them up to put them on a bus and take them across the border, probably, we'll say, at El Paso they'd take them down to Juarez. Maybe the next night they'd wade back across the Rio Grande.

Somebody in Immigration decided that the way to handle this would be to load these boys on a ship and take them way down the coast, these Wetbacks, take them way down probably to Vera Cruz. That, I think, is about 1,000 miles down the coast. It would be a long walk back, so at least they'd have a respite for a while.

This ex-general who was in charge of immigration was

apparently a very close friend of the President. They'd been classmates, as I recall the story. I can't say this for sure but I suspect what happened was that he went to the President and suggested that, in effect, they load these boys on LSTs and ship them down to Vera Cruz. They'd take them out of Brownsville, and this sounded like a very good idea. I haven't any doubt that President Eisenhower said, "I think that's a good idea. Let's go ahead and do it." Now, having made this decision, they go back and they call the Navy and, I suppose, tell the Navy to back up their LSTs for the first trip. Whereupon they immediately ran into difficulties because somewhere along the line the Navy decided that this was not the way to use an LST and refused to make their LSTs available.

I got into it when Neil Dietrich, with whom I'd been shipmates in London with, called me. I think at that time he was in MSTS and apparently the buck had been passed to Neil in this respect. I guess they told Immigration they couldn't use LSTs and nobody had the nerve or the initiative to go back to the President and say this was a good idea but, at this point, we haven't got the ships available. So they began to scrounge around to decide how else it could be done. So Immigration came up with some money and apparently chartered a Mexican vessel that had originally been a banana boat, carrying bananas out of Central America to the States. It had been built in 1915 and was designed to carry, I think, about twenty in its crew and had some passenger accommodations, could carry about 40 passengers - just a small vessel. They were going to carry these Wetbacks south from Brownsville to Vera Cruz on this vessel.

The way I first heard it was that they were going to carry about 1,000 Wetbacks - I don't think they ever carried quite that many because they'd have been hanging on the sides if they'd carried that many. That may have been the total that they planned to carry ultimately, I don't know. In any case, it was obvious that they were going to overload it far beyond the capacity of the vessel. Furthermore, it would be, in effect, carrying passengers I suppose you might say for hire - whether for hire or not, it was carrying passengers out of the United States, and at that time Mexico was not a signatory to the Safety of Life at Sea Conference. Therefore, they would be subject to inspection and the minute we inspected this vessel we'd say it was unseaworthy and therefore it couldn't go out, anyway.

But, the commandant has the power to waive the navigation laws under certain circumstances, and the request to me was would I waive the navigation laws in this particular case. My answer was a quick emphatic no, which got me into an immediate hassle as to what were we going to do. After much talking, I pointed out that there was a provision in the law that had been passed during the war and which permitted in the interest of national defense the Secretary of the Navy

Richmond #3 - 394

to waive all navigation laws. This was still on the books, by the way, but it was a pretty far cry. The purpose of this law had been to permit transports to carry soldiers with only these belt life preservers and various things. In other words, to violate the navigation basic laws in order to get troops to Europe.

Q: To expedite things?

Adm. R.: Yes. I pointed this out but I said I thought that if he did that he would be making a mistake. I said, "That's the only way it can be done. It won't be done by the Coast Guard." I was very much disturbed about this, but they eventually decided that the Secretary would grant this waiver. So, of course, the Coast Guard from that standpoint was out. However, I did go to the Secretary and I pointed out - the Assistant Secretary - that this was very dangerous because if anything happened to this vessel on the trip down and these people were lost - and I was sure from the descriptions that the conditions on the vessel would be worse than the slave ships and the ships that used to carry the prisoners out to Australia, if anything happened and this came out, it would be a terrible disgrace to the United States and reflect right back to the President because unless the President himself had directed it, why would the Secretary of the Navy take it upon himself to do it. Yet, I knew from what

I'd been told that the President hadn't directed this particular act. He had directed that they be taken down by LSTs. This is where so often orders in government get misconstrued.

Nevertheless, they went through with this. They made at least one or two trips and nothing happened. But it did have a peculiar aftermath in that I guess it was the following year - oh, and by the way, another argument I had at the time - it was just about the time of the U-2 incident and if you recall Khrushchev walked out of the Paris summit, so my argument was what better fuel right at this critical time for a real blow-up than something like this to point the accusing finger at the United States and at President Eisenhower.

Well, the following year, Immigration had to ask for money to keep this charter going and, I suppose before the Appropriations Committee, they described it in rather glowing terms. The way I heard it was that it almost appeared that the Mexican Wetbacks were getting a yachting trip down the coast of Mexico. Anyway, the Appropriations Committee dispatched one of its clerks down to Brownsville to look into this situation. And, rather than finding what he went to find, namely these boys riding down the coast in luxury, he came back appalled and came screaming to me and to his committee about these terrible conditions. These people, men and women, were being stuffed into holds with maybe one incandescent light, insufficient toilet facilities, being served box lunches, and packed, as I had anticipated, worse than the conditions on slave ships.

Actually, this one that he saw start out was the last trip they ever made because they got down off Tampico when apparently they had trouble with the engines and anchored in Tampico Harbor, and four of these boys couldn't take it any more and jumped overboard and drowned before they got ashore. There was a little article in the paper. It was hushed up and nothing more ever came of that part of it, except that I was in the middle because there was a Democratic congressman from West Virginia who the clerk had gotten agitated about this and they were calling almost daily to know how the Coast Guard could have permitted this to happen. It was rather difficult to explain without putting other people behind the eight ball how it did come about. I didn't want to put the Secretary of the Navy behind the eight ball because he was caught and it was going to bounce on the Republican President. So, I have to confess my answers were fairly evasive, along the line that we were looking into it and so forth.

Of course, the service was discontinued. It was just about election time and, fortunately, for me, this congressman who was round my neck was not reelected. So that was the end of that episode.

Q: There was one other item you told me about, the offshore

rigs?

Adm. R.: Oh, yes. Well, along with the oil-pollution problems that we had, especially during my second term, we were getting more and more involved with this offshore drilling proposition. This was long before the Santa Barbara spill-out which brought so much notoriety. We were having some trouble down off of the Texas coast, where most of the drilling was at that time.

Q: In the Gulf of Mexico?

Adm. R.: Yes, Louisiana, and so forth. There were problems, of course, of potential spills although, in fairness, the oil companies did their best to avoid that. There were problems of servicing the rigs, of the type of craft that were being used for servicing the rigs, some of them were chartered. The oil companies were working with us. The chartering companies were working with us.

Q: Most of these were international companies, weren't they?

Adm. R.: No. Shell, I guess, is an international company, but that was about the only one.

Q: I was thinking of the rig outfits. Most of them were?

Adm. R.: No. I think most of the rigs that were built were U. S.-designed. I could be wrong, but I don't remember any international aspect. Many of the details are hazy, other than that it was a continual conference give and take. A lot depended on where the rigs were. If they were up in the bayous, we had a lot more control than if they were offshore.

I attended any number of meetings with the various oil people, and, as I say, it's the old story, you have the interests working one against the other. Yet, of course, basically they were all interested in safety, from an economic standpoint, if nothing else.

At that time drilling out on the west coast, on the shelf, was just beginning. I remember, I think during the last year I was in the service, coming out to a conference in Santa Barbara and meeting with the oil people and the drillers and so forth.

We were in the process of drafting regulations from a safety standpoint on these rigs. It was an odd situation in that, in a sense, we were dependent on them for information as to the expertise to really draft these regulations. The Interior Department handled the oil rigs, to a degree, in the interior of the United States, so they came into it. Somebody would write something and then there'd be a big battle over whether it really ought to be this way or some other way.

Q: Well, in truth, it was a pioneer effort, wasn't it?

Adm. R.: It really was, and there was nothing to go on. As I say, it wasn't that they didn't want safety but they didn't want safety at the expense of restricting what they were doing or restricting their possibility of making money. You can regulate safety to a point. I mean if you want safety on the highways you can take the automobiles off the highway then nobody's going to get killed in an automobile accident. That's extreme, of course, and some way or another you've got to get in between. It was not a whole lot unlike the battle that's been going on over the Alaska pipeline. The ecologists say you're going to ruin Alaska. On the other hand, we need oil. Of course, now we're going ahead with that, but what did they do? They held it up for four or five years while they fought the issues.

Q: The scope of Coast Guard activities is simply amazing, I think. So much of it keeps pace with modern technology.

Adm. R.: Well, as I think I told you when we started this, I often facetiously said that when there were questions of putting the Coast Guard - whether the Coast Guard should properly be in the Treasury or in the Navy or where we should be, well, based on the functions assigned to the Coast Guard, I thought I could conveniently raise a plausible argument for putting the Coast Guard in almost any department of the government, with the possible exception of Agriculture, and probably, if I worked real hard, I could find a reason why we might properly be put in Agriculture. As a law enforcement agency, we could very properly belong in Justice, be the waterborne FBI.

The Hoover Commission had one argument for putting us in Commerce. It was a rather ridiculous argument, I thought. It was based on this. Actually, it was the agency that worked for the Hoover Commission that made the recommendation, after studying the thing - it's that research group on Lafayette Square in Washington.

Q: You mean Brookings?

Adm. R.: Brookings - it really stemmed from the Brookings group, I understood. But this essentially was their argument. It was the old if Mohammed can't come to the mountain, bring the mountain to Mohammed approach. They reasoned this way. The Coast and Geodetic Survey is in the Commerce Department. The Coast and Geodetic Survey makes charts. Charts are aids to navigation. The Coast Guard maintains aide to navigation. Therefore, let's put the Coast Guard over in Commerce with the Coast and Geodetic Survey. Essentially, that was the basic argument.

Q: You'd better watch out, you might get into agriculture even so, with mariculture or something of that sort!

Adm. R.: It could have been. Of course, from what little I know about it, I understand the Coast Guard is now more and more involved in oceanography and things like that. For years, we had conducted the ice patrol. That had been a standard duty for years. And more and more interest was being aroused at the time I retired about the possible implications of the Coast Guard getting into oceanographic work. That was, of course, before this what do you call it, National Administration of Oceanography or something. I'm out of it so I don't know the titles.

There were rumblings of this coming in, I'd say, 1960, 1961. Everybody now and then gets an idea for the Coast Guard. Senator Claiborne Pell, of Rhode Island, who had been in the Coast Guard during the war and was a Coast Guard reserve officer - I guess he's still a reserve officer unless they've retired him, he had an idea, I don't think it ever got very far - I think he even broached it several times in the Congressional Record and presumably on the floor or something like that - that if the United Nations needed a waterborne peacekeeping force, probably the Coast Guard would be an ideal - with our white ships and so forth - agency to be lent to that. I never thought we'd ever get to that, but it indicates some of the ramifications that you occasionally ran into in this thing. I think he's long since given up this idea and there's been no need for a waterborne peacekeeping force, but I suppose there might be some merit in it.

As far as I know, until after World War II and the Japanese set-up, there was never any other agency quite like the Coast Guard. It's true it sort of grew up like Topsy. Yet, if you really analyze it, the way it finally evolved with the four agencies that I mentioned previously, it's really a rather logical development. Maybe it's happenstance and all that. The only other agency that might have been added, and I'm not so sure it would have been a good idea although they do operate ships and therefore might have fitted in and might have been a little more economical, is the Coast and Geodetic Survey. That was considered, I think, a number of years ago, in Admiral Waesche's time, but it was discarded as probably not being desirable.

I might just conclude by saying that when I was serving in England on a number of occasions I was stopped by British servicemen who knew something of our insignia and they were always intrigued by the fact that I had a shield, not a Navy star. Nevertheless, in their eyes, I was wearing a Navy uniform. The usual question was that, in effect, he couldn't understand what it was and wanted to know what insignia it was. I would say I was in the U. S. Coast Guard, whereupon they would shake their heads because the British coast guard was really comprised of retired Navy or customs people. They were usually given a cottage and their job was that of sort of watchmen. They would look out to sea and if anybody was in distress they would inform the Royal National Lifeboat Institution. It was, in effect, a passive organization, and I would be told, "Well, I don't understand because our coast guard is different."

I used to have a stock answer which was to the effect that if you took your coast guard and the Royal National Lifeboat Institution and part of your RNR and your RNVR plus some of your air force and a couple of other things that they had around at that time and rolled them all in one, they'd sort of approach the U. S. Coast Guard. Whereupon the person would usually look at me like I was crazy and walk away shaking his head. But that was about what it amounted to.

Q: But you didn't add the Warden of the Cinque Ports, did you?

Adm. R.: No, I didn't put that one in, but I had practically everything else.

And it is a fact, I think, that the Coast Guard has developed into a unique organization. I've always opposed going into the Navy. People have asked me recently what I thought of the Coast Guard going into Transportation. From a prestige standpoint, I would have preferred to see the Coast Guard stay in the Treasury Department. But I always did say that if any department was ever created which covered transportation - and most foreign governments have transportation departments, we were the only major nation in recent years that did not have a transportation department - I frankly thought it would be a long time before it came. I didn't expect it to come quite so soon because I thought one of the requirements would be that they would take in the ICC, and I felt that the ICC, by virtue of having at that time some seventy years of a fairly enviable record - the ICC is one agency that has pretty well weathered a lot of criticism over the years and has done a good job, I really believe - I assumed that they would be taken into Transportation. As it turned out, they created a Department of Transportation without taking in the ICC. But I said that as long as the Coast Guard went into this Transportation as a unit, I thought it would be the inevitable answer and, sure enough, four or five years after I retired we were moved into Transportation and basically I think it probably now is the most logical home for the Coast Guard because in our modern-day operation we are more allied to transportation - maritime transportation perhaps - than anything else.

I think, through it all, you've got to remember, as I often facetiously said, the Coast Guard, regardless of what department it's in, is sort of like the handyman you have around the house and, if you need the grass cut, he cuts the grass, if you need somebody to be a butler, he's the butler. I think basically we had fourteen or fifteen definable functions to perform. Of course, as I always said, our paramount duty was the saving of life and property at sea, but it was not our primary duty.

Q: And, as the head of that glorious organization for such a long period, you came to your retirement on the 31st of May 1962. I do thank you very much for giving me all this concentrated time in recounting the events of your very notable career in the Coast Guard.

Adm. R.: Thank you, Sir, it was a pleasure. I tried to remember as best I can. I've been confused on some points, I'm sure, but at my age events sort of telescope in together and you can't always remember just exactly how things happened. Generally, I think you'll find it's reasonably accurate.

Q: Thank you very much indeed.

This is an addendum report to the tapes made with Dr. John Mason. This report pertains to the matter of Negroes in the Coast Guard.

Adm. R.: During my entire service in the Coast Guard, integration, or the use of Negroes in the service, never presented a particular problem.

In the early days, we had a number of Negroes, most of whom were in the stewards' branch, although occasionally you would find a Negro, sometimes even a pretty officer, in the other branches, particularly in the firerooms - engine-room group.

During the war, an attempt was made to utilize Negroes more extensively, and, in fact, there was an attempt to have an all-Negro-manned ship, that is, except for officer complement. There were not at that time available officers to completely man a vessel. A frigate was put in commission and, as I recall it, the entire enlisted personnel was colored. The frigate was under the command of Carlton T. Skinner, who later became government of Guam and who wrote quite a report on his experiences in command of the frigate. Generally, I think he felt it was a complete success and demonstrated that Negroes could man and properly operate a vessel, if given adequate support topside. His main criticism seemed to be that, as a colored-manned vessel, they were subject to critical inspection every time they were operating with other vessels, largely because everybody expected them presumably to do something wrong, and every maneuver was watched intently by other ships who might be operating with them.

I remember reading the report after the war and being greatly impressed by it, and I remember one comment of his was that he had found with his officers, that, even though he had some white southern officers who you might expect to have a certain antagonism, if it came to a question of being double-bunked and having to take an upper bunk, they would rather be in a room with a colored man who might be junior to them than have an upper bunk and be with a white man and they themselves have to take an upper bunk.

This report presumably is somewhere in the files at headquarters and would be very interesting, I think, to anyone who was making a study of the colored question.

The Coast Guard had not to my knowledge ever had an application for a colored cadet until I would say the late fifties, when a boy from Philadelphia took the examination and went to the Academy. Being the first one, it obviously caused some problems - that's not the word, but there were adjustments for the fourth-class dance which were made to arrange a date with a colored girl from Connecticut College. I remember hearing that there was a little anticipated consternation when they had what they called a shoe dance, where the girls threw one shoe into the center of a circle and the boys rushed in and whatever shoe you got you danced with its owner. But nothing arose. It was more pre-consternation. The situation went off very naturally, as I understand it, and there were no problems.

Unfortunately, I believe in the second year this cadet contracted a kidney infection which they felt could not be corrected during the period he was in the service, and he and his family agreed to his release from the Academy. I recall that the superintendent at the Academy at that time and the instructors were so impressed with this boy that they indicated that is, at a later date, this ailment should be overcome with medical help or otherwise, the boy would be allowed to reenter the Academy in the second or third class, I'm not quite sure which. In other words, at the same place where he had unfortunately had to be terminated.

The boy did, as I recall go on to Temple University and never did come back to the Coast Guard.

The situation that caused so much trouble, however, or caused a degree of trouble for me, arose at the Kennedy inauguration - President Kennedy's inauguration. I might mention at the outset that, before this happened, while the President was still a senator he had written a very commendatory article concerning appointment of cadets to the various academies and had cited the Coast Guard favorably because, as one knows, our examination was entirely competitive as distinct from the appointment system in other academies.

At the inauguration, I understand that as our cadets

passed in review he commented that he did not see any colored cadets. He had flanked himself, as one may remember, with a number of young, enthusiastic fellows who, hearing the President make this comment and remembering that the President had been elected on a bit of a - well, one of his platforms or pronouncements in various speeches had been more equality for the colored race, immediately took it up with the Coast Guard through the Treasury Department - we were then in the Treasury Department - as to why there were no colored cadets at the Academy. I might say this was done in a rather arbitrary manner.

It was pointed out to them that the difficulty was that we had a competitive examination for the Academy and, very frankly, there were two things. One was that the competition was very rough - my recollection was that that particular year we had from 6,000 to 7,000 applicants and we were only going to appoint 250 cadets, at the most. Furthermore, the colored boys who had the mental capability to pass high enough in the examination to be considered probably were not interested in a military career where the rewards, at the outset, were reasonably limited. Boys of that caliber would probably be more interested in the legal profession or the ministry or the medical profession.

By that time, incidentally, we had given our cadet examination for the forthcoming year and were in the process of having the examinations graded. The exams at that time were being given, except for the adaptability mark, by the Educational Testing Service - I think that was the name - at Princeton.

The young man particularly who was forcing this issue accused us of discrimination and indicated that we were prejudiced against colored people and we ought to do something about it. He wanted to know how many colored boys had taken the examination. I discussed it with him and told him there was absolutely no discrimination and said, "I can't tell you how many colored boys took the examination because in the application blank there is no indication of color or creed." However, he argued that this was a sure mark of discrimination. Finally, somewhat in desperation, I agreed that we would circulate the larger points of examination like New York, Philadelphia, where, in fact, most of the exams had been given by Civil Service examiners, anyway, and ask them if they could remember how many colored boys might have been present taking the examination.

I think we got reports from about ten places and we figured out that probably somewhere between 200 and 300 colored boys had taken the examination. That didn't satisfy the White House representatives, who then wanted us to find out who the boys were and appoint a number of them.

Backing up just a moment. I had pointed out that the only way possible that we would ever know whether a colored boy had taken the examination was when the adaptability marks were assigned and then only because on the application would be a picture. Even that was a dangerous way to judge because you might have a white boy with a dark complexion whose picture might indicate he was colored, and you might have a colored boy with a light complexion. So there really was no fair way of finding out. I further argued that the idea of cutting out a number of white boys to put in arbitrarily, irrespective of where they stood, these colored boys would be ridiculous. It also politically would be very bad for the President because any insertion of boys simply because they were colored into the list would deprive certain ones, because we could only take so many cadets - certain white boys, it might deprive them.

If they were really adamant about having colored boys at the Academy, which we did not object to, the best way to do it would be for the President to, you might say, exercise executive privilege and simply appoint arbitrarily x number of colored boys above the number that we presumably were going to take in, anyway, of course, from the examination and assuming that they had passed the examination. However, they did not want to do this, and it was finally agreed that the exam would stand and, hopefully, we would get some colored cadets on the next examination.

But that did not end the matter at that point because it was then felt that we should make every effort to get boys to take the examination for the following year.

Some of this leaked out into the papers, unfortunately. As a matter of fact, my point about the more talented boys wanting another profession was borne out by a newspaper article that appeared at that time. A colored boy down in Hampton Roads or Norfolk had an outstanding record scholastically and had been offered a number of scholarships and all, and he was asked what he would like to do. This was a newspaper article describing his reply. Basically, it was that he would like to do to the Coast Guard Academy and then practice law. In other words, let Uncle Sam educate him for private practice - not a career in the Coast Guard.

To carry out the effort to drive for qualified candidates for the next examination, I had a colored officer, a lieutenant aviator integrated from the reserve, I believe, brought in and assigned to travel around the country visiting high schools and colleges, hopefully drumming up interest among colored students in the Coast Guard Academy. I particularly urged him to concentrate on first year students in engineering colleges or universities on the theory that among such a group he might find some boys with mathematical or engineering bent who were having difficulty financially and the Academy might offer a way to continue their education. Also with one year of college behind them they might have a better chance of competing in the examination for entrance. I am not sure how successful our effort was, however. The following year, we did obtain one colored cadet, as I recall it, but I believe his father was an Army colonel, so possibly the boy was already service oriented.

That same year on an inspection trip to the west coast, a young Presidential assistant went along for transportation. He was going to travel up and down the west coast talking to officials of schools in an effort to arouse interest among colored students in a Coast Guard career. On the way out I voiced my opinion that with few exceptions, colored boys were not interested in a Service career. They were mainly interested in law or medicine because with the then state of development that was where the positions of leadership, power and money were. He pooh-poohed my thesis but on the way home after several weeks on the coast he was converted to my idea. He admitted that he was surprised to find in one university with over 15,000 students and a fairly large engineering department, only one black student.

About this time another problem arose. We had a vacancy for a chemistry professor at the Academy. Now for a number of years we had had minimum requirements for filling such positions. As I recall it, one of the requirements was a master's degree in the particular science involved, and ability to go for a doctorate as advancement in grade was indicated. Possibly these requirements were arbitrary, because possession of a degree does not necessarily indicate a good teacher or educator. However, you have to have some standards and these were ours. Anyway one applicant was a negro. He had done undergraduate work at North Carolina State, I believe, and was either working for or had just completed his work for a masters degree in chemistry at Howard University. His record at both schools was only average and I was dubious about appointing him for this reason. In other words, I would have been doubtful of him irrespective of color. Putting it another way, had he been white, I would have eliminated him on the spot just on the basis that on the record he was marginal by our requirements. However, in order to avoid any possible charge of discrimination, Assistant Secretary Flues and I set up an appointment with the then President of Howard University to discuss the applicant. Basically he confirmed what I suspected from the record. That the applicant was not an intellectual giant but a good average middle of the road student. He questioned whether the applicant could ever sit for a doctorate but did state that the applicant had done some instructing of undergraduates at Howard and did appear to be able to communicate with them as a teacher in an effective manner. So it was decided to appoint him. I am happy to say that it was apparently an excellent choice. I later met him at the Academy, he fitted in well, and by report was doing an excellent job teaching chemistry to the cadets. As far as I know he is still at the Academy.

This concludes all I recall about the negro situation in the Coast Guard. As I said earlier, I recall no particular problems arising at any time other than that brought about by President Kennedy's observation at the inaugural parade and the attempt by over zealous young assistants to carry out what they thought was the wish of the Boss. Parenthetically, after I retired I had a short meeting with the President and he thanked me for the effort of the Coast Guard in the field of race relations.

APPENDIX

4105 La Junta Drive
Claremont, California
July 2, 1976

Professor John P. Lovell
Department of Political Science
Indiana University
Bloomington, Indiana

Dear Professor Lovell:

First, let me apologize for my delay in answering your letter of May 21 st. My wife and I were in Europe until the 29th of May, and having had a bout of flu in Paris, I did not arrive home in tip top shape. I have been a month trying to pick up the pieces.

Giving you specific information to the questions you posed will not be easy. As you know, I retired fourteen years ago and kept few records or papers. So the best I can do is to give you a general picture of the situation as I recall it and hope that will serve your purpose.

You are aware, I am sure, that the Academy came out of World War ll with a permanent physical plant built in the early thirties to accomodate approximately 100 cadets with possible expansion to 200. During the War, a number of temporary wooden buildings had been built for the training of reserve officers. These builings were a fire hazard, but were retained because it appeared that the post war Coast Guard would require a minimum graduating class of 50 to 100. With the normal rate of attrition experienced in pre-war years, this meant an entering class of approximately 200 cadets, or a total enrollment for the four classes of 400 to 600 cadets.

The practices and curriculum at the Academy was as indicated in your article similar to that of pre-war years, modified only to reflect technological changes brought on by the war. The Academy had been accredited a number of years before the War by the ECPD (as I recall it, this stood for the Engineering Council for Professional Development) and the boast of the Service at this time was that the Coast Guard Academy was the only Service Academy so accredited. As I will explain later this accreditation boomeranged and in fact did, in my opinion, contribute to our attrition rate in the officer corps. The Board of Visitors had been inaugerated under Admiral Waesche prior to the War and continued throughout without much change in membership. I mention this because two members that I recall, Dr. Ted Barker (who was I believe, Dean of Engineering, Columbia University) and a Professor Seward (from Yale University as I recall) regarded themselves as part of the permanent scenery at the Academy and were not too happy when we put membership on the Board of Visitors on a rotating basis after the War.

The documents which you have reviewed have already undoubtedly indicated the above to you but I thought it best to review the situation not only to insure that you were aware of these matters but also to give you an understanding of how these conditions affected the decisions made at the time. To this end, I think it wise to review my interest in the Academy and how my assignments from 1946 through 1962 impinge on my involvement in the affairs of the Academy. From 1946 to 1950, I served as Chief, Planning and Control (now referred to as Chief of Staff) and during this period visited the Academy several times a year, usually with the then Commandant, Admiral Farley. Quite often these visits were to accompany the Congressional Board of Visitors or to meet with the Academic Board of Visitors. I became Assistant Commandant in March, 1950 and served as such from then to May, 1954. During this period, I visited the Academy a number of times, although possibly not as frequently as before. I sometimes accompanied the then Commandant, Admiral O'Neil, or was delegated by him to accompany the Congressional Board of Visitors or to sit in on the meetings of the Academic Board of Visitors. During the eight years from 1946 to 1954, I collaborated in all decisions relating to assignments of Superintendents and principal officers to the Academy as well as all problems relating to the Academy.

From 1954 to 1962, as Commandant, I visited the Academy at least four or five times a year for graduations, Congressional Board of Visitors, Academic Board of Visitors, and occasional visits for other purposes. Also, during the period from 1957 or 1958, the Superintendent came to Washington several times a year, and starting about that time we initiated the practice of convening the Board of Visitors (Academic) in Washington once a year. Summing up the situation, I think you can see that for 16 years, I was very close to the developments at the Academy.

Probably the biggest problem during the whole period was attrition, parricularly among graduates after their three years of service. During the late 40's and early 50's, we were losing more than 50% of a graduating class after three years and since we then estimated that it cost from 70 to 90 thousand dollars to put a cadet though the Academy, this was a high price to pay for three years service. In fact in the late 40's, Captain Joseph Bois (a Reserve Officer, who was a management specialialist on duty in the Commandant's office) made a persuasive argument for closing the Academy and drawing officers from colleges and universities. Fortunately after some argument, the idea was rejected. However, the economic situation on the outside being so much more favorable than that in the Service (especially with engineering companies running adds in the New York Times to employ Coast Guard officers) our attrition problem was serious.

While we explored the attrtion rate among cadets, it was not appreciably greater than before the War and was accepted as the penalty of a strictly regimented life, coupled with a difficult technical curriculum. Actually, I found that our attrition was not really much worse than that of any good engineering school, if compared with 4 year graduates. Many starting engineering students in universities were taking 5 or 6 years to graduate as engineers or switching to other specialties.

Trying now to give more specific answers to your questions, I did hand pick Admirals Leamy and Evans. Evans retired shortly after I did, and the choice of Admiral Smith was up to Admiral Roland who succeeded me, although I may have consulted with him on the choice, since he was Assistant Commandant during the period when the choice would have been made.

As to whether there were particular aspects of their careers which contributed to their choice, the answer is, in general yes, specifically no. You should understand the conditions under which the Service was then operating. Because of percentage limitations on the number of flag billets, there were insufficient flag officer to fill all of what were considered key billets. Properly we had about 22 billets that merited flag rank but from 1948 to 1962 we ranged from 11 to 18. All key assignments, whether Academy, Office Chiefs at Headquarters, or District Commanders were my final choice while serving as Commandant, although recommendations might be made by the Chief, Office of Personnel, and final decisions often made after consultation with that officer, plus the Assistant Commandant.

At the time, we were usually selecting one or two flag officers each year, whose term of service could be estimated as an average of six to seven years. Thus each yearly selection board initiated what might be called a game of "musical chairs". The situation was complicated somewhat by the fact the District Commanders of the 3rd District (New York) and the 12th District (San Francisco) wore an additional hat as Area Commander to coordinate search and rescue operations for his respective coast with command authority over other districts. Thus if it was necessary to fill either of these billets, it was necessary to fill it with a flag officer senior to other District Commanders in the Area to avoid possible conflicts in command authority. All of this contributed to the fact that assignments to key billets seldom lasted more than three years, although in the case of the Superintendent of the Academy, we did attempt to look ahead and choose an officer who would be assured a minimum of this period and possibly longer. As for other attributes, since all of the senior officers were known to me individually, personal judgment on my part as to the ability of the officer to successfully discharge to job of Superintendent was a big factor. Prior service at the Academy was considered. Frankly, the distaff side was a factor, since the social side of the job of Superintendent is most important. As far as particular problems which the selectees might be well fitted to meet, I don't recall that to be a special factor in their selection. The choice was largely based on available personnel and chosing the best man for the job. There were no special instructions that I recall other than, go in-run a tight ship-maintain Academy standards-improve anyway you can. Within these limits, it was their show. Parenthetically, I might addd that we always made every attempt to overlap the tours of the Academy Executive Officer and Engineer Officer with that of the Superintendent in order to maintain continuity of effort. Further I considered these positions key positions and usually made the final decision on assignments.

As I recall it now, I may have given Admiral Leamy some special instructions because his predecessor had not been too agressive and shortly after I became Commandant in 1954, word came to me indirectly that morale at the Academy was bad,—first class men were advising under classmen that the Coast Guard so needed officers that they could slough off, more or less get away with murder, graduate, and do three years, resign, and get a good job on the outside. I promptly went to the Academy and called for the cadets to be assembled in the Auditorium for a "bull session". I talked for about an hour on Service problems, ended by saying that although we had problems, we didn't need officers so badly that we were begging anyone to stay, and if any cadet wasn't satisfied, he could head for the door and hand in his resignation on the way out. Then I threw the floor open for questions and fielded them for two and a half hours. The meeting which started at eight was finally broken up by the Superintendent at 11:30. I think the meeting cleared the air a great deal but I recall telling Admiral Leamy about it and suggesting that he keep a close watch on the mood of the cadets, and if he felt at anytime they wanted to air griefs or gripes, I was available.

For the last five or six years that I was Commandant, I used to go to the Academy and discuss with the officers and the first class cadets, the budget of the Coast Guard for the coming year, the problems involved in clearing our requests through the Treasury Department, the Budget Bureau and finally Congress, plus the possibility of having to sequester 5 to 15% of appropriated funds as happened once or twice during the Eisenhower years.

One problem that arose, I believe, during the Leamy regime, about which you might be interested. The ECPD, which I mentioned earlier had accredited the Academy for a number of years, got into a dispute with the Department of Defense over accrediting engineering schools with ROTC and a four year course leading to an engineering degree. The claim was that the time spent in ROTC courses prevented the proper presentation of the required engineering courses. Therefore ROTC students should be required to go five years for a degree. Naturally the engineering schools didn't like the idea. They neither wanted to jeopardize their accreditation or lose the support of the Government money. The Defense Department didn't like the proposal because candidates wouldn't join the ROTC if it took 5 years against 4 to get a degree. The ECPD was embarassed by the fact that the Academy was accredited with a 4 year course and since we were due to come up for a review (the policy of the ECPD was to review the curriculum every so many years) there was a good chance that the Academy might lose its accreditation not necessarily because the curriculum or training had deteriorated but to remove an embarassment to the ECPD. Dean Barker wrote and suggested that the Academy voluntarily surrender its accreditation and he, being acquainted with some of the ECPD accreditation committee members, assured me that in a year or so after the ROTC flap was resolved, the Academy would be reinstated. That struck me as sort of "plea bargaining" and not being sure that the accreditation was an unmixed blessing, especially since the Academy was accredited by the New England Association of Colleges, made the decision to waive the accreditation.

You asked about the details of the letter which I wrote to the resignees from the class of 1954 or 1955. I can't give you too much information on that now. As I recall it, there were about 40 resignees out of a graduating class of 85 or 90. I had a letter prepared to each one after their resignation was accepted, and asked them to write me and give me their reasons for resignation. The results were disappointing. I think only 15 or 20 replies were received and from these it was not possible to draw any firm conclusions. In most cases they gave no specific reasons, only glittering generalities. I recall that one young man wrote and said that he couldn't put it down on paper but would like to talk to me. He came to Washington and spent about two hours with me one afternoon. When he left I still was not sure why he had resigned and I am not sure he knew. It appeared that during his second class year at the Academy some incident arose which soured him, he decided to resign but his father talked him out of it, but from then on he never intended to make a caree of the Service. But for specific gripes against Service life his arguments were all trivial. For instance, he had never met the District Commander at New York where he had been stationed because the District Commander had never come aboard his ship for lunch. When I asked whether the District Commander had ever been invited he didn't know. Incidentally I forgot to mention that he could not recall what the incident at the Academy was that had soured him in the first place. Summarizing the results of the letters, my conclusions were that the resignations came about because the resignees never intended to make the Service a career.

You ask about the tour of duty as Commandant as compared with the tour of duty of the Superintendent of the Academy. The tour of duty for the Commandant is fixed by law at four years. In my case I was reappointed to a second term so of course served eight years.

Secretary Flues was a very enthusiastic supporter of the Coast Guard in all aspects and his interest extended to the Academy naturally. He enjoyed visiting the Academy and probably displayed more interest in the institution than any of his predecessors. He also gave me considerable support in getting appropriation funds for the management study that was made of the curriculum and plant at the Academy. It was that study which led to the expansion of the Academy into what we have today.

I believe I have covered most, if not all of your questions, and I hope that the little bit of information that I have been able to provide will be of some help to you. I am sure that by now you have reached to conclusion that I am no typist, so please accept my apologies for a very sloppy letter.

Sincerely,

A. C. Richmond

INDEX

to

Series of Interviews

with

Admiral Alfred C. RICHMOND
U. S. Coast Guard
(Retired)

ALASKA: p. 131-5; p. 207 ff; see also entries under USCGC HAIDA; JAPANESE IN ALASKA: CORDOVA:

USCGC ALEXANDER HAMILTON: p. 80; p. 87-88; p. 90.

USCGS AMERICAN SAILOR: new ship building in Seattle, p. 184; destined to service the Maritime Administration Station at Port Hueneme, California, p. 182; Richmond prepared for assignment with cruise on merchant ship, p. 182-3; the first quota of 300 trainees, p. 185; drawbacks to training on her, p. 185-6; early graduation for training contingent (Dec. 1941), p. 191; p. 196; her difficulty in making Port Hueneme - an all night anchor along the coast, p. 197-8; delayed permission to paint ship a war-time grey, p. 199-200; Richmond becomes commanding officer at Base in Port Hueneme as well as skipper of American Sailor (Feb. 1942), p. 200; gets an armed gun crew, p. 200-1;

AMMUNITION, DYNAMITE: Problems involved in transportation - a responsibility of the Coast Guard, p. 331 ff; the Perth Amboy explosion, p. 331; a discussion of the problems and difficulties involved, p. 331-335; poison gas, p. 335-6; ammonium nitrate, p. 336-7;

BERING SEA PATROL: (1933) part of the Seattle District Command, p. 131 ff; duties of the Coast Guard on this patrol, p. 132-3; p. 135; p. 144-6;

BILLARD, Rear Admiral F. C.: Commandant of C.G. (1924-32), p. 45; Richmond becomes his junior aide, p. 45; a description of headquarters, p. 45-8; p. 50; p. 162;

BOARDING SHIP: comments on procedures, etc. p. 101-2.

BRITISH CONFERENCE TACTICS: p. 175-7;

BROCKWAY, Comdr. Benjamin L.: p. 70-1;

BUREAU OF MARINE INSPECTION AND NAVIGATION: Coast Guard takes over full time administration (1942), p. 216; procedure for dealing with infractions of rules, with accidents, etc in Marine Inspection at time the Coast Guard assumed control, p. 217; Coast Guard expedites matters by setting up HEARING UNITS, p. 217 ff; Richmond ordered to New York to head experimental UNIT (1943) - he acted as examining officer and hearing officer, p. 219;

SS BURROUGHS - collier of the Mystic Coal Co. - collision with the CG DD HERNDON, p. 116 ff.

CANFIELD, The Hon. Gordon: Member of Congress from New Jersey - becomes known as the father of the U. S. Coast Guard Reserve, p. 282-3; p. 311; p. 313-14;

CASEY OF THE COAST GUARD - Pathe film: gala showing by Coast Guard at Wardman Park Theatre, p. 56 ff.

CHALKER, Vice Admiral Lloyd T.: heads delegation (Apr. 1943) to U.K. to study possibility of setting up Merchant Marine HEARING UNITS, p. 221-3; in charge of headquarters during final illness of of Admiral Waesche, p. 274-5;

COM NAVEUR: Coast Guard unit in London assigned to ComNavEur-Richmond on the staff, p. 236-7; Richmond serves on a committee to investigate accidents in convoy, p. 252-3; British system of using retired officers for jobs of a lesser rank, p. 253-254; Committee to interrogate survivors of ships sunk in convoy, p. 254-5; Richmond accompanies Admiral Stark on visit to OMAHA Beach, p. 255-6;

CORDOVA, Alaska: becomes a Coast Guard station, p. 145-6;

CURRY, Capt. Ralph R.: enters law school with Richmond, p. 154; p. 162;

DECCA: Name for British system competitive with Loran, p. 296;

DEMPSEY, Jack: becomes commander in Coast Guard - his trip to England, p. 240.

DERBY, Vice Admiral Wilfred N.: p. 77; as head of Maritime Service - gives Richmond command of the new AMERICAN SAILOR, p. 182; p. 199;

DOG TEAMS - SENTRY WORK: Coast Guard organizes teams for work in South Pacific, p. 293;

DUTCH HARBOR: base for Coast Guard ships on Bering Sea Patrol, p. 145;

EBASCO MANAGEMENT COMPANY (Electric Bond and Share Co.): gets the task of studying various functions of the Coast Guard, p. 286 ff. p. 290-1;

EISENHOWER, The Hon. Dwight D.: p. 391-2; p. 395;

ENSENADA, California: p. 141-2;

FARLEY, Admiral Joseph F. Jr.: becomes Commandant on Jan. 1, 1946, p. 275; hearing on the Coast Guard Budget for 1946-7 Fiscal year, p. 275-6; his patience in dealing with post war problems, p. 279;

FLUES, The Hon. A. Gilmore - Assistant Secretary of the Treasury: Richmond takes him (1961) in a C-130 for an around the world inspection trip, p. 372; p. 414;

GEARY, The Hon. Vaughn - Member of Congress from Virginia: an Appropriations Committee member who was very much interested in the Coast Guard Reserve, p. 283; p. 308; p. 311; p. 314.

GERMAN V-1 and V-2 bombs over London: p. 245-47.

GORMAN, Rear Admiral Frank J.: in charge of Enlisted Personnel Office in headquarters, (1924), p. 48-9; skipper of the USCG HAIDA, P. 145: in command Planning and Control Division, 1945 - p. 272; p. 27-56; retires in 1945 as Richmond takes over Planning and Control, p. 278;

GREEN, The Hon. Theodore: Senator from Rhode Island, p. 306-7;

USCGC GRESHAM: p. 70;

USCGC HAIDA: Richmond becomes Executive on her in Alaskan waters (1932), p. 131; on the Bering Sea Patrol, p. 132; p. 134-5; patrol of seal fisheries and halibut fishing, p. 136-7; p. 140; part of picket line off California coast (1933), p. 142; plan for supplying canned goods to enlisted men while on duty in Cordova, p. 147-9; rescue of Alaskan Steamship Company vessel VICTORIA, p. 150-2; Richmond takes command of HAIDA (1942) stationed at Juneau, Alaska, p. 207; convoy duty from Pleasant Bay to Kodiak, p. 208-9; the HAIDA and the Navy order to strip paint, p. 212; p. 214-5;

HEBRIDES; three Loran stations set up there for the invasion forces, p. 243;

HELICOPTERS: p. 352-4;

USCGS HERNDON - DD: p. 109-110; episode involving an engineer officer and command, p. 111-112; quarantine aboard, p. 113-4; collision with a collier, p. 116 ff; her guns, p. 122-3; overhaul in Boston Navy Yard - difficulties with GAO, p. 124-5;

HINCKLEY, Captain Harold Dale: Superintendent of CG Academy, p. 33-5; p. 90; p. 99; District Commander in Seattle, p. 131; an Alaskan hunting/fishing trip, p. 134-5;

HIRSCHFIELD, Vice Admiral J.A.: p. 178-80;

HUMPHREY, The Hon. George - Secretary of the Treasury: difficulty in obtaining his approval for additional moneys for Coast Guard vessels to be used in port security, p. 328-9; approves Coast Guard Aviation Report - asking for C-130s helicopters, p. 376;

HOT PURSUIT Doctrine: I'MAH ALONE case, p. 100;

IMCO (International Maritime Consultative Organization), p. 356; p. 363; p. 364;

INTERNATIONAL ASSOCIATION OF LIGHTHOUSE AUTHORITIES (IALA): p. 364-5; desire to have U.S. as a member, p. 365-6; the Washington conference, p. 366-8;

INTERNATIONAL SAFETY OF LIFE AT SEA CONFERENCE (1960); called to revise provisions of earlier Treaty, p. 356-7; prior preparations p. 358 ff; ratification by the U. S. Senate, p. 362-3;

INTERNATIONAL WHALING CONFERENCE (July 1939): Richmond attends conference in London, p. 171 ff;

JAPANESE IN ALASKA: p. 135-6; p. 207 ff;

JUNEAU, Alaska: home base for Coast Guard ships engaged in convoy duty, p. 208; p. 210-11;

KENNEDY, The Hon. John F.: his anaugural remark about lack of black cadets, p. 408 ff;

KENNER, Rear Admiral Frank T. (Frankie): p. 33-5; p. 39; takes Congressional Committee on visit to Alaska, p. 313-14; p. 322;

KERRINS BOARD: a special board set up to study question of selection out and to devise legislation, p. 387-8;

KHARTOUM: p. 232-4;

KILGORE, The Hon. Harvey - U. S. Senator from West Virginia: p. 315-7;

KODIAK, Alaska: p. 207; p. 210-211;

LAND, Admiral Emory Scott: p. 181; p. 188;

LAW ENFORCEMENT - indoctrination: Richmond and team develop a brief course of instruction on maritime law for Coast Guard commanders involved in law enforcement, p. 162-3;

LEGAL OFFICER - Coast Guard: Richmond serves temporarily as legal officer, p. 55-6;

LIGHTHOUSE SERVICE: comes into the Coast Guard in 1939 - aids to navigation system, p. 288-9;

LORAN: Richmond learns about Loran - its use in connection with the invasion of Normandy, p. 242; stations established in the Hebrides, p. 243; p. 274; p. 288; p. 291; p. 295; its value for commercial shipping, p. 296; p. 297; summary of Loran installations in 1947-9, p. 304-7; Loran and the Senate Committee, p. 306-8; personnel problems at Loran stations (1950), p. 320.

MACAULEY, The Hon. Edward: (U.S. Maritime Commission, 1941-46) (War Shipping Administration, (1942-46) - instrumental in taking training of merchant seamen from Coast Guard and putting it under War Shipping, p. 187-8;

MacLANE, Captain Gordon W. (Don't Know): Coast Guard Academy Instructor, p. 36-7; his exacting way as Commandant of Cadets, p. 38-40;

MARRAKESH: p. 85-6;

McCARTHY, The Hon. Joseph - Senator from Wisconsin: trouble with his committee over Personnel matters, p. 323-4; over Port Security p. 323-4;

MEALS, Captain Frank: Coast Guard Officer on staff of General MacArthur in Japan, p. 300.

MEXICAN WETBACKS: the proposal of the Bureau of Immigration - position of Richmond and the Coast Guard, p. 391 ff; Immigration Bureau charters a Mexican vessel, p. 392 ff;

MILLS, The Hon. Ogden: Under Secretary of the Treasury, p. 62; p. 64-5;

USCGC MOJAVE: replaces ALEXANDER HAMILTON (1927) for cadet cruise, p. 80;

MORGANTHAU, The Hon. Henry: Secretary of the Treasury coopts Coast Guard officers to give clearance for incoming merchant ships - and to monitor radio for news scoops, etc., p. 178-9;

MOTORBOAT NUMBERING ACT: outboard motor improvements in World War II, p. 343 ff; passage of Act, p. 345-7;

MURMANSK - : destination of U.S. - U.K. convoys to Russia, p. 224;

NARCOTICS: Richmond comments on, p. 103.

NASH, Commander W.J. (class of 1876): Richmond delegated by C.G. Commandant to remain in his Washington home until funeral services were over, p. 50-53;

NOME, Alaska: p. 138; panning for gold, p. 138-9;

NORMANDY INVASION: Coast Guard role in providing patrol boats for rescue purposes, p. 237-8; base established at Poole, p. 238; miscellaneous problems for the Coast Guard, p. 238-41; Richmond's visit to Coast Guard units established on the Continent after invasion, p. 247-8;

USISV NORTHWIND: in Bering Sea Waters, p. 139;

OIL POLLUTION: a problem for the Coast Guard, p. 369 ff; Oil Pollution Conference, 1962 - Richmond heads U. S. delegation, p. 371;

O'NEILL, Admiral Merlin: designated by Adm. Waesche together with Richmond and John Myers of Lifesaving Service to write regulations for a Coast Guard REserve, p. 168 ff; recommends Richmond (1950) to serve as Assistant Commandant and Chief of Staff, p. 319 ff.

ORTAUGS (Organized Training, Augmentation of ships) - see entries under US COAST GUARD RESERVE. p. 281; p. 283;

ORTUPS (Organized Training Units Port Security) - see entries under U.S. COAST GUARD RESERVE. p. 281;

PERTH AMBOY EXPLOSION; see entry under AMMUNITION, DYNAMITE - Problems of transportation,

PONTA DELGADA, Azores: p. 88.

USCGC PONTCHARTRAIN: p. 91; LAKE class - characteristics p. 92; at Mobile, p. 97-9; p. 103; her demise, p. 110;

POOLE, England: Coast Guard base for patrol boats established there p. 238; p. 249; picture taking of 83-foot patrol boat at different speeds for identification purposes, p. 250-1;

PORT HUENEME, California: Maritime Administration builds a station on Coast Guard property, p. 181; Commissioner Macauley comes to celebrate Coast Guard day (Aug. 4, 1942), p. 188; background history of this base, p. 189-191; Pearl Harbor jitters at Port Hueneme, p. 194-5; erosion of land at Port Hueneme - a Wakefield bulkhead constructed, p. 202; p. 203-4; p. 205;

PORT SECURITY: a post-war Board established by Navy evaluates needs for future war - assigns Port Security as task of the Coast Guard, p. 278;
Problems in the McCarthy era, p. 323-4; evolvement of 24 hour system, p. 325 ff; difficulty with Secretary of the Treasury Humphrey in getting money for additional port security vessels, p. 328-9; p. 330; ammunition, p. 331 ff.

PRIBILOF ISLANDS: included in Coast Guard Bering Sea Patrol, p. 136-7;

RICHMOND, Admiral Alfred C. USCG (Ret.): personal data - school experiences - Massanutten Academy, p. 1-10; George Washington University, p. 11-24; examination for C.G. Academy, p. 24-25; becomes editor of class yearbook, p. 41; his marriage, p. 126; p. 126; p. 144; his wife joins him in Cordova, Alaska, p. 146;

RUM RUNNERS and the Coast Guard: p. 66; Richmond becomes aide to Captain Wheeler (Wm. J.) on the Cutter TAMPA, p. 67-71; thd beginning of the syndicate and rum running, p. 72-74; difficulties in apprehending - and in convictions, p. 74-5; p. 76-7; rum runners (1930) and Coast Guard techniques, p. 104-109; rum runners on the west coast, p. 140-1; after repeal of the 18th Amendment problems with liquor smuggled in by the syndicates, p. 141-2; a new Coast Guard picket line concept off California coast, p. 142; request to the HAIDA for water from a rum runner, p. 143-4;

SALTONSTALL, The Hon. Leverett: p. 282;

SCOTCH CAP, Alaska: Coast Guard maintains navigation light there, p. 312-13;

SEABEES: Navy makes inquiry about Port Hueneme as training base for Seabees, p. 205;

SEARCH AND RESCUE EXERCISES: Coast Guard conducts such exercises for benefit of airline personnel, p. 348-52; question of Coast Guard responsibility in sea areas - aviation study board deals with problem, p. 373-4;

SEA SCOUTS and EXPLORERS: Coast Guard problems with inspection of boats they acquire for use, p. 340-2;

SHAEF: p. 243; Richmond's account of a reserve officer on the staff who dealt with finances of occupied countries, p. 244-5;

USCGS SHAW - DD: participates in cadet summer cruise (1928), p. 87-8; p. 90.

SHEPHEARD, Rear Admiral Halert C.: p. 355 ff;

SKINNER, Carleton T.: member of USCGR - commanded an all black manned frigate in the Coast Guard, p. 406;

SPARS - see entries under US COAST GUARD RESERVE

SPENCER, Vice Admiral Lyndon: p. 33-4; p. 37; p. 120;

STEPHENS, I.J.: Coast Guard officer assigned to Ebasco Management Co. for study of Coast Guard duties, p. 291;

TABOR, The Hon. John: Chairman of House Appropriations Committee, p. 275-7; p. 290;

USCGC TALLAPOOSA: stationed at Juneau, p. 145; p. 151;

USCGC TAMPA: flagship of Capt. Wm. J. Wheeler of the rum runner patrol, p. 67; p. 80;

THE GEORGE WASHINGTON UNIVERSITY: p. 11-12; p. 14; the football team, p. 15-23; engineering course, p. 23;

THE GEORGE WASHINGTON UNIVERSITY - LAW SCHOOL: Richmond enters law school (1935), p. 154; his previous experience as defense council in a court martial case excites his interest in law, p. 155-160;

THOMPSON, Commander Warner Keith: at headquarters, p. 48-9;

TRINITY HOUSE - United Kingdom: a private organization with government sponsorship - in control of U. K. Lighthouses, p. 364-5;

TROJAN HORSE THEORY: name given by Secretary George Humphrey to the measures adapted by the Coast Guard to protect U. S. ports, p. 330;

USCG TUSCARORA: the loss of personnel at Shelby, N.S., p. 53-4;

TWENTY-FOUR HOUR SYSTEM - for Port Security: see entry under PORT SECURITY.

VICKERY, Vice Admiral Howard Leroy: p. 181; p. 188;

WAESCHE, Admiral Russell R.: p. 77; his plan for indoctrination of commanding officers of small boats in better understanding of maritime law, p. 162-3; as Commandant wanted regulations drawn up for Coast Guard Reserve (1939) - instrumental in getting an Act of Congress to create the Reserve, p. 168-9; sends Richmond on tour of U. S. Insurance companies to unravel problem of insurance coverage on boats taken into C.G. in wartime, p. 260-2; his interest in formation of a Coast Guard League, p. 269-70; final illness, p. 274-5; p. 384;

USCGS WAINWRIGHT - DD: Richmond reports for duty (July, 1930), p. 103-4; p. 109; p. 155;

WALSH, Commander Quentin R.: on staff of Richmond in United Kingdom, p. 225;

WAR SHIPPING ADMINISTRATION: takes over Port Hueneme from the Coast Guard - Navy takes it from War Shipping for training of Seabees, p. 205-7;

WEASEL: an amphibious jeep, p. 313-14;

WHEELER, Rear Admiral Wm. J.: p. 67

SS YANKEE: The case involving her and the Coast Guard, p. 339-40;

YEANDLE, Stephen S. Capt. USCG: Aide to Admiral Billard, p. 46-7;

U. S. COAST GUARD; ENTERS THE U.S. NAVY (Nov. 1941): p. 191; wartime regulations on wearing uniform, p. 193-4; families permitted in Alaska, p. 210-11; Navy order to strip paint from ships - difficulties in Alaskan waters, p. 211-212; Richmond comments on difficulties with inflexible orders, p. 213-214; Coast Guard returns to Treasury Department in 1945, p. 272; Congress perplexed by various new duties in postwar era - Loran, weather stations, etc. p. 286 ff; Congress orders a study of Coast Guard (1948), p. 286 ff; results of the study - impact on the Congress, p. 291-2; scope of its activities - proposals for it, p. 399 ff; logical for it to be under TRANSPORTATION Department, p. 404;

U. S. COAST GUARD - ACADEMY: circumstances surrounding Richmond's appointment (1922), p. 24-25; attrition rate for entrants, p. 27-29; cruises, p. 31-3; Richmond's class graduates in a little over two years, p. 42; difficulties in awarding commissions, p. 42-4; Richmond returns in 1926 - teaches Math and English, p. 77-8; memorable visit to London, p. 81-3; visit to Casablanca, p. 84-5; early expectations of an enrollment ceiling, p. 300-2; efforts for increased appropriations for new buildings, p. 302; See also - letter of Adm. Richmond in APPENDIX (July 2, 1976) on C.G. Academy.

U. S. COAST GUARD - AVIATION: Richmond's brief try at aviation exams, p. 130-31; questions about Coast Guard responsibility in Search and Rescue - Aviation Study Board investigates, p. 373-5; Richmond's decision to ask for C-130s, p. 375-6; single C-130 adapted for passenger service by adding a pod, p. 377-8;

U. S. COAST GUARD - ASSISTANT COMMANDANT AND CHIEF OF STAFF; Richmond named to post in 1950 - duties, p. 319-230; Richmond makes a number of inspection trips to Loran stations in Pacific area - their value, p. 320-2; trouble with Senator McCarthy Committee over personnel, p. 323-4; over Port Security matters, p. 323-4; p. 359;

U. S. COAST GUARD - AUXILIARY - see entries under U. S. COAST GUARD RESERVE

U. S. COAST GUARD - BLACKMEN: p. 406; p. 415; attempt at a black manned frigate, p. 406; incident at Kennedy inaugural, p. 408-12;

U. S. COAST GUARD - BUDGET: hearings for 1946-47 budget, p. 275-6; Richmond assigned the task of presenting budget before Congressional Committee by Admiral Farley, p. 276; Richmond has task of presentation for next sixteen years, p. 277; Budget presentations to the Congress simplified by the EBASCO Study, p. 293; Richmond continues Budget responsibilities as Asst. Commandant and Chief of Staff, p. 319-20; Richmond supports aviation needs in budget, p. 352-3;

U. S. COAST GUARD - BUDGET PRESENTATION: p. 306 ff; the use of travel as a means of educating Committee members, p. 308-10; p. 312-313; problems with time for presentation of budget, p. 309-11; a European trip with a Congressional party, p. 314-7;

U. S. COAST GUARD - BUREAU OF MARINE INSPECTION AND NAVIGATION: p. 354 ff; former Steamboat Inspection Service becomes permanent part of Coast Guard (1946), p. 354;

U. S. COAST GUARD - CONSTRUCTION CORPS: p. 93; work of the Coast Guard in design of small boats, p. 96-7;

U. S. COAST GUARD - CONSTRUCTION PROGRAM (1938): Richmond given task at headquarters of clearing titles for construction program, p. 165-7;

U. S. COAST GUARD - HEADQUARTERS: a description in the year 1924, p. 45 ff; total Coast Guard complement, p. 49;

U. S. COAST GUARD - INSPECTIONS: under terms of Navigation laws - the Chesapeake Bay Bugeye, p. 338; the case of the YANKEE, p. 339-40; the problem with the boat of the Sea Scouts, p. 340-1;

U. S. COAST GUARD - LEAGUE: Admiral Waesche advocated formation of a League patterned after Navy League - reasons for its lack of success, p. 269-70;

U. S. COAST GUARD - LEGISLATION: p. 383 ff; re-codification of Coast Guard laws, p. 383; legislation to boost rank of Coast Guard Commandant to full admiral, p. 384-5; legislation to permit selection out, p. 385-6 ff; the KERRINS Board, p. 387-8; question of desirability to get authorization for new equipment from Congress before asking for an appropriation, p. 389; attempt to get legislation for mandatory pilotage on the Great Lakes, p. 389 ff;

U. S. COAST GUARD - MEMORIAL STATUE: the saga of the World War II memorial now mounted in the Battery, New York City, p. 378-81;

U. S. COAST GUARD - MERCHANT MARINE HEARING UNITS: See entries under Bureau of Marine Inspection and Navigation; Richmond heads first experimental HEARING UNIT (1943), p. 219-221; in post-war period practice of being an Examining Officer and Hearing Officer was ruled in error, p. 221; Richmond and a delegation sent to London (Apr. 1943 - Ass't. Commandant lloyd T. Chalker heads delegation) to investigate feasibility of setting up HEARING UNIT, p. 221-3; Richmond sent on investigative tour of North African ports, p. 223; Richmond ordered to visit India, p. 231-35; unit established at Colombo and one at Bahrein, p. 236; Richmond named to head U. K. units, p. 224 ff;

U. S. COAST GUARD - MERCHANT MARINE HEARING UNIT - UNITED KINGDOM: Richmond named to head UNITS (July 1943) in London, Liverpool, Bristol, Glasgow, p. 224 ff; London headquarters, p. 228; a miscellany of cases, etc. p. 228 ff; Command structure, p. 236-7; Richmond's supplementary role in preparations for invasion of Continent, p. 237 ff; V-1 and V-2 bombs, p. 245 ff; p. 255;

U. S. COAST GUARD - OFFSHORE OIL RIGS: p. 396-8;

U. S. COAST GUARD - PLANNING AND CONTROL DIVISION: established summer of 1945 - Capt. Frank Gorman in command - Richmond principal assistant, p. 272; drastic postwar reduction in personnel strength of Coast Guard, p. 273 ff; Richmond succeeds Capt. Gorman (1945), p. 278; Richmond deals with very urgent need for a Reserve complement geared to question of Port Security, p. 278-9; the EBASCO study, p. 286 ff; disbands sentry dog teams, p. 293-4; new devices for Search and Rescue, p. 298; Weather Stations, p. 298-9; cooperation with General MacArthur in Japan on a Defense Command patterned after U. S. Coast Guard, p. 300; Richmond named (March 9, 1950) as Assistant Commandant and Chief of Staff - leaves Planning and Control, p. 319 ff;

U. S. COAST GUARD - RESERVE: in 1939 Richmond and others given task of writing regulations for the Reserve, p. 168-171; a more complete story on development of the Reserve - problems and difficulties encountered, p. 257 ff; original of the term "temporary reserve", p. 258-9; problems of caste, p. 259; problem of insurance to cover boats taken into Coast Guard, p. 260; a solution arrived at, p. 262-3; a natural progression to the present Coast Guard Reserve during and following WWII, p. 265 ff; Wartime SPARS a part of the new Reserve, p. 266; temporary Reserve status, p. 266-7; plant guards in wartime become "temporary reservists" in the Coast Guard, p. 267; difficulties over postwar discharges and a "ruptured duck", p. 267-8; p. 270; attitude of members of the Pilot's Association, p. 271; great need for a Reserve after WWII, p. 274 ff; plans in 1948-49, p. 280; Coast Guard goes to Congress (1950) with request for money to establish a Reserve, p. 281; finally evolves into ORTUPS (Organized Training Units Port Security) and ORTAUGS (for augmentation of ships), p. 281; proven value of new Reserves in Korean conflict, p. 284; Academy used for training reserve officers in WWII, p. 301; p. 303;

U. S. COAST GUARD - RIFLE TEAM: Richmond becomes captain of the team, p. 129-130;

U. S. COAST GUARD - SEARCH AND RESCUE: new postwar devices, p. 298;

U. S. COAST GUARD - WARTIME ART: Richmond causes a photo index to be made of the Coast Guard collection of Combat Art, p. 382;

U. S. COAST GUARD - WEATHER STATIONS: p. 298-9;

U. S. MARITIME ADMINISTRATION: delegates the training of merchant marine officers to the Coast Guard, p. 181 ff; expansion of training facilities, p. 181; Commissioner Edward Macauley influential in taking training from the Coast Guard and putting it under War Shipping, p. 187-193; Richmond obtains three old whaling killer boats for use in training, p. 201; p. 205;

U. S. NAVAL OBSERVATORY: Richmond works there at the end of World War I, p.10-14;

www.ingramcontent.com/pod-product-compliance
Lightning Source LLC
Chambersburg PA
CBHW080623170426
43209CB00007B/1505